Michael Newman
New York City English

MW01094196

Dialects of English

Editors
Joan C. Beal
Karen P. Corrigan
Bernd Kortmann

Volume 10

Michael Newman

New York City English

DE GRUYTER
MOUTON

ISBN 978-1-5015-0889-9
e-ISBN (PDF) 978-1-61451-212-7
e-ISBN (EPUB) 978-1-5015-0060-2
ISSN 2164-7445

Library of Congress Cataloging-in-Publication Data
A CIP catalog record for this book has been applied for at the Library of Congress.

Bibliographic information published by the Deutsche Nationalbibliothek
The Deutsche Nationalbibliothek lists this publication in the Deutsche Nationalbibliografie;
detailed bibliographic data are available on the internet at http://dnb.dnb.de.

© 2015 Walter de Gruyter, Inc., Boston/Berlin
Cover image: Michael Newman
Typesetting: PTP-Berlin Protago-T$_E$X-Production GmbH, Berlin
Printing and binding: CPI books GmbH, Leck
♾ Printed on acid-free paper
Printed in Germany

www.degruyter.com

This book is dedicated to my parents for bringing me to New York before I was born and to Paco for ending up here with me so many years later.

I also want to thank Dan Silverman for suggesting my name to the original editors of the Dialects of English Series; John Singler, a true mensch, for giving me ideas and letting me sit in on his New York City English Seminar at NYU in addition to the students attending the seminar; Miki Makihara for co-organizing our Voices of New York class, and the various students in that class who have contributed to book including Angela Wu, Lisa Fogelman, Kyle Khachadurian, and Andrew Crocker; the members of the BQ-16 and the teachers and administration of the "Urban Arts Academy," who must remain anonymous. Finally, I want to thank Emily Farrell, who balances support and advice in an ideal way as editor.

Contents

1 Introduction

1.1 New York City English and the approach taken in this book

A half-century ago, in what became the foundational text in the emerging field of variationist sociolinguistics and the best known examination of New York City English (NYCE), Bill Labov (1966/2006: 18) wrote the following:

> It is safe to say that the language of New York City is better known to the people of the United States as whole than the language of any other single city. ... On radio and television, stereotypes of middle class and working class New York speech have traditionally been used for comic effects. For many years several other features of working class and lower class New York City speech have been stigmatized under the label of *Brooklynese*.

Labov's study is called *The Social Stratification of English in New York City* (hereafter SSENYC).[1] The title reflects his then novel findings that dialectal variation was far from chaotic but was systematically organized by social factors, in this case exponents of socioeconomic stratification.

Take non-rhoticity or r-lessness – two terms meaning lack of a consonantal /r/ after vowels – as in words like *four* and *fourth*. Although stereotypical New Yorkers might be thought of as dropping their /r/s consistently, Labov notes that there is usually variation. As such, he describes this trait as a variable, which he labeled (r) – with (r-1) as the pronounced or r-ful variant and (r-0) the r-less one. Labov also examined two other characteristically NYCE variables – also indicated in parentheses – in detail:

- (oh) the vowel in *thought*,
- (aeh) the vowel in *bath*,

Finally, he analyzed two pronunciations associated with a vernacular versus standard distinction not only in New York but in many other English dialects as well:

- (dh) the initial sound of *this*, and
- (th) the initial sound of *think*.

New Yorkers treat the three more characteristically New York variables in similar ways to the more widespread (dh) and (th). The higher their socioeconomic status (SES) and – holding SES constant – the more attention they pay to their speech – the less frequently they use the locally marked variants in each case. This rejec-

---

1 It is cited so often in this book that it will be referred to with those initials rather than the usual name date reference as given in the quote above.

tion of local pronunciations is so strong that Labov asserts that "the term linguistic self-hatred is not too extreme to apply to the situation" (SSENYC: 329–330).

Bonfiglio (2002) observed that this reaction is surprising. Inhabitants of comparable cultural capitals – say London, Paris, Mexico City, Tokyo or even Los Angeles – do not systematically try to sound like they are from elsewhere. It is the inhabitants of their respective hinterlands that are embarrassed about their speech. Bonfiglio traces the different behavior of New Yorkers to the racialization of late 19th and early 20th Century immigrants from Ireland, Italy, and Eastern Europe, who were heavily concentrated in the city. Although we now mostly think of people of these origins as White, at the time their Whiteness was highly questioned. Since Whiteness is to a large extent conflated with American identity, even the immigrants' children were considered at best only partly American. Their English, although native, Bonfiglio claims, was consequently felt to be out of the mainstream and funny, if not just bad.

Although the construction of Whiteness in America has become more inclusive and racism less overt generally, Niedzielski and Preston (2003) find that NYCE still only compares with southern varieties in provoking dislike among Americans. Moreover, NYCE continues to draw interest and attention as somehow quirky as best. A 2008 movie by Heather Quinlan called *If These Knishes Could Talk* (http://newyorkaccentfilm.com) documents NYCE and its relationship to the city's culture. It is hard to imagine such a film about any other urban US speech variety. New media – which allows us to easily gauge interest in contemporary popular culture quantitatively – tells the same story. The search term "New York accent" on YouTube yielded more about 12,900 results in July 2013.[2] Contrast that with a mere 1,960 for "Chicago accent," 1,911 for any of "Los Angeles accent," "LA accent," "SoCal accent," and "California accent."[3]

The reference to *knishes* (pastries containing potato or other savory fillings of Eastern European origin) in the title of Quinlan's movie provides a culinary connection between NYCE and Eastern European Jews as presumably the most archetypical speakers. Nevertheless, Jews are not the only group represented in the film, and so-called Brooklynese is more properly associated generally with the ethnic Whites who dominated the city demographically from the late 19th Century to the 1970s. Since then, a more recent wave of immigrants from all over the world has altered the population of the city and, to a lesser extent, the surrounding area. Now well over a majority of New Yorkers are either immigrants or children of immigrants (Kasinitz, Mollenkopf, Waters, & Holdaway 2008). The

---

2 In quotation marks, without the quotes, the result is much higher.
3 Note that the term accent is imprecise and often avoided by sociolinguists, but we can stipulate here that it means the phonology of the dialect.

2011 US Census American Community Survey, for example, reports that for 49.1 %
a language other than English is spoken at home. The characteristics of recent
immigration have also led the city to become far more racially diverse than at
any time in its history. Although "Brooklynese" may remain the most iconic form
of NYCE, the ways New Yorkers actually speak English has multiplied with this
diversity. Therefore, it is necessary to define NYCE plurally; any form of English
distinctive of any of the many New York identities counts and so is fodder for the
descriptions that follow in this book.

The focus of the book is primarily descriptive, to give an account of the story
of NYCE including geography and demographics in Chapter 2, and phonology,
morphosyntax, discourse, lexicon, and history respectively in Chapters 3 to 7.
Nevertheless, the stigma of NYCE and the racial and ethnic diversity of the city –
even in its less extreme state half a century ago – have played an important role in
the progress of sociolinguistics itself. This is the case not only for Labov's original
theoretical insights in SSENYC but also important advances by interactional sociolinguists and linguistic anthropologists, whose work is discussed in Chapter 5.
So developments in sociolinguistic and linguistic anthropological theory form
part of the story of NYCE too.

Moreover, there is no such thing as atheoretic description, which makes it
hard to avoid addressing a current challenge to the variationist paradigm. This
dispute arises from the work of Vertovec (2007), who argues that contemporary
post-industrial urban areas are characterized by a "diversity of diversity." This
so-called *superdiversity* involves destabilization of social categories like gender,
class, subcultures and forms of communication in addition to ethnic and racial
groups that variationists have traditionally relied upon in analyses. Blommaert
(2010) claims that variationists' use of those macrosocial categories and their
focus on linguistic structures consequently provide only superficial accounts
of the sociolinguistic reality in superdiverse societies. Perhaps the changes that
characterize New York at the beginning of the 21st Century spell the limits of the
approach Labov developed in the middle of the 20th. The discussions in the following chapters of can be read as implicit responses to such claims, and the question itself is addressed briefly in the conclusion.

1.2 The data used

Dialectologists – who describe and analyze dialects in mostly geographical
terms – began systematic studies of NYCE with a short but remarkable work by
Babbitt (1896) followed by a number of studies of varying quality and importance
discussed in Chapter 7. Although Labov has never claimed to have superseded

the dialectological framework so much as complemented it (e.g., Labov, Ash, and Boberg 2006), SSENYC marks a break from that approach. That book is less concerned with characterizing NYCE comprehensively – as a dialectologist would do – than systematically connecting variation with social factors. Therefore, the dialectologists' work provides a wider range of NYCE features, but those examined by Labov, such as the five variables mentioned above along with a few others, have been studied more in depth in particular with respect to their social and linguistic roles.

SSENYC was largely derived from fieldwork on the Lower East Side (LES) of Manhattan and focused mainly on White speakers although data from African Americans were collected and included in some analyses. Later Labov, working with some collaborators, examined the English spoken by Black and a few Puerto Rican youths in Harlem (Labov, et al. 1968 a, b). These studies along with a number of follow-ups in which Labov reexamined the original LES and Harlem recordings appear over and over again in this book.

Unfortunately for the study of NYCE, Labov left for the University of Pennsylvania in 1971, and local universities were slow to pick up the slack, although important work in interactional sociolinguistics and linguistic anthropology appeared from time to time. The most well-known of the interactional studies are Tannen's (1981) inauguration of research on conversational style and Urciuoli (1996) and Zentella's (1999) examinations of bilingualism and identity. Yet apart from Wolfram's (1974) important account of Puerto Rican English, hardly any variationist research on NYCE appeared for over 25 years. Variationist research resumed with a major expansion in the New York University Linguistics Department beginning in the 1990s. The first research in this line is Cutler's (1999/2003) examination of AAE variants and identity among White youth associated with Hip-Hop, which although largely interactional was informed by variationist insights. A more classically variationist study is Kara Becker's (2010) dissertation and a shorter article (Becker 2009), which reprise much of the work in SSENYC on the LES. Several sociolinguists are currently working on NYCE, and they (or better we) will be providing more data on variation. Also, interactional sociolinguists and linguistic anthropologists continue to provide useful findings about identity and discourse.

Yet New York is such a sociolinguistically rich place that NYCE remains considerably understudied. It is impossible here to fill in all the remaining gaps, but any book with the title *New York City English* must take at least a first stab at doing so, and I provide some new, although tentative, historical and discourse analyses in subsequent chapters. The largest new contribution concerns variation. These data are derived from analyses of sixteen research participants I call the BQ-16 due to their homes in Brooklyn and Queens. The BQ-16 represent a cross-section

Table 1.1: The BQ-16 with Macrosocial Categories and affiliations

Pseudonym	Race	National Heritage	Approximate SES Origins*	Childhood Neighborhood	Immigrant Generation	Birth Year	Sex	Source
Mandie John	East Asian	Chinese	UMC	Flushing, Queens	3rd gen.	1990	F	QC
Chang John		Chinese	LMC	Flushing, Queens	2nd gen.	1959	M	Outside
Clara Chin		Chinese	MC	Middle Village, Queens	Arr. <1 y.o.	1988	F	QC
Rashid Lewis	Black	Af. American	LI	South Jamaica, Queens	n/a	1983	M	UAA
Kendrick Pierre		Haitian	WC	Canarsie/Flatbush, Brooklyn	2nd gen.	1985	M	QC
Diondre Davis		Af. American	LMC	Springfield Gardens, Queens	n/a	1975	F	Outside
Darryl Hanson		Jamaican	WC	East Elmhurst, Queens	2nd gen.	1984	M	UAA
Delia Figueres	Latino	Ecuadorian	WC	Elmhurst, Queens	2nd gen.	1992	F	UAA
Colton Vega		Puerto Rican	LI	Bushwick, Brooklyn	3rd gen	1988	M	Outside
Missy Ibáñez		Dominican	LI	Williamsburg, Brooklyn	2nd gen	1976	F	QC
Johan Aranda		Venezuelan	LMC	Richmond Hill, Queens	Arr. 3 y.o.	1989	M	QC
Carl Pisapia	White	Italian-Irish	MC	Flushing, Queens	3rd gen.	1988	M	QC
Laura Feldman		Italian-Jewish	WC	Howard Beach, Queens	3rd gen.	1992	F	QC
Andy Sullivan		Italian-Irish	WC	Howard Beach, Queens	3rd gen.	1992	M	QC
Janet Krebbs		German-mixed	LI	Glendale, Queens	n/a.	1983	F	UAA
Sharon Rosen		Jewish	UMC	Flushing, Queens	4th gen.	1988	F	QC

* Based on parents' reported professions: UMC = Upper Middle Class, MC = Middle Class, LMC = Lower Middle Class, WC = Working Class, LI = Low Income.

of New Yorkers of different racial and class backgrounds. The lack of Manhattanites can be justified by the fact that much recent major work (e.g., Becker 2010) focuses on that borough. Yet the Brooklyn/Queens bias is mainly due to questions of availability to a researcher based at Queens College. However, as discussed in Chapter 2, limited borough diversity is less important than it might seem, although naturally research based in the Bronx, Staten Island, and suburban areas would certainly be welcome.

Nine of the BQ-16 were Queens College students, and four were students at "The Urban Arts Academy" (UAA), the pseudonym for the research site in my prior studies on NYLE and Hip- Hop (e.g., Newman 2001, 2005). I also worked at UAA as a teacher before beginning sociolinguistic research there, and my fascination with the speech of my students was a prime motivation for engaging in this research in the first place. Two of the BQ-16 (Rashid Lewis and Janet Krebbs) were former students of mine, although I interviewed them years later. I interviewed ten of the BQ-16, and the rest were interviewed by Queens College students participating in course projects. All the members are listed in Table 1.1 on previous page, which provides some demographic information about them.

Table 1.1 describes the BQ-16 in terms of social categories, but short biographical descriptions of each can be found in Appendix A. These more complete descriptions can be referred to to contextualize their usage in terms of more individual qualities. Also, Rashid Lewis, Johan Aranda, Laura Feldman and Andy Sullivan have excerpts transcribed in Appendix B.

The BQ-16 were selected to address the largest demographic gaps in the research, but they still leave some significant groups like non-Chinese Asians, Middle Easterners, and New Yorkers of recent European and African origins unrepresented. Another set of remaining gaps is class related, including the local elites such as those who attend or attended non-religious private schools. Age is also skewed in the sample, with only Chang John born in the 1950s and Diondre Davis and Missy Ibáñez born in the 1970s. The rest are young adults.

Yet the BQ-16 do accomplish the task they have been set: to provide initial new data missing in prior research. It is best to view these data as an illustrative not a scientific sample: as snapshots of diverse individuals' variable usage identified by racial and class-related categories. My hope is that the resulting dialectal collage can serve as a starting point for establishing the range of speech patterns that can be found in New York and as fodder for hypotheses to motivate future research.

1.3 What non-specialists need to know

This section is designed for non-specialists, and anyone familiar with basic linguistics can therefore skip ahead to Chapter 2. The reason it is here is because reading serious writing about language requires background knowledge that many people interested in the subject do not have. Those without specialized training who nevertheless wish to understand NYCE will therefore require a guide to some of the basic principles.

1.3.1 Variationist studies

SSENYC develops the first major systematic effort to explore how social and linguistic factors interact in language variation and change in a large speech community. For those interested in a more complete understanding, Gordon (2013) provides an excellent exposition aimed at non-experts of the significance of that work, its historical roots, and methods used. Here I only make a depiction of the core ideas needed to make sense of the rest of the present book.

The central concept is the sociolinguistic variable. It is worth noting that the notion of variable is not limited to pronunciation but is found at all levels of the language. For example, *was* and *were* function as variant forms of a single variable in the following snippet of discourse from a teenage rap artist I call MalCo in (Newman 2005: 421):

> MalCo: Like every day, all of us, we **were** in a circle cipher, all of us. ... And we **was** doing it constantly. ... And I mean we **wasn't**, we shoulda gotten that consistent building of the peace and everything. I was giving it. ... I remember that 'cause we **was** all together. We **were** all making a beat; we **were** all rhyming together.

Before SSENYC, dialectologists and linguists usually referred to this kind of alternation of forms as "free variation," but that label represents a kind of scientific surrender because it assumes no possibility of further explanation. Labov's innovation began with employing the mathematical term, *variable*, which allowed him to develop the idea of variation as not erratic and unpredictable but as "orderly heterogeneity."

To understand how seemingly random variation can be orderly involves refocusing attention away from the individual example to the rates at which each variant appears over larger stretches of discourse. With sufficient examples – the little snippet above is way too short – proportions of *was* and *were* or instances of r-ful or r-less pronunciations can be calculated. The proportions of each variant can then be correlated with different linguistic contexts, with stylistic conditions, or with individuals or groups of speakers. For example, it would be possible to calculate MalCo's rates of *was* and *were* and compare them to other individuals from similar versus different backgrounds. It is also possible to compare the rates of different social groups or for linguistic factors such as for different grammatical subjects, *we, you,* and *they* or when there is negation (as in *wasn't* versus *weren't*). We can also compare the rates in different styles of speech and writing, with different (types of) interlocutors and so on. In the end, although we cannot predict the motivation for each instance, we can begin to theorize about the factors motivating the usage of *was* versus *were*. Because these rates turn out to be consistent and predictable, the heterogeneity is indeed orderly.

In the case of (was/were) a major social factor is prestige. Linguists sometimes express this evaluation by saying that *we was* is non-standard or vernacular and *we were* is standard. Of course many English speakers who hear *we was* and *we were* would just say that *we was* is incorrect and *we were* is correct, with the same true for *you was/were* and *they was/were*. But for linguists, this kind of condemnation or approval is just data about social prestige or lack of it. In other words, as scientists of language linguists see through the idea of correctness to its social sources and social and linguistic effects. The different forms are ultimately arbitrary, and the justifications given for preferring one form over are *post hoc* and spurious. This dismissal of such rationales, of course, infuriates people invested in the notions of correctness and incorrectness of different linguistic forms. Yet there is nothing to be done; there is no way to study language scientifically and take assertions regarding correctness at face value however widespread and heartfelt they may be or how smart the people who hold them.

A common retort to claims like the one just made is that linguists themselves tend to follow the very rules they ridicule in their own writing and even in most cases their speech. However, linguists are not hypocritical in doing so. More formal registers or styles are marked as formal by mostly following the *prescriptive rules* that are used to determine what is considered "correct," and academic writing is a formal genre. A linguist kickin' it back with some friends will rarely if ever make an effort to follow prescriptive rules; in fact, many prescriptive sticklers do not make much effort in this direction either. There is evidence that Malco was aware of this stratification of use on a stylistic level. I know this because he had been a student of mine a couple of years before I recorded this excerpt, and I am pretty sure he never wrote non-standard *was* in his assignments.

Malco's use of *we was* in speech is not however only a question of speaking casually; it is also related to social identity. *We was* is much more common in the speech of Blacks and Latinos in New York than among Whites or Asians, and MalCo's heritage was mixed African American and Puerto Rican. Moreover, he was also a rap artist, and so a participant in a culture closely identified with those ethnic heritages, and in this case he was talking about rapping to other rap artists, although they may have been his teachers. So his usage of *we was* fits his ethnic background and the context of situation he was in. In fact, it is emblematic of them.

One more point: *we was* appears more frequently in lower socioeconomic status (SES) groups than higher ones, and MalCo was of middle class background. Not surprisingly a low- income classmate of his, Rashid Lewis, a member of the BQ-16, has higher rates of *we was* than MalCo. Note that Rashid was also considered a *thug*, an identity associated with a lifestyle outside the law as in gang membership, selling drugs, and/or being involved in violent crime. MalCo, by contrast, went on to college the following year. Labov's discovery in SSENYC involves exactly this kind of patterning. He was the first to observe that the use of variant forms and the rates of their use tell intricate, subtle, and most importantly revealing stories about language and society.

The point linguists make about appropriate use of forms is therefore subtler and more based in actual usage rather than merely notions like *correct* and *incorrect* can capture; thus the linguists' position is sometimes called *descriptivism*. The use of prescribed forms is, as I implied above, characteristic of the genre of academic writing, which is why I mostly follow them here. One exception is the case of singular *they* as in "a student is concerned with *their* future." This form remains condemned by many prescriptive accounts, but Baranowski (2002) shows it is common in written English, and in my earlier work I argue that avoiding it – as prescriptivists recommend – reduces expressive possibilities (Newman 1997, 1998). So I use singular *they* here.

1.3.2 Appreciating NYCE

More importantly, the issue of prescription is particularly important when discussing a stigmatized variety like NYCE. There are, sadly, New Yorkers who believe that their pronunciations reflect badly on them (Meseck 1992). There are some who even believe that their speech is an obstacle to their professional success and spend considerable sums in an effort to change it (Roberts 2010). Nevertheless, the anti NYCE prescriptions fail the descriptive test just as the prohibition of singular *they* does. It is not hard to find successful New Yorkers from billionaire bankers like Jamie Dimon to politicians like Governor Andrew Cuomo and to entertainers like Regis Philbin and Fran Drescher who regularly use NYCE features. It therefore seems more likely that anyone who blames their New York accent for career disappointments is not addressing the real problem.

The continued presence of supposedly low status forms like those that characterize NYCE can serve a purpose too through what is sometimes called "covert prestige." The notion refers to non-standard forms as tacitly indicative of socially desirable qualities. A New Yorker who uses stigmatized NYCE variants can seem cooler, more down-to-earth, more one of us, and/or tougher than one who does not. In this way, (r-0)s can give elite Wall Streeters an aura of toughness, street smarts, and regular guy status that can work for them businesswise. Similarly, the same features make politicians sound less removed their constituents and so more likely to fill in potholes.

The upshot is that there is no reason to condemn any form or any dialect. To do so in the case of NYCE interferes with appreciation of the dialectal richness of the city and larger dialect region, which, after all, reflects the diversity New Yorkers routinely celebrate. Condemnations blind us to how each glorious NYCE variant echoes a piece of the history and demographics of our fascinating city and region. You cannot fully love New York unless you also love our English!

1.3.3 Comprehending NYCE

I used (*was/were*) and (r) as illustrations of variation because the alternations of forms are so transparent. By contrast, much variation in pronunciation is challenging to display in writing. Our spelling system can represent speech only just well enough to begin to characterize it but not to do so consistently, clearly, or accurately. Although (r) works quite well, the case of (dh) – the first sound in *that* – is not as obvious. If (dh) stretches the limits of traditional orthographic based renditions of sounds, the respective variants of that variable, along with those of its pair (th), break it. Traditionally, the vernacular (dh) and (th) variants are rendered in popular writing through what linguists call *phonetic respelling* as *dat* and *tink* for *that* and *think*. Actually, however, the *d* and *t* are not exactly equivalent to the sounds usually rendered with those letters in standard English. Moreover, there is a common variant intermediate between the standard and the vernacular (called an affricate) that is impossible to phonetically respell. There is no letter or combination that captures the sound, although maybe '*ddh*' and '*tth*' would come closest. Another limitation is that phonetic respelling only works if the reader is already familiar with pronunciation indicated and the relevant respelling convention. 'Tawk,' for example, is often used to represent a characteristically NYCE pronunciation of *talk*. However, 'aw' indicates no special pronunciation in standard orthography. The word *awe* has the same vowel as *talk*, *bought,* and *caught;* if a New Yorker gives a characteristically NYCE spin to one, they invariably do to the others as well. The spelling has nothing to do with it.

Dictionary writers have to render pronunciation graphically, and although their efforts are more systematic than popular phonetic respellings, they do not solve the problem. Take the word *sure,* which varies dialectally even leaving out the question of r-lessness, and for which standard spelling is a poor guide to any pronunciation. The *American Heritage Dictionary* provides *shŏor* and *shûr* as possible variants and *Merriam-Webster's* has "\ˈshủr, especially Southern ˈshȯr\." To make sense of these renditions requires consulting the dictionary's pronunciation key because each set of conventions is specific to that dictionary, and none is readily transparent. In fact, only after some digging does it become apparent that American Heritage's first variant and Merriam Webster's second are actually entirely different pronunciations. Each dictionary leaves out one of the pronunciations given by the other!

The on-line *Wiktionary* (http://www.wiktionary.org), by contrast, uses symbols from the International Phonetic Alphabet (IPA), the most widely used system for representing pronunciation graphically. For what linguists call *phonemic transcription* IPA symbols are placed between slashes. As of June 2013 the Wiktionary provides /ʃʊɹ/, /ʃɔɹ/, and /ʃɝ/ as the "General American" (i.e., r-ful) pronunciations for *sure.* This entry makes clear the upside of the open-source wiki principle since the three variants cover all those found in the two dictionaries. However, it also shows the downside of IPA. Unless a reader has learned it, symbols like ʃ, ʊ, ɔ, ɝ, and ɹ are awfully obscure. For many people, the sight of a bunch of unfamiliar symbols like these causes instant shut down.

Fortunately, most words do not require as many unusual symbols as *sure.* Many IPA symbols reflect common English pronunciations associated with the respective letters. For example, *so* is transcribed as /so/ and *zoo* is /zu/. Also phonemic notation allows some wiggle room, and I will use /r/ to represent the (r-1) variant in *sure:* /ʃʊr/ in my pronunciation. It should be obvious (since readers already know how the word is pronounced) that the IPA symbol /ʃ/ stands for the sound normally represented by 'sh' in spelling. The convention just needs to be remembered, like learning how ñ is pronounced in Spanish. Finally, IPA guides are available on line, including with sound files attached.[4]

---

4 For more information on IPA, the Wikipedia entry is a good place to start (http://en.wikipedia.org/wiki/International_Phonetic_Alphabet). An interactive site that allows the reader to hear the sounds associated with each symbol is also available at (http://www.phonetics.ucla.edu/course/chapter1/chapter1.html). Also, the International Phonetic Association has an excellent site, with all the relevant information at http://www.langsci.ucl.ac.uk/ipa/ipachart.html.

Like other books in this series, I employ IPA in phonemic transcription mainly for consonants because for vowels a more transparent form of representing pronunciation exists via the *lexical sets* or *keywords* developed by Wells (1982). Wells established 24 sets, each of which represents the vowel sound used in that word across most dialects of English. For the Wiktionary's three pronunciations for *sure*, the keywords are CURE, NORTH or FORCE, and NURSE respectively; NORTH and FORCE contain the same vowel sound in most varieties of American English including NYCE. As in the examples, Wells' keywords are traditionally written in SMALL CAPS. Nevertheless, also as in other books in the series, I will provide phonetic respellings indicated by single quotes (e.g., 'singl kwotes') whenever feasible, although this is not always the case.

Another obstacle to understanding pronunciation is more conceptual in nature. It involves distinguishing between phonology and phonetics. Phonology studies the sound system; how sounds are organized. This includes how many phonemes there are and how they are permitted to go together. Phonetics is the physical side of sounds; for example how similarly different vowels and consonant sound to each other and how they are produced. IPA is also used for phonetic distinctions – it is the International *Phonetic* Alphabet – and phonetic transcription is indicated by placing symbols not between slashes but square brackets []. To see the difference, I can write /r/ for all the General American r-ful pronunciations of *sure* because I am indicating whatever the differences, they all count as the same sound. It is much the same as how <a>, <*a*> and <A> count as the same letter even though they are actually quite different shapes. I cannot do the same when I am transcribing phonetically because those picky details are the point. It must be [ʃʊɹ], [ʃɔɹ], and [ʃɝ], with only the first two really having a consonant and the last having the "r-colored" vowel NURSE. The symbol [r], by the way, is reserved for the rolled Spanish or Scottish /r/. These differences will appear along with related details such as how the sounds are produced and acoustic similarities and differences between them in Chapter 3, which highlights NYCE pronunciation

You do not need to learn IPA or master the difference between phonetics and phonology to follow much of Chapter 3, although the understanding will be deeper if you do. For readers who have difficulty, I suggest simply skipping over the parts that are confusing or referring to resources in footnote 4. How deep you go depends entirely on how much you want or need to know.

2 Geography demography and cultural factors

2.1 The New York City Dialect Region

The *Atlas of North American English* (Labov, Ash, and Boberg 2006) shows the New York Dialect Region as comprising the central portion of the New York City Metropolitan area, all of which is shown in Figure 2.1:

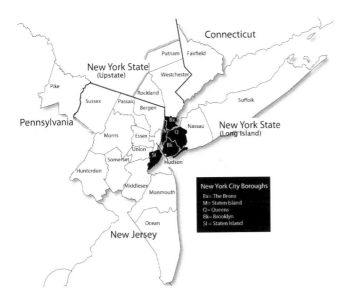

Figure 2.1: The NY Metro Area, black lines=state borders, gray lines =county borders, white lines in black background=NYC borough borders[1]

By contrast, the dialect regions associated with many other East Coast cities such as Boston, Philadelphia, and even Richmond, Virginia extend well beyond their metropolitan areas. As Labov, et al. (2006: 232) put it: "One of the most startling facts about New York City is the narrow extent of its influence in the surrounding area." The reasons for this lack of regional influence are mysterious, but Labov, et al. (2006: 233) cite an unpublished paper by the dialectologist Raven McDavid as claiming that the limits coincide "with the limits of the occupation" of New York City by "British troops in the war of 1812." The claim (which actually should

---

1 The Metropolitan Area as defined by the 2010 Census plus Fairfield County, which although not included by the Census is commonly assumed to be part of the region.

have been to the Revolutionary War) could only reasonably be accurate with regards to the western border and probably had little or nothing to do with troop positions directly. Selesky (2006: 796–797) locates the northern limit of British presence in the southern Bronx, which is well within the dialect region and the southern one from the Amboys to New Brunswick, which are outside it. The case of Long Island to the east is unclear. The western limits to British occupation and the dialect region border line up with the Hackensack River Valley. Much of the valley actually coincides with the Meadowlands, an extensive area of swamps that form a natural barrier to this day, as anyone who has driven west from the Holland or Lincoln tunnels can attest.

Looked at more closely the dialect border turns out to be not as abrupt as the above depiction might make it appear at first but follows a dialect transition pattern – i.e., a gradual change in features – commonly found in long settled areas. Cohen (1970: 86) looks at the distribution of one representative character-istic of the traditional NYCE dialect: the complex feature called the *short-A split* Gordon (2004). This feature – discussed in detail in Chapter 3 – refers to the fact that words like *cab, (tin) can, bath, pan, tram* are pronounced in traditional NYCE differently than words like *cap, (yes, I) can, bat, pang, trap,* and *am.* The pronun-ciation of the 'a' in first set is called *tense* and that in the second *lax.* By contrast farther west, both *cans, pan, tram, am,* and *pang* are tense and *cab, bath, bat, trap,* and *cap* are lax; because tense vowels are limited to before the nasal conso-nants: /n//m/ and /ŋ/, this pattern is called *the nasal short-A system.*

Cohen found patterns of short-A usage in New Jersey could be divided into "three roughly north-south strips." In the one closest to the city (i.e., east of the Hackensack Valley) the tense vs. lax words are identical to New York. In the one farthest away, the nasal system is used. The central strip shows a mixed pattern. At some point before arriving at the nasal system – in Passaic County – the dialect also becomes r-ful (Labov 2001, Coye 2009). Similar transition patterns are found by Coye's (2009) self-report surveys taken by high school students around New Jersey. To mention just one well-known feature, Coye found that the word *hero* for baguette sandwiches clustered only quite close to the city, whereas others, such as the classic NYCE pronunciation of THOUGHT 'thawt', expanded further west and south. Figure 2.2 illustrates this transition by overlaying two data sets on one map. Cohen's (1970) three strips, are indicated by lines called isoglosses in dialect geography – in this case dashed – with the rightmost one at the Hackensack river. Black circles are towns where NYCE-like short-A systems are found, the gray ones hybrid patterns, and the circles with crosses reveal the nasal pattern. The second data set shows results of a web-based survey I conducted in 2010 on baguette sandwich names. Filled stars mostly on the east side of the solid isogloss show delis, restaurants, and pizza places with *hero* as the term for this kind of sand-

2011 Sandwich Names and 1970 Cohen Short-a Data

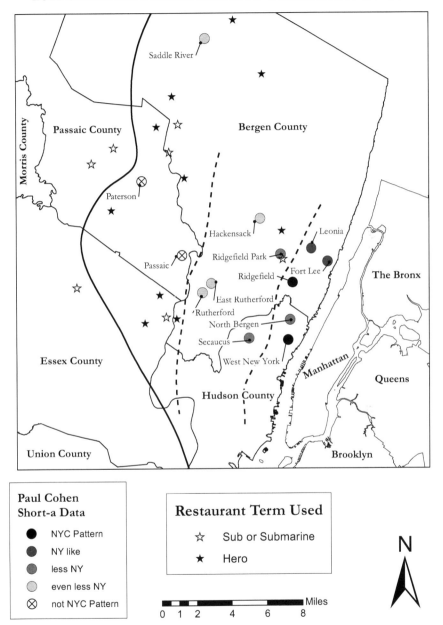

Figure 2.2: Dialect Map of Cohen's (1970) strips and 2010 survey of baguette sandwich terms.

wich in their menus and signs. To the west and south of that line are found mainly empty stars showing places with *sub* or *submarine,* the most common American name in their menus. Note that a few exceptions can be found too, but this is typical of dialect transitions. The sandwich isogloss is farther away from the city than the short-A pattern. Yet the data sets agree on a rapid transition away from NYCE.

The other limits of NYCE are less well studied. Thomas (1947: 30) places the eastern border at the Nassau-Suffolk County line on Long Island in Figure 2.1. At first glance this claim seems plausible; the Dutch versus English names of the counties reflect different colonial roots. Eastern Long Island was settled mainly from Connecticut and retains a cultural and dialectal identification with New England to this day (Bakht 2010, Olivo 2013). By contrast, western Long Island was part of New Netherlands along with the city. However, looked at more closely, it seems doubtful that the current county line ever approximated the dialect border. For one thing, the political line has shifted east (Shorto 2004, Strong 2011 cited in Olivo 2013: 44); for another, even under Dutch administration, some settlers were from New England (Scheltema & Westerhuijs 2011). In any case, since Thomas's writing NYCE speakers have moved eastward in such large numbers that western and central Suffolk County now appears dominated by them (Olivo 2013). Also, some former New Yorkers and inner suburbanites moved into a patchwork of exurban developments farther east, and these communities remain surrounded by speakers of the autochthonous dialect.[2] Therefore, it seems unlikely that any coherent dialect boundaries can be established.

To the north, Thomas describes the presuburban dialect of Westchester and Rockland Counties as transitional with what he calls "Upstate," but this claim is also problematic. *Upstate New York* usually refers to the entire state north of the metropolitan area, and this includes at least two major dialect areas as shown in Figure 2.3.

Dinkin (2010), who investigates Hudson Valley English, has his southern-most research site at Poughkeepsie, which leaves the area between there and the city unexplored. Still, Thomas's observation about a transitional zone is not unmotivated. Pederson (2001) considers the Hudson Valley as closest to NYCE dialectologically. Similarly, Labov (2007), Dinkin and Freisner (2009), and Dinkin

---

2 A childhood friend of mine – a NYCE speaker – spent his adolescence mainly with other former city and inner suburb dwellers in Lake Panemoka eleven miles west of where the island
splits into two forks. The area was developed in the 1960s and is still surrounded by farmland
and woods, where many descendants of long time inhabitants of eastern Long Island still live.
This recording of a teacher provides an example of their speech, clearly not NYCE: http://www.
youtube.com/watch?v=gqxCDqNpgvI.

Figure 2.3: Regional situation of NY Metro Area with traditional dialect regions indicated.

(2010) discuss the short-A split as having diffused into that dialect region. This link with NYCE is also supported by a number of dialectologists (Kurath 1949, Romaine 2001) who mention long-standing commonalities in lexicon. These linguistic connections follow from the tight demographic, political, and commercial links that the Hudson Valley has maintained with the city since Dutch settlement.

This transition is symptomatic of a larger regional pattern by which NYCE is in some ways transitional between northern dialects like Eastern New England, Western New England, and the Hudson Valley and the Mid-Atlantic. The producers of the major 20th century dialect atlas of American English, Kurath and McDavid (1961) emphasize lexical commonalities and consider NYCE Northern. By contrast, the *Atlas of North American English* (Labov, et al. 2006) produced 40 years later emphasizes its connections with the Mid-Atlantic through similarities in vowel systems. Despite these commonalities, the New York Dialect Region has its own character and identity (Gordon 2004).

Although small, the region is certainly populous. The 2010 US Census gives the population of New York City at 8,175,133. Nassau County, which is entirely within the dialect region, adds 1,339,532. The remaining counties are only partly inside. They include Suffolk (1,493,350), Westchester (949,113), and Rockland (311,687) in New York State and Hudson (905,113) and Bergen (905,116) in New Jersey.[3] Since the greatest population densities in these counties lie close to the city, it seems safe to say that over 11,000,000 people live in the NYC dialect region.

Specifying where people speak NYCE is important to dialectologists, but popular attention lies more in how New Yorkers' English may vary within the region. A humorous YouTube video featuring a native New Yorker giving impressions of the supposed accent of each of the five boroughs that compose the city received nearly half a million views in four years. This video (McNally 2009) reflects a widespread belief that not only does the accent vary by borough but that there are different accents for the NYCE speaking parts of New Jersey and Long Island. New Yorkers often speak of a Bronx accent, a Long Island accent, or a Brooklyn accent as if differences between these areas were the stuff of common knowledge. Urban legend even has it that certain particularly sensitive Gotham Henry Higginses can specify a speaker's origins down to the block they grew up on.

Some differences are indisputable. For example, the pronunciation of the first syllable of Schermerhorn Street as [skɪm] ('skim') is limited to those familiar with Downtown Brooklyn where it is located. The Dutch name provokes mostly puzzlement elsewhere, not that anyone's version approaches anything like an actual Dutch pronunciation. More systematically, Johnson (2010) reports that more teenagers from Queens perceive LOT and THOUGHT (i.e., the vowels in *cot* and *caught*) to be the same – thus the disappearance of one of the most emblematic NYCE features – than those from Brooklyn and other boroughs. Nevertheless, Labov (2001: 226–227) asserts that this kind of difference is really class and ethnic based:

> No empirical studies have been carried out in and across the borough of Brooklyn to determine whether there is a *Brooklynese* distinct from the speech of other boroughs. Every feature attributed to this local dialect corresponds to the features of working class New York City speech as described in the literature with no reference to Brooklyn.

Labov is not claiming that New Yorkers all speak alike regardless of where they live. Johnson's data, for example, shows that there is variation. Furthermore, it seems indisputable that certain local features tend to be diminishing much more rapidly in core areas like Manhattan and nearby neighborhoods in Brooklyn – so called *Brownstone Brooklyn* – than in more peripheral communities. By contrast, forms traditionally associated with "Brooklynese" appear most densely in the

---

3 Labov, et al. (2006) found that Newark, in Essex County, also had NYCE features.

speech of New Yorkers from certain specific neighborhoods. These include Howard Beach in Queens, Gerritsen Beach in Brooklyn, Country Club in the Bronx, along with much of Staten Island and parts of Long Island.

The contrast, however, involves demographic changes that have largely changed the population makeup in much of the core of the city. Olivo (2013: 106) cites one Long Islander whose awareness of these changes creates in his mind a hierarchy of authenticity based on culture, ancestry, and language primarily and that is only secondarily geographic:

> SM: When people say New Yorkers now, Manhattanites, I think of people that grew up in Idaho, [that] get an apartment in New York, and think they're New Yorkers.... They're not New Yorkers. (...) Like I always say, when people wanna know what ethnic New York was like, you come to Long Island because you have, the true New York accents, it's the Italians, Polish, German, Irish, now Puerto Ricans.

2.2 Social Class and Prestige

As discussed in Chapter 1, Labov's great innovation in SSENYC consisted in creating a workable theory that explained variation as principled and orderly mainly by showing that it followed clear predictable patterns in terms of social stratification. That stratification was defined stylistically by attention to speech and demographically through social class. Class, in turn, is generally understood as a person or type of person's position of status in a society. That status is, however, notoriously hard to determine. For example, although no one would dispute that income is a key factor, it is not the only one. Compare, for instance, a teacher versus a plumber. The plumber might have the higher income, although plumbing is typically considered a working class occupation whereas teaching is usually considered middle class.

In SSENYC, Labov took advantage of a three-factor index developed for a sociological study that his participants had already been involved in to assign them to different social classes. The index included family income, education, and occupation with points assigned on each dimension. Becker (2010) partially replicated Labov's study two generations later. In the absence of a prior study to piggyback on, she had to develop her own way of organizing her participants by social class. Becker developed her own index that like Labov's included education and occupation, but she replaced income (which is difficult to ask about) with housing. It is worth examining how points were allotted in Becker's housing component because it provides a window into how housing is stratified in New York:

1   = low-income public housing
2   = renter of some type of rent-controlled housing
3   = middle-income public housing
4   = renter of market-rate housing
5   = owner, but grandfathered in to ownership
6   = owner of a market-rate apartment (from Becker 2010: 76)

Becker also tweaked the rest of her index with some important peculiarities of class in New York. For example, she raises the score of graduates of selective public schools over non-selective schools putting them at the level of similar private schools. Becker's study, like Labov's, was limited to the LES. However, a study involving more than one neighborhood would certainly add neighborhood or suburban town as a factor too. However, the neighborhoods would in many cases assign very different index scores in the 2000s than the 1960s!

In the 1960s, although the LES included low-income to upper middle class people, the lower end predominated. In Manhattan, really only the Upper East Side – particularly that part near Central Park and between 60th and 79th Streets, and up 5th Avenue – along with far eastern parts of Midtown were predominantly elite. Surrounding those areas were middle to upper middle class communities. Also, there were well-off neighborhoods in the outer boroughs such as Forest Hills, Douglaston Manor, and Jamaica Estates in Queens, Riverdale in the Bronx, Brooklyn Heights and parts of Flatbush in Brooklyn, and Todt Hill in Staten Island. However, probably, the bulk of the region's upper and upper middle classes could be found in suburbs such as Scarsdale or Larchmont in Westchester and along the north shore of Long Island and parts of New Jersey. Other large swaths of the city and suburbs were predominantly lower middle to upper middle class. Working class to low income New Yorkers – mostly but not entirely Black and Puerto Rican – lived in northern Brooklyn, Harlem, and scattered areas of Queens and the south Bronx.

This pattern has changed radically over the subsequent generations particularly in Manhattan and nearby areas of Brooklyn. The Black and Latino areas first expanded then contracted and became somewhat less segregated at least in certain cases. Many once working-class areas, including the LES, have become increasingly out of reach to those with moderate incomes of whatever race as mostly White transplants moved in. Those recent changes and the tensions they cause form the social and linguistic context of Becker's studies in the area.

Theoretically, there have also been changes in the way class is approached. Becker was partially replicating Labov's 1960s study, so she took an old-fashioned approach to achieve comparability. Nevertheless, most recent variationist research looks at class in a less rigid way. Eckert (1988), for instance, showed that speech can reflect class trajectory and aspiration more than origin particularly for adolescents. After all, high school students who are successful academically and plan to go to college are at least constructing middle class futures whatever their background. Trajectory-related effects on variation were actually already implicit in Labov et al.'s (1968a) Harlem study. That study shows that speakers' use of vernacular linguistic forms track with their social acceptance in mainstream Black working class peer culture and correlate inversely with school engagement and so social mobility.

Rashid Lewis, the most vernacular BQ-16 participant, who was a reputed gang member and drug dealer, provides an example of someone who is clearly aware of being on a trajectory that has kept him and will keep him thoroughly marginalized. He expresses those expectations this way: "I am only 18 and I almost done been through it all. This was the game that was left for me to play, and I gotta play it. It's gonna be bad, namean [=know what I mean]." By contrast, another Black BQ-16 participant Darryl Hanson, who was a rap artist, saw himself on a different track. When asked whether his imagined future included rap, he stated the following:

> Darryl: I ain't gonna be no broke ass rapper. Ain't gonna be none of that. Ain't gonna be none of that. Either I'm makin' some cheese, or I'm just getting a straight job. By then, if I'm not making money off my music, I'll probably still do it, but it ain't gonna be like number one in my life, ... be like some hobby type shit. Yo, I can't be making music and be broke, starvin'. That is not happening. That don't work for me. Ends gotta meet. I don't want ends just to meet; I want my ends overlappin'.

In fact, Darryl would go on to be accepted at and graduate from a prestigious state university, the first in his family to go to college. Evidently, although he maintains nonstandard AAE in the interview, he had control of standard registers when he needed them. Yet as will be shown the next chapter, even at his most vernacular he was less non-standard than Rashid.

2.3 A City of Immigrants

New York, of course, has famously always been a city of immigrants and it is possible to divide the various historical influxes that made it so into seven groups based on chronology, demographics, and points of origin:
– New Amsterdam settlers: A mix of mainly Dutch, Huguenots, Walloons, Germans, Sephardic Jews, English, and Africans who arrived from the 1620s to 1660s when Dutch was the language of administration.

- British colonial and postcolonial settlers: Predominantly English speakers from southern and midlands of England but with other British and Germans included.
- Pre-1924 immigrants: Primarily Europeans including Germans, Irish, Italians, and Jews and other Eastern Europeans who arrived from the mid 19th Century to the cutoff caused by the 1921 and 1924 Immigration Acts.
- The Great Migration: African Americans mostly arriving from the Carolinas and Georgia from the early 20th Century to just after WWII.
- La Gran Migración: Puerto Ricans who arrived largely from 1930s to the 1960s.
- Post-1965 Immigrants: Groups who came from all over the world after the 1965 Immigration Act reopened large-scale immigration.
- Transplants: Mostly White professional class migrants from all over the US who have come to the city in increasing numbers in recent years.

The first two groups are the ancestors of only a sliver of the current population of New Yorkers. The largest group is now comprised of Post-1965 Immigrants (Kasinitz, et al. 2008: 66) and their descendants, as mentioned in Chapter 1. Their arrival has had led to an enormous increase in the racial diversity of the region. This impact can be appreciated in Figure 2.4, which shows the racial distribution for 1970, just as this migration was getting underway, and 2010 for the city and Nassau County. That county was chosen as representative of the suburbs because it is located entirely within the Dialect Region.

The total number of residents has changed little over the four decades – with Nassau losing a small portion and the city gaining some – but both juris-dictions move towards greater diversity albeit with Nassau lagging considerably. The demographic churn is actually greater than it appears in the chart. Although

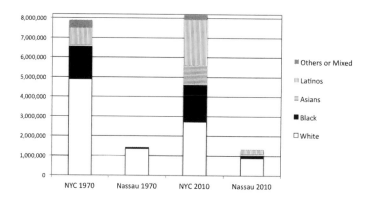

Figure 2.4: Census Data on racial diversity in NYC and Nassau County in 1970 and 2010

there is little change in the proportion of Blacks, the composition of this group has altered with Great Migration African Americans leaving and other African diaspora groups arriving. Whites diminish in both jurisdictions, but European immigration and transplant arrivals mask a portion of the outflow of pre-1924 immigrants. The effect of immigration is most visible in way that the proportion of Latinos more than doubles in the city and emerges as significant minority in Nassau. Also, Asians emerge as a significant category in 2010, although only in the city.

The loss of White pre-1924 immigrants actually began in the 1950s if not earlier, and it is often termed "White Flight." A personal anecdote can illustrate some of the causes. Even though I was only a child growing up in the Queens neighborhood of Jackson Heights in the 1960s, I witnessed a great deal of anxiety surrounding race and community. There was a tension between an ideal of a stable racially mixed community expressed by adults who closely followed the civil rights struggles occurring at the time, and their simultaneous belief that such a result was impractical in our neighborhood. There was also tension within the White group between overt racists and those who felt racism was wrong, although as the previous sentence implies it is obvious looking back that they too were struggling with prejudice. The contradiction revolved around the assumption that an influx of minorities – particularly Blacks – would lead to wholesale community degradation and especially decline in school quality. The cliché image of the time was the White person who justifies opposing Blacks' moving into their neighborhood because of worries about property values and then denying any personal prejudice. Perhaps, "some of their best friends," were, so they claimed, Black.

Fears of neighborhood degradation were certainly victim blaming and at best self-fulfilling, but they were increasingly bolstered by visible urban decay. The South Bronx was the largest area in New York to undergo socioeconomic degradation and to suffer it most extensively. The area began the 1960s largely as the domain mainly of working to upper middle class pre-1924 immigrants and their descendants. Over the years, it shifted first to upwardly mobile African Americans and Puerto Ricans and then to successively lower income groups of the same ethnic origins. These movements accompanied by institutional racism and economic marginalization led to a spiral of decline of schools, infrastructure, and housing. Many buildings were burned for insurance money after they ceased to be productive income sources for landlords. The eventual result was announced to the nation in what became an iconic phrase uttered in 1977 by sportscaster Howard Cosell during the baseball World Series at Yankee Stadium in the southwestern part of that borough. When scenes of a nearby fire intruded upon a game, Cosell announced, "Ladies and Gentlemen, the Bronx is burning."

The southern Bronxites reacted to the destruction with more vitality and creative energy than could be appreciated farther downtown. What came to be called "the Boogie-Down Bronx" was the place that gave birth to Hip-Hop at just about this time. Finally, about the late 1980s, coinciding with the spread of that great Bronx cultural innovation around the world, a substantial reversal of the demographic flows began. Former suburbanites or their children looking for a more urban lifestyle and lower property taxes began to come to the city in every increasing numbers, as they continue to do. Transplants, who resemble the suburbanites racially and socioeconomically, also came for the New York life or economic opportunities. These twin influxes gave rise to *gentrification,* a term that had been coined to describe a similar population change in London. As in London, well-off newcomers concentrated in central areas of the city, in many cases displacing lower-income residents. Effects on the southern Bronx were delayed and indirect as New Yorkers moved from increasingly expensive more stable neighborhoods to cheaper more marginal ones. Also, the city began to support development through direct investment and by supporting the work of local groups and *urban homesteaders* – individuals whose *sweat equity* gave them title to decrepit property they rehabilitated.

The dialectal effects of gentrification include a pattern of hollowing out, i.e., the loss of NYCE features in affected core areas. Not surprisingly a similar pattern has been reported for London English (e.g., Fox 2007, Torgersen, Kerswill, & Fox 2006) under the name *deregionalization.* At the same time, immigrants have continued to arrive and had children further diversifying the city and increasing its population and helping rehabilitate blighted areas. The Bronx remains the second poorest county in New York State, but it has recovered considerably since the days of Howard Cosell.

2.4 Racial and Ethnic Identities

It will be clear in the course of this book that race provides the most significant factor in the dialectal diversity of NYCE as in other areas of the US. Not coincidentally, it is also, by far, the most problematic demographic factor in the country's history and present. Finally, it is impossible to entirely disentangle from class, and in different ways other macrosocial categories, such as gender, and affiliative ones like religions, professions, and subculture. Although, a comprehensive account of race in New York is well beyond the scope of this book, it is impossible to understand NYCE without a relatively extensive discussion.

2.4.1 Racial nomenclature

The terms used to refer to racial categories are historically changeable, invariably controversial, and ultimately unsatisfactory. So even before delving into the question of what race is, what it means, and how it affects NYCE, I will justify the ones I choose. The criteria are first of all clarity of reference and then a combination of continuity with other academic treatments, predominant naming practices in the community, and my own preferences. I apologize in advance to those who are unhappy with how they are referred to. My only defense is that their preferred alternatives would inevitably produce negative responses from others.

I use *Black* for groups that orient to an African diaspora identity, including (1) African immigrants and their offspring, (2) African descendants from the Caribbean basin who identify as West Indians, (3) Haitians, and (4) African Americans. This last term is reserved for American slave descendants following Baugh (1999) and Becker (2010).[4] Descendants of Latin Americans with phenotype (i.e., body characteristics) indicative of African ancestry are not included for reasons to be given later.

White is used for people who trace their family roots to Europe. In some academic treatments, *European American* is used for this group, but I do not use it here because it appears to parallel *African American*, which refers only to *some* Blacks. A competing academic term *Anglo* is not usual in New York because it is taken by many New Yorkers as implying British heritage, which clashes with their typically more recent immigrant roots. I personally find it difficult to reconcile with my identity as a Jew. *Caucasian* is, by contrast, widely heard in public and in the press, but it has a euphemistic quality and disreputable origin in biologistic 19th Century "scientific racism" (e.g., Coon 1939/1962). I personally cannot get beyond my discomfort with these origins and again avoid it.

East Asian is used to refer to individuals whose origins lie within the pentagon from Japan, Tibet, Burma, Indonesia and the Philippines. *South Asian* means those from the Indian subcontinent, India, Pakistan, Bangladesh, Sri Lanka, and potentially Afghanistan. Of course, the cover term *Asian* encompasses both groups, although in North American usage it often refers only to East Asians. This ambiguity will be addressed in more detail later.

Even given the general difficulties surrounding racial terms, those used to describe people from Latin America are notoriously controversial and politicized (Kasinitz, et al. 2008). *Latino* overwhelmingly dominates academic treatments, and for that reason it is adopted here, but in daily conversation *Hispanic* tends to

---

4 Many people of this origin also claim Native American descent in New York.

alternate with *Spanish* in New York. *Spanish* suffers from the fatal flaw of having a standard reference to people from Spain, but *Latino* has a number of drawbacks. One is the sometimes-strong preference of many New Yorkers of that background for *Hispanic*. Also, *Latino* is ambiguous about the status of Brazilians, who, after all, consider themselves Latin Americans but who share a different linguistic and colonial heritage.

Unfortunately, this dicing and slicing leaves out many New Yorkers, including Middle Easterners and Western and Central Asians, who are rarely if ever considered Asians in New York. Their English, along with that of people of mixed backgrounds, South Asians, and non-Chinese and Korean East Asians has rarely if ever been the subject of sociolinguistic research in New York. I hope their absence represents more of a stimulus for research than a cause for offense.

2.4.2 Defining race

Fought (2006) in a study devoted to the intersection of language and ethnicity explicitly declines to define *race* implying that doing so would cause more confusion than clarity. However, researchers in other fields have attempted definitions, all on the basis of the axiom that race is a social construction. Their interest lies in understanding why that construction takes the forms it does.

A common approach taken by anthropologists (e.g., Sanjek 1996), sociologists (e.g., Omi & Winant 1994) and historians (Painter 2010) is to anchor race in historical experience. This history is crucial because, as Omi and Winant (1994:53) observe, "the racial legacies of the past – slavery and bigotry – continue to shape the present." So powerful are they that race remains "a fundamental axis of social organization in the US" (Omi & Winant 1994: 13).

To understand race, Omi and Winant develop what they call "Racial Formation Theory." On this account race serves as a vehicle for often competing "projects," which use it for specific purposes. Because these projects differ, they instantiate different definitions of race; because they compete, these different definitions are also in competition. There is, however, a common thread through the various definitions, they claim: a grounding of social differences through reference to differences in the human body.

In earlier times a "biologistic and social Darwinist" (Omi & Winant 1994:12) definition that conflated racial groups with different species or perhaps animal breeds was used to undergird a rigid social hierarchy. This conflation of human and animal differences is useful for that project because it naturalizes the hierarchy via purported innate endowments. As Painter (2010: xi) explains "Work plays an essential part in race talk because people who do the work are likely to be figured as inherently deserving of the toil and poverty of laboring status." Those essentialist views were challenged in the 1920s and ultimately dethroned from dominance, although they linger on in sporadic strained efforts to find genetic sources for mean differences on such cultural artifacts as IQ tests.

Omi and Winant contend that the biologistic project was mostly replaced by understandings that assimilated race to ethnicity. This project downplays phenotype differences without challenging the basic reference to the human body as constitutive of race. In other words, groups like Whites, Blacks or Native Americans may be racially differentiated because of appearance and ancestry. However by seeing race as a form of ethnicity, supporters of this view consider those differences to be superficial. There is no essential difference, they argue, between Blacks and Whites than, say, between German Americans, Anglo-Saxons, Jews, Italians, or Irish. On the one hand, this definition has the virtue of supporting equal civil rights for all. But on the other hand, it promotes the notion that racialized groups can and should assimilate and advance in the melting pot pattern ascribed ideologically at least to pre-1924 immigrants. The ultimate effect is to blame social stagnation on the members of groups who can be accused of refusing to assimilate and clinging to cultures purportedly not compatible with American middle-class norms. Omi and Winant argue that although this view has been challenged by those who see races more in terms of class differences or national ones, the conflation of race to ethnicity still dominates our discourse on the subject.

Racial Formation Theory impels researchers to accept both a degree of ill-definition and circularity in the notion of race. In other words, a race is whatever is considered a race by social consensus, and it is only a race to the degree to which that consensus exists. Although race may appear to be naturalistic and permanent, this is an illusion; the history of changing racial assignments actually shows it to be quite changeable. To take one group, Brodkin (1999) describes how Jews were considered White in pre-Civil War America but had that status questioned during the periods of increasing xenophobia around the turn of the 20th Century (see also Bonfiglio 2002). Then, after the holocaust made anti-Semitism unacceptable, a consensus about Jewish Whiteness returned. Yet I can attest to some surprisingly spirited discussions in my ninth grade social studies class in UAA (the school I worked at, see p. 6) about whether Jews should be considered White. It should be said that non-White status was seen as positive by these mostly Latino and Black teenagers. A claim that Jews are not White may reflect an understanding regarding similar historical experiences of oppression or marginalization or perhaps just sympathy with individual Jews.

2.4.3 How New Yorkers define race

To show my students the complexities involved in defining race, I have been conducting in-class anonymous surveys and holding follow-up discussions as reflective learning tasks for a number of years. The objective is for students to see just how emergent, varied, and ill-defined racial categories are, and that their classmates may or may not agree with their own constructions of what constitutes a race. Although the wording of the task has changed over the years – rendering the results not comparable – I gave a single version over three semesters from 2010 to 2011, and the results of these provide a window on what New Yorkers think of as races. After all, if race is truly a social construction, the only way to find out what constitutes a race is to ask members of the society doing the defining.

That version of the survey asked 85 undergraduates of various majors and 25 graduate students in an education program were to anonymously list what they thought were "all the groups New Yorkers consider the races that exist in the city and metropolitan area." The undergraduates highly diverse and tended to be from the city whereas the graduates were mostly from Long Island and were predominantly White. Yet the results were essentially the same, and they are aggregated here. Figure 2.5 shows all groups receiving more than two mentions.

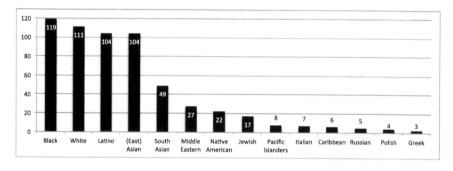

Figure 2.5: Number of mentions greater than two of "races" in open-ended survey.

Four groups appear by a dominant consensus ranging from almost 99 % to 87 % rate of being mentioned.[5] However, a major breakdown in the consensus involves

---

5 A similar four-racial composite of New York appears in the *New York Times* as a successful entry in a contest for New Yorkers' personal subway maps. Drawing on Census data, the artist (O'Hare 2010) drew the subway as connecting neighborhoods largely segregated by these four groups, each illustrated by dark brown, lighter brown, pink, and yellow faces for Blacks, Latinos,

East and South Asians. Half the students named this group as a unitary racial category, mainly using the term *Asian*. A small minority, however, provided other names such as *Koreans and Chinese*, just *Chinese*, or *Asians and Pacific Islanders*, a phrase probably picked up from official forms or the US Census. The other half also provided a separate category for South Asians, although the main name here was *Indians*, with *Indians, Pakistanis, Bangladeshis*; *Hindus* (a probable calque from Spanish); and *South Asians* also appearing. Of course, it is unknown how many of the students positing a single Asian racial group meant to include South Asians within it and how many simply did not think of South Asians, erasing them completely. The high proportion of these non-mentions is curious given the notable presence of South Asian diaspora students at Queens College.

Another omission affects those whose origins lie in North Africa and the Middle East, who are also present although in smaller numbers at Queens College. This group was identified by only about 20 % and was described in terms of two highly inappropriate names by all but four students. The most common misnomer was *Muslim*, which is of course a religious reference. The other was *Arab*, which excludes Iranians, Kurds, Israeli Jews, and Turks, all of whom are at least potentially considered Middle Easterners. This category is closely followed in number of mentions by Native Americans. Their low number almost certainly follows from their small demographic presence in the city.

Following are four groups mentioned by small minorities of students; the Jewish group's relatively larger number is likely a product of class composition. The survey was anonymous, but the class with the largest number of Orthodox Jews returned the highest rates of identifications of Jews as a race. These smaller groups and the rare mention of nationalities such as Korean and regional ones like West Indians – both with only two mentions and so not shown – reveal that some of the students conflated race with ethnic, national, or regional origins.

The partial mixing of South and East Asians into a single racial category diverges from Omi and Winant's reliance on appeals to the body as determinative of racial status in the US, and the status of Latinos presents further counterexamples. Latin Americans, like North Americans, Haitians, and West Indians have historical experiences of conquest, colonialism, slavery, and cultural syncretism. Like people from those other areas Latin Americans descend from indigenous communities, Europeans, Africans, or various mixtures of all three. Of course, there are also differences in the nature of the historical experiences and proportions of group origins and particularly the relationships between the various groups. For example, in many Latin American countries particularly in South

---

Whites, and Asians respectively. The following link, accessed May 5, 2014, is to O'Hare's personal page: http://www.kmohare.com/drawing.html, where the map appears under "maps."

America and Mesoamerica the nominally mixed White-Indigenous *Mestizo* identity constitutes the majority. In others, particularly the Caribbean, that place is taken by an again sometimes nominal Black-White mixture that goes by various names.

What is important is that race plays out quite differently in Latin America than it does in North America. One result of this difference is a clash regarding the treatment of Latinos on the 2000 US Census detailed by a Kasinitz, et al. (2008). On the Census form, Latinos were expected to indicate "Hispanic Heritage" and then also identify as a member of traditional US racial group such as Black or White. Kasinitz, et al. report that many New York Latinos felt that they should be considered a race of their own, and Figure 2.5 suggests that this construction is widely accepted by New Yorkers.

Sociolinguists have generally taken two approaches to Latinos' discrepancy from traditional US racial categorization. Bailey (2000a, 2000b, 2002) and Toribio (2000, 2003) discuss issues facing second-generation Dominican immigrants with visible African ancestry. Their focus is on their participants' use of Spanish to resist efforts by non-Latinos to categorize them as Black. They also point out the historical roots in the Dominican Republic for this desire in good part in contradistinction to Haitians.

Urciuoli (1996), Zentella (1997), and Mendoza-Denton (2008), by contrast, locate the reluctance to fit into US racial categories in terms of the fine-grained construction of race that predominates in Latin America. They point out how Latin American racial assignment is bound up with cultural allegiances and corresponding indexes of those allegiances. In many Latin American countries it is possible, for example, for someone to be born and raised indigenous but by shifting to Spanish and changing hairstyle, clothes, and other cultural behaviors, come to be considered Mestizo. This flexibility and choice is incompatible with Omi and Winant's notion of appeal to the human body as inherent in the US construction of race.

These two approaches to Latino resistance to traditional US racial formation are not incompatible, but neither entirely accounts for the emergence of the assumption of a pan-national Latino racial status. Although idea of a Latino race exists in Latin America, it is somewhat marginal (Urciuoli 1996, Zentella 1997, Mendoza-Denton 2007). Yet in New York elements of a separate racial status began to emerge immediately upon the *Gran Migración*. Labov and Wolfram (1974) assume a non-White/non-Black category for Puerto Ricans, which concords with my own perceptions as a teenager in the city at that time. A Puerto Rican was identified either as Puerto Rican or Spanish and not considered Black or White whatever their skin color, hair type, or facial characteristics.

This pan-ethnic or pan-national identity became more significant with the arrival of non-Puerto Rican post-1965 immigrants from Latin American and has been identified as arising out of the idea of "latinidad," (Dávila 2000). New York, unlike most urban centers in the US where one group (e.g., Cubans in Miami, and Mexicans in the South and West) dominates demographically, has a widely diverse population of immigrant Latino origins. Alongside Puerto Ricans are Dominicans, Mexicans, Ecuadorians, Colombians, and Salvadorians, to mention just the largest groups. These otherwise quite different Latino groups focus on commonalities that distinguish their experience from that of other coterritorial communities and relegate differences to a second order status (see Potowski and Mats 2008 for a discussion of *latinidad* in Chicago). This process even occurs to Latin American immigrants in Spain, where evidently language is not the defining characteristic (Trenchs-Parera & Newman 2009, Newman 2011, Newman, Patiño-Santos, & Trenchs-Parera, 2013, Corona, Nussbaum, & Unamuno 2013). The suggestion here is that *latinidad* becomes racialized in the US because it is viewed in terms of its similarities to other pan-ethnic groups that are already defined in racial terms. Black, White, and Asian also serve as superordinate categories for people of heterogeneous national, regional, or ethnic heritages. The crucial point here is that the arrival of Latino groups and probably other groups who decline to accept the traditional US racial system as explicated by Omi and Winant have altered racial formation in New York. As it stands, race has evolved to be conceived of as superordinate categories and so inclusive of subordinate national or ethnic categories. Phenotype has not entirely disappeared as a significant defining element, but it can be overridden by assumed cultural commonalities and/or (sub)continental origins.

Which subcategories belong where is not always clear because the superordinate categories are themselves not well defined; witness for example the discrepancies over the position of groups like South Asians. However, the argument going forward is that there is in New York an expectation at very least that language variation will correlate primarily with superordinate racial categories and secondarily if at all with the subordinate ethnic or national ones. In other words racial status, understood in this way, ideologically governs the dialectal panorama of NYCE. This language ideology is grounded in a more general process identified by Kasinitz, et al. (2008: 82): "Average New Yorkers ... have a folk theory that different groups have different cultures that explain their attitudes and behaviors." In other words, the expectation that there will be an association of race with language variation forms part of a larger folk theory about the significance of race and ethnic identification.

Examples of these folk beliefs in their linguistic and general cultural forms appeared fairly frequently in my fieldwork at UAA. The linguistic examples are discussed shortly, but here a brief mention of the more general cultural associations is in order. Purported cultural attributes of ethnic identities were common fodder for jokes. A striking example occurred at a mock award event for and by that year's graduating seniors before their commencement ceremony. At that event – with parents in attendance! – each student was given a mock award such as *Sassiest Senior, Worst Joker,* and so on. One quiet and somewhat socially awkward White boy was awarded the prize *Whitest Senior.* The winner gamely walked up to the stage to general cheers and picked up his plaque from the two White students who were serving as MCs. Evidently, the award responded to as it made fun of the purported social uncoolness associated with Whites and, given the way it was done (the awards seemed all evenly humiliating!), the acceptance of this boy's persona among his peers. Yet the larger pattern behind the joking was often revealed in the form of imagined common sense assumptions, a point made by Omi and Winant (1994). For instance, one Latino ninth grader remarked as an aside that Black students beat up Latino students as if that were a kind of common and known type of event. The boy simply assumed that Blacks were more aggressive and better fighters than Latinos and picked on them despite many friendships and enmities that both crossed and remained within racial lines. I saw no evidence for this kind of race-based bullying at the school.

The impact of race on sociolinguistic variation can be seen in the BQ-16, which contain four Black participants. AAE is the first dialect of only two, but the others a Jamaican American and a Haitian American also spoke what is identifiably AAE. This assimilation to AAE by Blacks of immigrant origin is not limited to New York or even the US. Ibrahim (1999, 2001, 2004) studies African immigrants in an Ontario high school, who in some cases did not see themselves as Black in their homelands. He refers to their adopting AAE as an important part of the process of what he calls "Becoming Black," i.e., responding to their racialization in Canada by adopting a Black identity in North American terms. Many Latinos also picked up features of AAE, but they never would have been considered speakers of that variety since there were always some features that distinguished their speech, as will be discussed in the following chapter.

Returning briefly to the more general cultural pattern, Kasinitz et al. (2008) noticed this form of acculturation to an imagined racial category among second generation New Yorkers. They see the process as mediated by a "reference group," by which they mean a pre-existing group constructed as being of the same race. In the case of African diaspora West Indians, Africans, and Haitians, that reference group is African Americans. In the case of Latinos, it was originally, at least, Puerto Ricans. For European immigrants, it is the descendants of pre-1924 immigrants. Other groups lacked a substantial pre-existing community before 1965; even the number of Chinese Americans at that time was relatively small.

Nevertheless, accepting the linguistic patterns associated with a given race does not entail linguistic erasure of ethnic differences among groups within that broader category. In SSNYC, Labov found subtle differences between Jews and Italians. More recently, Blake and Shousterman (2010: 41) find differences in /r/ usage between African Americans and Black West Indians in New York. However, they add, "[Black] West Indian Americans add a layer to what it means to be African American, as well as to speak African American English." Further evidence from the BQ-16 will be presented below.

2.4.4 Sociolinguistic treatments of race and ethnicity

According to Eckert's (2012) influential historiography of the field, variationist approaches to social identity can be divided into three basic types, what she calls "waves." However, rather than waves with their implications of succeeding theoretical advances, I will examine them using the metaphor of zooming in or out.

Eckert describes SSENYC as paradigmatic of what she calls the "First Wave," which provides the most zoomed out view. It is zoomed out because it looks at macrosocial categories – race, ethnicity, class, age, or sex – as explanatory social variables. Individuals are grouped into such a category, and that category is correlated with the use of linguistic variants. Variable use of one group can be compared with that of other groups by comparing the different correlations. Labov's main focus, as discussed earlier, was on social class. Nevertheless, he did pay attention to ethnicity, as discussed above and race since he eliminated Blacks from some analyses because of the differences in production and particularly evaluation of variants with White groups. He also examined age and sex as factors in language change.

Immediately after SSENYC, Labov, et al. (1968a) and Wolfram (1974) produced what Eckert would later call "second wave" studies on African American and Puerto Rican New Yorkers respectively. Those studies zoomed in from large social categories to locally constructed *microsocial* categories including peer groups, communities of practice, and other social networks. An important insight driving that research is that microsocial groups construct and give meaning to macrosocial categories in different ways and are the mechanism by which variants spread.

Delineating relevant microsocial categories requires examination of local social dynamics through ethnographic methods as opposed to the more survey-like methods used in first wave studies. However, the contrast between the approaches can also be seen in their different treatments of outliers even by the same researcher. In SSENYC one Black speaker is depicted for all intents and purposes as White on the basis of his linguistic and social behavior. By contrast, Labov, et al. (1968a, b) describe boys who do not participate fully in the AAE vernacular system with the local term for them, *lames*. These individuals were invariably isolated socially from the dominant peer groups, but being a lame is not racial reassignment.[6]

A different construction of the relationship between racial and microsocial groupings can be found in Wolfram (1974), also a second wave study. Wolfram's division is between Puerto Rican teenagers with and without many African Americans in their social networks. Their cross-race socializing is not constructed as problematic, but it does have linguistic consequences in terms of rates of variant use. My own much later studies of New York Latino English (NYLE) can also be classified as second wave because they look at the role of peer culturally-defined groups such as rap artists, rap fans, nerds, or skaters and so on (Slomanson & Newman 2004, Newman 2010). These cases are discussed in terms of the relevant variation in Chapter 3.

When the focus zooms maximally inward to examine individuals and their relationship to micro and macrosocial categories, the study is considered "third wave." These studies examine the tension between individuals and groups and particularly large-scale macrosocial identities. They also connect language use with other expressive stylistic elements such as clothes, music, and forms of discourse because language forms part of a stylistic whole of self-presentation that plays off those identities. This is the approach taken by Cutler (1999/2003, 2008, 2010) in her studies of White Hip-Hop affiliated youth in New York. Style is certainly prominent in Hip-Hop, and Cutler's studies are quite revealing about the role the peer culture plays in the (re)construction of racial identity in contemporary New York. An example of what Cutler's approach can offer is a depiction of how Hip-Hop's ideology of authenticity interacts with the locally high status of African American culture and the consequentially high status of AAE. Cutler (2003, 2008, 2010) notes that successful White rap artists negotiate the use of some AAE variants but avoid attempting to adopt the entire AAE system. By contrast, those who miss this balance can get accused of "wanting to be Black" (Cutler 1999/2003, 2008). Also significant is Cutler's (2008) discussion of Kin, an Armenian-Bulgarian immigrant, who was accepted within Hip-Hop. Kin reports being told he was insufficiently White by a White non-Hip-Hop oriented peer, a criticism that he interpreted as racist. This kind of criticism of a person's speech is called *linguistic policing*.

---

6 Admittedly, there may have been substantive differences between the cases. The lone African American in the LES study may have had no AAE features, but the lames were defined as speaking a less vernacular AAE.

A fourth type of approach to language and ethnicity and race combines aspects of all three waves. This is the case of recent work in London (e.g., Torgersen, Kerswill, & Fox 2006; Kerswill, Torgersen, & Fox 2008) and Toronto (Hoffman & Walker 2010, Nagy, et al. 2014). In this type of study relatively large samples are analyzed as in first wave and degree of ethnic orientation as in second or third wave is obtained either via interview questions, ethnography, or social psychological instrument. The results are then correlated. The only example of this kind of study in New York is Wong and Hall-Lew's (2014) examination of Chinese Americans.

2.4.5 New Yorkers' associations of race and variation

Linguistic policing is particularly interesting because it provides prima faciae evidence for language norms including covert ones that operate in a community. I heard a number of reports of it at UAA. The following example is from an African American student called Nyesha. Just before the excerpt, Nyesha was describing how she lived in a mostly White area and, prior to transferring to UAA, she had attended an equally White private school. When she arrived at UAA, she felt out of place linguistically.

> Nyesha: But when I started going to this school, [hearing] slang and everything, I went "what? Huh?" And I would not understand, and...
>
> Int: What didn't you understand?
>
> Nyesha: Slang words. You know, Ebonics. I didn't know Ebonics. You know, I knew I knew a few words, "yo" but I learned more better sometimes, so I could communicate more better sometimes, you know. But I could get made fun of sometimes, you know. I could get made fun of, called a Cauc..., White girl, whatever. .... My mom tells me when I go home, "you seem different Nyesha, you don't talk the way you used to. You don't use correct English anymore."

Nyesha shows what is probably the most common response by the object of policing, conformity to expectations, with AAE forms like *more better* appearing even in the interview. Note that as she tells it, the policing occurred alongside the desire to integrate into the group. This kind of response forms a plausible explanation for the maintenance of ethnolinguistic boundaries along racial lines even in the face of racially heterogeneous social networks. Nyesha, for example, had a

White boyfriend for a number of months, although she reported being criticized for that as well.[7]

The opposite response was provided by Evan, an African American, who grew up in the low-income largely Black neighborhood of South Jamaica. Evan did not describe being policed, but he showed signs of efforts to change his speech, in his case away from AAE. At points in his interview he appeared to be trying to avoid AAE pronunciation, once actually self-correcting *ask* from [æks] ('ax') to [æsk]. The key factor is his locus of identity as a self-described nerd. In the following quote, he affiliates with a principle of individualism common to nerd culture by describing himself as independent of the values and practices of his inner-city neighbors. Moreover, he paints those neighbors as conforming sheep-like to a narrow collectively constructed set of stylistic options:

> Evan: I grew up in an area that was largely, the large majority of people who live there, listen to hip-hop and rap and etc., etc., and I grew up in that area, and I really didn't like any of that, you know; that was something. And they weren't really finding what they really like. As I went around, I met different people. I was surrounded by different people, and I found all these different forms of music that I liked, and I also noticed that none of them were the same type of music, you know. So when, usually, people ask me what do I like, [incomprehensible], but I listen to jazz, industrial, uh, metal, techno, uh, trance.

Jazz and to an extent trance, techno, and some metal can be more associated with an intellectual orientation and are largely, though hardly entirely, associated with White followings. A final twist to Evan's story was that he defied any expectation that his dissociation with African American vernacular culture or his nerd identity implied acquiescence to mainstream middle class norms. Evan not only consistently failed most of his classes but he was eventually expelled from UAA for hacking the school's grading system.

The final account of racial-linguistic ideology from UAA involves the self-report of a perpetrator of linguistic policing: a White girl Janet Krebbs, who is included in the BQ-16. The incident she recounts took place through a program in which older students were assigned to mentor entering 7th graders. She was interviewed together with a Puerto Rican friend, John, who provides his own insights on race and language variation:

> Janet: Michael, this one girl she's like really, really tall, she came in one day, she's twelve. She came in one day a skirt up her ass, a shirt where she showed her breasts, ... and she came in to school like that, and I'm explaining to her, you don't come in to school dressed

---

7 I heard about complaints about interracial relationships as arising from only from one group of Black girls, although none repeated them to me. I heard about no similar complaints by boys.

as something like that. That is inappropriate, and she's all "oh yeah what are you talking about?" this and that and all up in my face, trying to talk slang. I'm like, "you're White, deal with it; you're not Black, you're not Puerto Rican; talk like a White girl."

John: That's gotta be hard for her, cuz a White girl talks a certain way like Spanish or with a ghetto accent, she gets called a poser, because she's trying to be something she's not, but when she acts like a typical White girl, she gets made fun of.

MN: I mean you're a White girl.

Janet: But it's different with some people; I mean they don't talk with a White accent. I mean most White people do have a certain accent. I mean it's really all depends on who you hang out with. Like all my life I have never hung out with White people. I just never got along with them. So, I just got the accent from the people that I hung out with, but...

MN: What's your accent?

Janet: I don't know what's my accent; I talk differently, every day.

John: Brooklynese, Yiddish.

MN: That's not the White accent? What's the white accent?

Janet: White is like

John: Like you know, [high pitch, fronted GOAT, and creak]

MN: Preppy?

Both: Yeah

This quote provides a view that diverges from the common understanding of White speech (and indeed White identity) as *normal* and so *non-accented*, an expectation discussed by Fought (2006). However, Janet and John take the idea of White markedness further. Note that Janet's own speech is not considered White even by John although he accurately identifies it through the traditional term *Brooklynese*. In fact, he associates her NYCE ethnically with Jews through the term Yiddish, although Janet is not Jewish. By contrast, in its most iconic form – given the vowel quality John produces in imitation – "sounding White" takes on associations with stylized California English, which would be heard by John and Janet mostly through the media (see Eckert 2008a). Although, I am the one to introduce the class-related term, *preppy*, that descriptor is embraced by both.

A similar construction of Whiteness and NYCE was expressed by Andy Sullivan, also of the BQ-16 and also a strong NYCE speaker. He was interviewed along with his friend and fellow BQ-16 member, Laura Feldman:

> Andy: My cousins are from Franklin Square [MN: a suburb in Nassau County, Long Island] and they like, they sound like more proper and more White than like I do. And like my brothers, they all sound like, you can tell, like an accent like.
>
> MN: You mean sound white. What is White? Can you imitate it at all?
>
> Andy: Can I? I can't imitate I'm terrible with... You, know more proper, like you know
>
> MN: OK
>
> Andy: Like kinda Connecticut, like that.
>
> Laura: Yeah
>
> MN: Yeah, I understand. You mean more preppy?
>
> Andy: Yeah, more preppy.

Like Janet and John, Andy identifies sounding White with my suggestion of *preppy* after struggling a bit for a descriptor beyond another class-related term *proper*. Andy adds an interesting distancing element that was only implicit in Janet and John's non-NYCE GOAT fronting. He associates Whiteness with non-New York speech through the reference to the stereotypically rich state of Connecticut.

Janet, John, Andy and Laura's descriptions suggest that racialization of pre-1924 immigrant New Yorkers as non-White, and the resulting stigma described by Bonfiglio (2002), lingers. Certainly, that distancing from stereotypical Whiteness should not be taken as indicative of an entirely non-White identity. There is a consensus that Andy and Laura's neighborhood, Howard Beach, has advanced a long way from a racist incident that led to the death of a Black youth chased onto a highway about 15 years before. However, the area remains overwhelmingly White.

Be that as it may, Andy reported, with some annoyance, being policed for his strong NYCE at his high school, which attracted students from across Queens and Nassau County. At the same time, these references to "sounding White" show that class-based definitions of race discussed by Omi and Winant (1994) are at least right below the surface and interact with the social stratification uncovered by Labov in SSENYC. Sounding White and sounding Black appear as opposing points on a class-related continuum. Yet John, a Nuyorican, also refers to "Spanish." It is unlikely that he meant speaking the Spanish language, which he could not speak and was rarely heard at UAA. Similar expectations that Latinos also have a distinct form of English also came up in interviews at UAA and in class numerous class discussions I have had at Queens. For example, it is not hard to find Latinos in college classes who describe being policed for "sounding White" by peers and family members. However, there is no evidence of correlation between academic orientation – and so class trajectory – and density of Spanish substrate features (Slomanson & Newman 2004).

The odd category out dialectally is Asian. New Yorkers show consensus about Asians' racial identity – without being entirely clear about the contents of that category – but I heard no mention of Asian linguistic distinctiveness in my research in New York. Wong (2007, 2010, 2012) and Wong & Hall-Lew (2014) show that Chinese American New Yorkers use traditional NYCE traits, though in ways that reflect their orientation vis-à-vis their Chinese identities. Wong does not, however, find distinctively Chinese or Asian features, a finding repeated in most research on East Asians' American English. The consensus is that there is insufficient evidence for postulating the existence of "Asian American English" (Lo and Reyes 2009).

Nevertheless, in Newman and Wu (2008), we found evidence for a degree of Asian distinctiveness. In that study, Queens College students raised in New York listened alternatively to either eight male or eight female New Yorkers including two Chinese Americans, two Korean Americans, two Whites, and one each Black and Latino. Figure 2.6 shows the results of their identifications for male speakers and Figure 2.7 shows them for female speakers. In those figures, mC1, mC2, fC1, and fC2 represent the male and female Chinese American speakers respectively, with K standing for Korean, W for White, B for Black, and H for Hispanic in the same way. The quantities shown in the bars are the total racial identifications for each category for each speaker by the judges.

It is evident that Latinos and African Americans were accurately recognized most consistently at rates of 90 % or above. The Whites were less consistently recognized, with three of four were also at rates above 67 %, but the most vernacular speaker was only recognized by 41 %. These rates approach that of the four Asians. Again, three of the four were recognized by a plurality, at rates ranging from 28 % to 78 %. The lowest rated one was again the most vernacular. Interestingly, when I have played the sound files at conferences or in classes, some New Yorkers have been able to pick out the Korean from the Chinese heritage voices in the sample. Yet the Queens College judges were not able to do so. The differences between successful and unsuccessful identifications of this intraracial difference did not even approach significance.

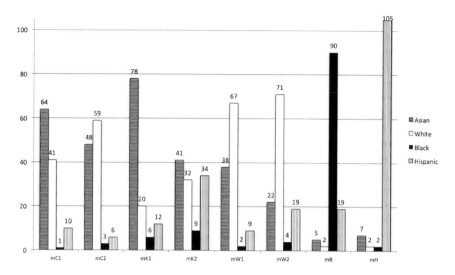

Figure 2.6: Bar graph of racial identifications of male speakers by judges $\chi^2 = 997.6$, dF = 21, p < 0.001

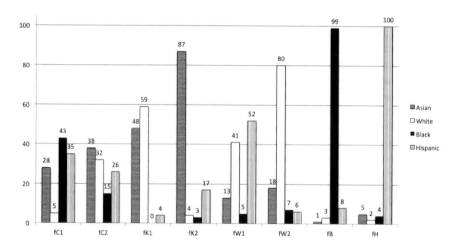

Figure 2.7: Bar graph of racial identifications of female speakers by judges $\chi^2 = 0.1012$, dF = 21, p < 0.001

2.4.6 Racial Segregation and Dialect Development and Preservation

In the previous subsections, it was made clear that race, as it defined by New Yorkers, correlates with detectable linguistic differentiation and often with expectation and enforcement of such differentiation. However, little reference was made to the truly cruel realities racialization imposes primarily on Blacks and Latinos. Arguably, Whites are also hurt in a much more minor and abstract way by the blindness associated with our own privilege.

Labov (2008b) argues that racism through pervasive racial residential segregation across the US maintains AAE as a separate dialect while endangering its speakers. There can be little doubt that New York remains highly segregated. Logan and Stults (2011) using 2010 Census data find that the New York-White Plains-Wayne, NY-NJ area (a somewhat artificial portion of the metro area, admittedly) is the third most segregated such region in the US after portions of Detroit and Milwaukee. Nassau-Suffolk clocks in at number 10.[8] Residential segregation is crucial for dialect preservation following a longstanding claim in the field that linguistic isolation is necessary for a dialect to develop and be maintained (e.g., Sapir 1921; Trudgill 1992).

Labov's point about endangered African Americans growing up in segregated communities was powerfully and sadly illustrated by Rashid Lewis, the most vernacular AAE speaker in the BQ-16. Rashid had been a former student of mine, but since I had left the school as a teacher and returned as a researcher he acquired a *telephone scar* across his face from having been *sliced*, a gang punishment.[9] In the following excerpt from his interview, he provides a nuanced view of residential segregation:

MN: When you talk with the older generation of Black people do you think the situation with the races has gotten better?

Rashid: It depends on the community. Namean [=know what I mean]. I found it growing up. Like see me personally, I am from South Jamaica, and that's a low-income neighborhood, and I am not afraid to say it. Some people are. ... Now in my neighborhood for a twenty-block radius, they probably be like five White kids. Now that's between about fifty sixty houses, a couple of projects, namean. So that's crazy. Those white kids there, they be just

---

8 This topic has engendered considerable journalistic interest, and a visualization of the segregation in New York and other segregated cities was produced by Business Insider (Jacobs, Kiersz & Lubin 2013) http://www.businessinsider.com/most-segregated-cities-in-america-2013-11. See also Fessenden (2014) for a series of graphics on New York Public Schools, also according to the reporter the third most segregated in the US.
9 The term *telephone* refers to the fact that the scar starts at the ear and ends at the mouth, paralleling the places one holds a phone.

like us, cuz that's the way they raised, and there is no love lost [=no hatred]. I grew up with you; you may be a little white, but I am a little black too; it's the same difference, namean. ... And I was basically a prisoner of the ghetto. I never left my neighborhood; I went to junior high school in my neighborhood; I almost went to high school in my neighborhood. I mean I stayed in my neighborhood. I never really came to Manhattan or the Bronx, Brooklyn. Never really went out there. Stayed in that lil' area of Queens, and it was crazy in there [...because] in my neighborhood it's do or die; you make money if you got to; there is nothing bad with selling drugs, and marijuana is barely even illegal nowadays in my neighborhood. I mean if police see you smoking marijuana they be like "Ah, let 'm live ya know. I used to do it too; it's not even 'worf' the paper work. I mean let's catch somebody selling it or let's get the shootout or something." Then they go crazy. That's how it is in my neighborhood.

At the time of the research for Labov, et al. (1968a,b) the authors note that their participants had no White friends and saw no possibility of having any. However, later in the interview, a longer excerpt of which is provided in Appendix B, Rashid contrasts his childhood with his experience in a mixed school like UAA. He discusses his interracial acquaintances and one close friendship with a boy he calls "White Mike" (to distinguish him from a classmate "Black Mike"). Also, he said that the diversity in that school opened his eyes to different ways of doing things, different lifestyles, and different types of people, which he described as

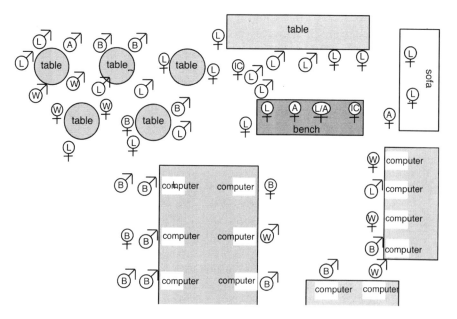

Figure 2.8: UAA students' seating by racial identity during free library period.

"beautiful." It certainly exposed him to peers whose speech was very different from his own.

Figure 2.8 illustrates the kind of interacial contact that typified the school. It was taken from my field notes in June 2002 and depicts the seating arrangements of a class of 11th grade (16–17 year old) UAA students in a free library period. Each student's sex is marked by the traditional male and female symbols ♂ and ♀ with racial and sometimes ethnic identities marked by letters inside those symbols: B for Black, L for Latino, W for White, A for Asian, and IC for Indo-Caribbean.

Students sat wherever they liked, which meant usually with friends or at least *ad hoc* social networks for this class period. A few of the resulting groups were made up of clusters that were racially mostly homogeneous: Latinos with one Indo-Caribbean girl at the top rectangular table, two Latino girls at the round table below and to the left of them, a nearly all Black group with one White boy at the bottom center computer table. The remaining groups are ethnically heterogeneous without even a pattern of combinations.

Figure 2.8 is a snapshot of a single moment in one class and in one school; but it documents a pattern that I found was typical of the interactions that occurred over the course of my fieldwork. Similar distributions occurred at lunch, in class, and in groups that left school together. Participants also described their current and childhood social networks in similarly varied terms in interviews. Some like Rashid depicted growing up in largely single-race communities whereas others described childhoods in neighborhoods and with networks that were biracial – e.g., Latino and Black – or multiracial – e.g., Latino – Indo-Caribbean – Black.

If these histories are accurate, it is hard to see how those individuals could have maintained racially defined dialects. Fix (2014), who studies White women with African American social ties, suggests that interracial childhood and adolescent social ties promote feature spread. Her findings also suggest that use of the features is highly bound up in personal identity construction. There is a lot of work that can be done in New York between people of different racial backgrounds, with different social networks at different life stages that can explore the questions Fix's research raises. However, extending her analysis, to a situation like the one found among the students at UAA we would expect widespread and prolific sharing of features and so a breakdown of ethnic speech patterns. Nevertheless, as will be clear in the subsequent chapters, we see across New York considerable maintenance of ethnolinguistic differentiation along with feature spread.

An obvious motive for dialect preservation may be found in the linguistic policing discussed earlier in this chapter. What is less clear is whether norms enforcing racial-dialectal distinctions are sufficient to provide the kind of orderly heterogeneity that characterizes true dialects. An individual may conform to expectations, after all, simply by using certain features which index (i.e., point to) identities associated with those dialects. In sociolinguistics, there is considerable questioning at present of the adequacy of viewing ethnic differences as differences in dialects versus less ordered repertoires of features (see e.g., Benor 2010, Hall-Lew & Yeager-Dror 2014). This difference is worth to paying attention to in the descriptions of NYCE in the subsequent chapters.

3 Phonetics and Phonology

3.1 I coulda been a contenda

Director Elia Kazan's classic 1954 movie *On the Waterfront* tells the story of Terry Malloy a New York area longshoreman played by Marlon Brando. Terry becomes a promising boxer, but his mafia-connected brother has him throw a fight costing him his one shot at a championship. In one of the most memorable scenes in movie history, Terry rebukes his brother saying, "You don't understand. I coulda had class. I coulda been a contender." Brando's performance is a tour de force of acting, and it is clear that he felt that giving Terry a New York accent was integral to the role. For instance, he ends the word contender with (r-0) as [kə̃nˈtʰɛ̃ndə] 'kuhntenda,' although he was a natively r-ful Midwesterner. Yet if you listen carefully (search for "I coulda been a contender" on YouTube), it is clear that Brando does not get the New York accent right.

A major slipup lies in the short-A split, mentioned briefly in Chapter 2 as a characteristic feature of traditional NYCE. According the NYCE pattern, the vowel in *class* is tense, meaning that it is pronounced [ɛə] 'cleh-uhs.' However, Brando uses the lax pronunciation – [æ] as in TRAP – following the nasal system because /s/ is not a nasal consonant.[1] Brando then goes on to make the opposite mistake in his pronunciation of the vowel in *am* in his next line: "I coulda been somebody, instead of a bum, which is what I am." That vowel should be the lax [æ] in NYCE, but Brando pronounces it with the tense [ɛ̃əm][2], 'eh-uhm,' again following the nasal system since the word ends in the nasal consonant /m/. In fairness it is hard not to be sympathetic to Brando. The NYCE short-A split involves a devilishly intricate set of patterns unlike the relatively simple nasal system, which is present in about half of the US (Labov, et al. 2006).

The term *split* refers to linguistic evolutionary process whereby what had once been one phoneme has become two, labeled TRAP for lax [æ] and BATH for tense [ɛə]. Without the split, TRAP and BATH are pronounced identically, and we can use only one key word (usually TRAP) to represent that larger class. An actor

---

[1] As discussed in Chapter 2, this book uses Wells' keywords to indicate vowel phonemes. These keywords and tenseness and laxness will be discussed more fully in Section 3.3.

[2] The difference can be hard to hear particularly for those who have Brando's system, which will be discussed later. However, it can be shown through acoustic measurement, although the sound quality and context after [kl] in *class* are not ideal for that purpose. The vowel in *class*, measured at the lowest F1, is F1=879. By contrast, *am* is F1=644, which are congruent with the phonetic description provided.

without the split who wants to sound like a New Yorker must therefore figure which words are TRAP and which are BATH and pronounce them accordingly. This task requires unfortunately considerable effort and a sophisticated dialect coach.

By contrast, (r) in NYCE is simple because (r-0) can appear anywhere except before a vowel in the same word. Brando's r-lessness may also be motivated by its social salience. In SSENYC (211) Labov considers that (r) "is the most sensitive and regular indicator of socio-economic status" of all the variables he studied. Brando's (r-0) therefore allowed audiences to imagine Terry Malloy as a New York dockworker even though he did not really sound like one. Because of its importance, this chapter begins with (r), followed by the remarkably complex NYCE vowel system including the short-A split. The section after that explores the remaining consonants and combinations of consonants. The last section deals with what are called suprasegmentals, like voice quality, intonation, and rhythm.

3.2 (r): the fourth floor

Although (r-0) is stigmatized in New York, it is highly prestigious in England and virtually universal in southern hemisphere varieties. The problem for New Yorkers is ultimately that few North American dialects – only parts of the south, Eastern New England, and AAE – exhibit r- lessness. It is also a very salient feature, and unsurprisingly it is discussed in virtually all dialectological studies of NYCE (e.g., Babbitt 1998, Hubbell 1950, Kurath & McDavid 1962). By far the best-known work on (r) is Labov's *Department Store Study*, which appears as a chapter in SSENYC. That study took place in three large stores, Saks, Macy's and S. Klein's, in descending order of prices and shoppers' average incomes. Labov went through each store asking employees for the location of items that he already knew were on the fourth floor. He then feigned not hearing the answer to elicit a repetition. In this way, he elicited four (r)s from each employee, two before consonants, two before pauses, each in a normal and a more careful enunciation. About 30 % of the employees at Saks produced all four possible (r-1)s. By contrast, only about 20 % did so at Macy's and less than 5 % did so at S. Klein's. Similarly, (r-1) was more frequent in the repetition than in response to the initial query and in the word final position of *floor* than in the preconsonantal one in *fourth*.

Despite its fame, the study was really ancillary to Labov's main project on the LES, which consisted of 122 full interviews plus 33 short ones. The idea was that the store workers came from all over the city. To the extent that their data matched the LES results those findings should be extendible to the whole dialect region. Indeed, both data sets matched exactly. Just as (r) usage tracked SES in the LES, so Saks employees used the most (r-1), Macy's somewhat less, and S. Klein's the least. Similarly, just as LESers used more (r-1) in tasks that required greater attention to speech than those that encouraged more spontaneous speech, so store employees used more (r-1) in the repetition than the initial response. Also, both groups used more (r-1) word finally as in *floor* than word internally as in *fourth*.

Naturally, the greater detail in the LES study led to more findings, one of which was an anomaly in the trend lines that Labov called "hypercorrection of the lower middle class." Whereas in relaxed styles lower middle class speakers used less (r-1) than those in the upper middle classes, as more attention was being paid to speech such as in the word lists the lower middle class surpassed the higher group in (r-1) usage. Labov interpreted this greater usage of (r-1) as overcompensation and so a sign of this class's deep linguistic insecurity (SSENYC: 151–153).

Labov also conjectured that New Yorkers' belief in the correctness of (r-1) set in motion a change in progress whereby r-fulness would increase over time. This kind of change, which takes place with a degree of awareness, he labeled a "change from above," meaning above the level of consciousness. Changes from below are those that proceed unconsciously, such as in response to internal linguistic or articulatory motivations or via automatic accommodation to other speakers.

Subsequent studies have shown a trajectory in NYCE of increasing rhoticity, as r-fulness is also called, although not nearly as rapidly as Labov first expected. Two careful replications of the department store study (Fowler 1986, Cited in SSENYC and Mather 2012) and Mather (2012) reveal this slow increase. Figure 3.1 shows the percentages of store workers who gave all four (r-1)s over those three studies. The order of the stores in (r-1) usage remains the same, with Saks at the highest and Macy's in the middle. The lowest class stores changes from S. Klein's for Labov, to Mays for Fowler, to Filene's and Loehmanns for Mather because the store used in the prior study had closed.

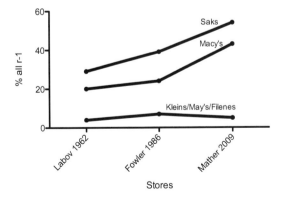

Figure 3.1: % of all (r-1) responses in three department store studies

The lowest store trend line defies the increasing rates (r-1) in Saks and Macy's. Mather plausibly attributes this stasis to the fact that virtually all the employees in those stores were Black or Latino. As Labov reported in SSENYC, use of (r-1) by New York Blacks is much lower than that of Whites when SES is held constant, but the steady state also suggests the pattern of increasing rhoticity is mainly a White or perhaps a White and Asian phenomenon. This difference anticipates a theme that will be found in a number of other places in this volume. The common use of a NYCE variant among different racial groups masks more subtle differences in the patterning between those groups.

Just as Fowler and Mather reprised the department store study, Becker (2009) returned to the LES to reexamine (r) forty years after Labov. Becker focused on "long-time" White LESers, meaning those who were either there in the 1960s or whose parents were. Becker's older White participants show a higher rate of (r-1) than those of the same approximate birth-year studied by Labov, and their children show even greater (r-1) rates. Becker (2009: 648) finds that the younger participants "have more than doubled the rate of (r-1) of their 1966 age equivalents, using it 55 % of the time." Most interestingly, Becker argues that despite this increase, r-lessness remains part of their repertoire, and both generations used (r-0) more when talking about the neighborhood than other topics. The point is that this increase shows that r-lessness is associated with these participants' identity as Lower East Siders.

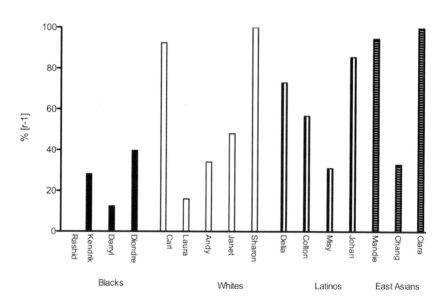

Figure 3.2: % of (r-1) usage from the BQ-16 with racial category marked

Because most of original White residents had moved away, Becker's restriction to "old timers" reduced her sample size to just seven speakers with the youngest born in 1962. Given the limitations in age range and numbers, the BQ-16 are useful in providing additional data. Figure 3.2 shows their percent r-fulness as based on between 80 and 100 (r) tokens taken from interview data although all cases with NURSE (e.g., words like *bird, Kurt, work*) are eliminated.

As in most previous work, the Blacks have the lowest (r-1) use; Rashid, the most vernacular speaker, is categorically r-less, and even Diondre, a middle class African American, produces under 40 % (r-1). This pattern repeats Mather's finding of little change in that racial demographic. It also is in line with a generalization of Thomas (2007) and Thomas and Wassink (2010) regarding a national pattern by which local AAE varieties are generally somewhat less rhotic than their co-territorial White varieties. However, it differs from Blake and Shousterman's (2010) finding of increased r-fulness in NYCE speaking Blacks of African American and West Indian backgrounds. The remaining racial groups show large ranges of variation, although a closer look provides some suggestive possible patterns:

First, the two youngest Asians are much more r-ful than the oldest, suggesting the possibility of an evolution parallel to that proposed for Whites, which would need firming up with data from more and a wider variety of Asians. Second, the White BQ-16 members were born about 30 years after Becker's youngest LES participant, but two of the BQ-16, Laura and Andy, have notably lower rates of (r-1) than Becker's participants do (16.0 % and 34.1 % respectively), and one, Janet, approaches their rate. Laura and Andy's (r-1) rates are actually in line with Labov's original speakers. For example, in the kind of interview style used to produce these data Labov (in SSENYC: 140) found between 10.5 % for his lowest socioeconomic status group to 25 % for his highest one. Laura and Andy show only a very small increase over half a century later. Decline in White (r-0) is, however, evident in Sharon's categorical and Carl's near categorical (r-1) usage.

Sharon is an Orthodox Jew, and Carl is mixed Irish and Italian, but both are upper middle class and from northern Queens areas that have received large numbers of immigrants mostly from East Asia. Laura and Andy, by contrast, are from Howard Beach, an area that Laura referred to as a "bubble." She meant by this that their mostly working class Italian American and Irish American community remains relatively isolated from cultural and demographic trends affecting the rest of the city. Janet is from Glendale, a racially mixed middle-income area, with a historically large German population, but her family was low income.

Finally, the Latinos show a wide range of (r) usage. Missy, the most r-less speaker shares a number of other characteristics of AAE, and her background – although not her trajectory because she is a college student studying to be a teacher – is low income. Colton has a similar background and trajectory, but his use of other AAE features is far less than Missy's. The other two Latinos come from working class backgrounds and show relatively little AAE influence in their speech.

Earlier, I described race-based differences in changes of rates in usage of (r) over time, but there are also differences in how (r) patterns synchronically between different racial groups. One difference involves the following sound in a different word. For all non-Black BQ-16 members when a word with a word-final /r/ was followed by a vowel (e.g., *care about, hair and*) the use of (r-1) – called *linking-R* – increases compared to contexts where it is followed by a consonant or a pause (e.g., *I don't care, hair stuff*). Labov, et al. (1968a) also found an absence of linking-R in their Harlem data, and Thomas (2007) points out there is little linking-R in Southern White vernaculars. Blake and Shousterman (2010) find a slight favoring of linking-R environments for (r-1). The data for the BQ-16 are shown in Table 3.1:

Table 3.1: % word final (r-1) before other words beginning with vowels vs. other contexts for BQ-16:

	Following Vowel	**Other contexts**	**Difference**
East Asians	97	72	25
Blacks	16	21	05
Latinos	85	50	36
Whites	88	53	35

Although it is a bit of a tangent, it is worth mentioning that linking-R is the main though not only source of so-called "intrusive-R," i.e., cases where an /r/ is pronounced but has no etymological source. Typical examples include saying *idea* as [aɪˈdiɹ] 'idear' or *law and order* as [ˌlɔɹə̃ndˈɔrə] 'lawrandawda,' which has the virtue of leaving two etymological /r/s unpronounced while adding a non-etymological one. Intrusive-R can seem bizarre because it involves saying /r/s that are not there while ignoring those that are. It is easy to see why it appears, however, in cases where r-lessness creates homophony between words like *lore* and *law*. When r-less, both would be identical or nearly so, e.g., [lʊᵊ], 'loo-uh.' However, in strings like *lore of old*, linking-R makes an r-ful pronunciation common, and if *lore* and *law* are homonyms, the same /r/ can appear in *law and order* (Uffmann 2007). Even though there is no such homophone for *idea*, the same principle applies. That's the idea*r* anyway. Since linking-Rs are rare in AAE, intrusive-Rs are likely to be far less prevalent for African Americans than the other groups, and there are no cases from the Black members of the BQ-16.

The other subtle racial difference occurs in the NURSE vowel, which was eliminated from the data from which Figure 3.2 was derived. Labov (in SSENYC) also eliminated this case because many New Yorkers who are heavy (r-0) users in words like *contender, four, forth, hair,* and *her,* are (r-1) users with NURSE. Rashid who is categorically r-less in Figure 3.2 was categorically r-ful in this class of words, as were the other Black speakers, a result more extreme but in the same direction as found by Blake and Shousterman (2010). Similarly, Andy was mostly r-less but was also categorically r-ful with NURSE, and Missy pronounced NURSE rhotically in 18 out of 20 tokens.

By contrast, Laura was non-rhotic in eight of nineteen NURSE cases, and Chang was non-rhotic in six of thirteen. The variant they used was a diphthong [ɜ^{ɪ}]. In SSENYC Labov (1966/2006: 213) describes this vowel as a having "come to symbolize New York City speech in folk mythology under the name *Brooklynese.*" It appears most famously in the phrase 'toidy-toid and toid' for *33rd and 3rd*, which has become such a stereotype that it appears three times only in the trailer for *If These Knishes Could Talk,* the documentary on NYCE.[3]

In the early 1960s 75 % of Labov's lower SES speakers between the ages of 20 and 39 (p. 214) used [ɜ^{ɪ}] for NURSE as did 35 % of his working class ones at least some of the time. However, it has sharply negative social associations as can be seen in Carroll O'Connor's prolific use of it in his depiction of Archie Bunker, the quintessential New York White working-class bigot in the 1970s television series *All in the Family.* These connotations led to a steep decline, and today it can be most commonly heard in recordings of New York voices of years ago such as Groucho Marx, the Three Stooges, and Bugs Bunny. O'Connor pairs this diphthong with a kind of intrusive-R, in words like *toilet* or *oil,* which come out as [tʰɜˑɪt˺] and [ɜˑɪ]. Labov (1995: 345) claims that that intrusive pronunciation is something of a myth, but Archie was probably even better known for saying 'terlet' and 'earl' than "that is man's woik" (from a 1974 episode titled *Archie's Helping Hand*). So rapid was the fall that the Labov in the second edition of SSENYC (216) describes it as extinct. Chang and, especially because of her youth, Laura, show that these death notices are premature.

3.3 Vowels

Labov (1966/2006: 346–7) and Berger (1968: 38) list nineteen vowels for what Labov calls the "maximum range of [vowel] distinctions available to New Yorkers."

---

3 http://www.youtube.com/watch?v=38tBuV2XsFc.

They are recompiled in Table 3.2. Later I will discuss two possible additions, but even these nineteen are already more than found in any other North American vowel system.

Table 3.2: Composite of Labov's and Berger's full paradigm of NYCE vowels using standard phonemic notation and Wells' Lexical Sets

	Lax	Tense		
Position		**Front Upgliding**	**Back Upgliding**	**Ingliding**
High-Front	/ɪ/ KIT	/i/ FLEECE		/iᵊ/ NEAR
Mid-Front	/ɛ/ DRESS	/ɛ'/ FACE		/ɛᵊ/ SQUARE
Low-Front	/æ/ TRAP		/æᵘ/ MOUTH	/ɛᵊ/ BATH
High-Back	/ʊ/ FOOT		/u/ GOOSE	/uᵊ/ CURE
Mid-Back	/ʌ/ STRUT	/ɔ'/ CHOICE	/ɔᵘ/ GOAT	/ɔᵊ/ THOUGHT
Low-Back	/ɑ/ LOT	/ɑ'/ PRICE		/ɑᵊ/ PALM

The table organizes the vowels horizontally first by whether they are lax or tense, a distinction discussed earlier only with reference to the short-A split between BATH and TRAP. As Table 3.2 shows, this distinction occurs across the vowel system. Labov, et al. (2006: 16) define *tense* as "a cover term for a complex of phonetic features: extended duration and extreme articulatory position with an accompanying increase in articulatory effort." Lax vowels by implication have shorter durations, less peripheral articulations, and consequently require less articulatory effort. Tense vowels tend to become diphthongal, and Table 3.2 uses the direction of the potential glides (i.e., the second part of the diphthong), front and up, back and up, or inward forms as the second level of distinction. The vertical organization is by position of the vowel or its nucleus. In part, the notions of position and direction used in Table 3.2 refer to the placement and movement of the tongue, and so supports a graphical depiction in what is called a vowel chart. Such a chart for the vowels in Table 3.2 is found in Figure 3.3. The simple dots represent lax vowels and dots with arrows tense vowels with the arrows pointing in the direction of the (potential) glide. The schwa [ə] at the center of the chart and is the target for what are consequently called inglides; [ɪ] and [ʊ] (the positions of KIT and FOOT) represent the targets for front and back upglides respectively except for /i/ and /u/, which begin above those levels.

One complication is that this maximal system assumes r-lessness because rhoticity reduces the number of ingliding vowels:

When /r/ is vocalized, [ingliding vowels constitute] a symmetrical set of six phonemes. When /r/ is fully constricted as a consonant, this sub-system shrinks to two main items: / æ³/ in *bad, ban pass, bath*, etc. and /ɔ³/ in *law, bought, sawed, lawn*, etc.[4] (SSENYC: 346)

In other words, with (r-1) NEAR, CURE, and SQUARE merge into neighboring vowels. *Car* and *cart*, when r-less, contain PALM,[5] but given (r-1), *car* has LOT, but *cart* joins STRUT, at least in my pronunciation. PALM is either reduced to a much smaller set of words, or it is merged entirely into LOT. PALM will be explored in detail later in section 3.3.2. By contrast, BATH and THOUGHT have many words that do not contain /r/ and so do not depend on r-lessness. These two vowels have received the lion's share of research attention.

3.3.1 The short-A split

According to Labov, et al. (2006: 146) NYCE is defined by r-lessness and its version of the short-A split. The split can be seen in the lower front area of the vowel chart in Figure 3.3, which shows tense BATH to the left of lax TRAP. Recall that a split is defined as the development of two phonemes out of what had historically been one. Different phonemes are diagnosed by the existence of minimal pairs, i.e., words that differ by only the sound in question. Minimal pairs of NYCE short-A include *can* in *tin **can*** versus *can* in *Yes, we **can***; *banner* meaning *person who bans* versus *banner* meaning *flag*; and *halve* versus *have*. In traditional NYCE, each of these pairs is pronounced differently, the first tense with BATH and the second lax with TRAP.

Different splits in short-A are found across a number of English dialects, but none are identical to the NYCE version. The most similar are found in neighboring dialects from Providence to Baltimore that also have tense BATH and lax TRAP; NYCE differs from these dialects mainly in the words containing lax and tense vowels. *Cab* and *cash*, for example, are tense in NYCE but lax in Philadelphia. A different type of BATH/TRAP split is found in Southern Britain, the southern hemisphere, and eastern New England. There, BATH is called *broad-A*, phonetically often [ɑː] or [ɒː] ('ah'), which is longer and farther back, giving rise to pronunciations like 'dahnce' for *dance* and 'bahth' for *bath* whereas TRAP – called *flat-A* – remains [æ], as it does in NYCE. The distribution between BATH and TRAP differ among these dialects and between them and NYCE.

---

4 I have altered the transcription to maintain consistency with the conventions used in this book.
5 Wells provides START as an equivalent pronunciation before /r/, but all research on NYCE shows that an r-less pronunciation is equivalent to PALM.

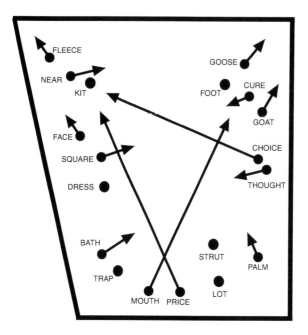

Figure 3.3: Vowel Chart of maximal NYCE vowels

The nasal short-A system mentioned earlier is not a split because the two pronunciations are not two phonemes but allophones (i.e., alternate forms) of the same phoneme; there are no words distinguished only by lax and tense short-As. Instead, there is a rule – i.e., tense always and only before nasal consonants, lax elsewhere – that predicts the distinct forms. Labov, et al. (2006) show this system is the most widespread in North America, but almost as frequent is a slightly different short-A distribution called a continuous system that has only a tendency for pre-nasal short-As to be higher than non-nasal ones. Another non-split outcome is found in the area around the US side of the Great Lakes from Syracuse to Wisconsin, which is the the Inland North. Here short-A is always tense.

The Inland North pronunciation can be heard in the speech of the actor Dennis Franz, who is from the Chicago area and was spectacularly miscast dialectally in his role of the hard-boiled detective Andy Sipowicz in the 1990s series *NYPD Blue*. To anyone paying attention to Sipowicz's speech, Franz's tense pronunciation of words like *back, cat, Spanish,* or *salad* undermined the supposed realism that the series had as a hallmark. The problem, of course, could easily have solved with a backstory giving Chicago origins and a move to New York, but it seems that the writers and producers were oblivious to the dialectal discord. As Labov (personal communication) has pointed out, the fact that they got away with it is testimony to dialectal deafness of much of the US television viewing audience.

The status of the NYCE short-A system has been a source of linguistic controversy because the distribution has some allophone-like characteristics. Some researchers have focused on the fact that rules can be adduced for most cases and claimed that the two sounds are best seen as allophones of one phoneme (Halle & Mohanan 1985, Benua 1995). Nevertheless, these rules are hardly simple. Labov, Yeager, and Steiner (1972: 48) – who then assumed an allophonic analysis – describe it as "the most complex conditioning rule that we know of." Furthermore, most researchers, including Labov later, have pointed to the minimal pairs and claimed that they are definitive diagnostics of separate phoneme status (Trager 1940, Labov 1994, 2001, 2007, Kaye 2012). Silverman (2002) describes the system as an *incipient* split. The complexity involved in describing the system by rules can begin to be appreciated in Figure 3.4 (adapted from Labov 2007: 354, 2010: 317). Short-A is tense before the consonants inside the polygon and lax before those outside it; the dotted lines enclose sounds with inherent variability:

	Bilabial	Labio-dental	Dental	Alveolar	Palatal	Velar
voiceless stops/affricates	p			t	ʧ'ch'	k
voiced stops/affricates	b			d	ʤ 'j'	g
nasals	m			n		ŋ 'ng'
voiceless fricatives		f	θ 'th'	s	ʃ 'sh'	
voiced fricatives		v	ð 'dh'	z	ʒ 'zh'	
liquids				l	r	

Figure 3.4: First level conditioning contexts for the NYCE short-A split.

The pattern is particularly difficult because the sounds inside the polygon cannot be described in terms of any single natural class such as "before all nasals" as in a nasal system. A further complication is that many constraints are added upon those already tricky conditions. The following list is taken with minor adaptations from Labov (2010: 317).

a. Function-word constraint: Function words with simple codas (*an, I can, had*) have lax short-*A*, while corresponding content words have the tense variant (*tin can, hand, add*); *can't*, with a complex coda, has the tense vowel, however.

b. <u>Open-syllable constraint:</u> Short-*A* is lax in open syllables, yielding tense *ham*, *plan*, *cash* but lax *hammer*, *planet*, *cashew*.
c. <u>Inflectional-boundary closing</u>: Inflectional boundaries close syllables, so that tensing occurs in *planning* as well as *plan*, *staffer* as well as *staff*.[6]
d. <u>Variable items:</u> Considerable variation is found before voiced fricatives (*jazz*).
e. <u>Initial condition:</u> Initial short-*A* with a coda that normally produces tensing is lax (*aspirin, asterisk*) except for in the most common words (*ask, after*).
f. <u>Abbreviations</u>: Short-*A* is often lax in abbreviated personal names (*Cass, Babs*).
g. <u>Lexical</u> <u>exceptions</u>: There are a number of lexical exceptions: for example, *avenue* is normally tense as opposed to lax *average, savage, gavel*.
h. <u>Learned</u> <u>words</u>: Many learned or late-learned words have lax short-*a* in environments where tensing would normally occur: *alas, carafe*.

Although an actor like Franz or Brando could argue that these complications are just too difficult to learn, it is possible to successfully portray an authentic traditional New Yorker even without getting all the nuances. Cohen (1970) reports on many New Yorkers who miss one or more constraints. A few do not even conform to aspects of the basic pattern, most commonly by tensing before the velar nasal /ŋ/ (as in *hang*). That said, the basic pattern held for most White and partially held for some Black Lower East Siders at the time of Labov's fieldwork (SSENYC, Labov, Yaeger, & Steiner 1972).

Although Labov describes the rules for NYCE short-A split, in SSENYC he was concerned only with the actual pronunciation of BATH, not which words it appears in. Consequently, BATH can be seen as a variable in and of itself, which Labov transcribed as (aeh). At the mid-level, *bad* comes to be homophonous with *bared* in it its r-less pronunciation. *Bad* and *bared* then can move together still further to the highest level, so these words become homonyms with *beard*.

---

6 Condition (c) is key to Silverman's (2002) argument. He describes it as the result of what he calls "a static complementary relationship" meaning that the allophone is established by rule in the stem, and it does not change when suffixation makes for a new phonetic context.

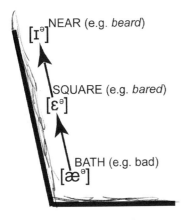

NEAR (e.g. *beard*)
[ɪ^ə]

SQUARE (e.g. *bared*)
[ɛ^ə]

BATH (e.g. bad)
[æ^ə]

Figure 3.5: Upward shift of BATH, modified from Becker (2010: 20)

Labov found in SSENYC that as with (r), increased formality and higher social class tended to reduce the height of BATH variants, although the split itself was not affected. Yet unlike (r), which was declining, BATH height was increasing over generations (Labov, et al. 1972) in an unconscious or *change-from-below* pattern. Also, there were ethnic differences: Labov found that Italians raised BATH more than Jews, and many African Americans, particularly younger ones, did not have a short-A split at all but used a nasal system. The last finding was confirmed and extended later by Becker and Wong (2009), Coggshall and Becker (2010), and Becker (2010) who find that among non-Whites the nasal system was pervasive.

The non-White members of the BQ-16 also mostly had nasal systems, an example of which is shown in Figure 3.6 which depicts the Haitian American Kendrick Pierre's short-A vowels. The numbers at the side refer to the frequencies in hertz of first and second formants used to plot the vowels and made comparable to other speakers through a process called normalization.[7] Triangles represent nasal and circles non-nasal contexts. Filled-in shapes are those that would be tense in the traditional NYCE short-A split, whereas empty symbols would be lax, and those that show variation in Cohen (1970) are half filled. The triangles cluster in the tense area above and to the left of the lax one, which is filled with circles, but whether the shapes are filled in versus empty seems to matter not at all.

---

7 Labov ANEA TELSUR – G normalization was used on Thomas & Kendall's (2007–2012) NORM suite http://ncslaap.lib.ncsu.edu/tools/norm/norm1.php

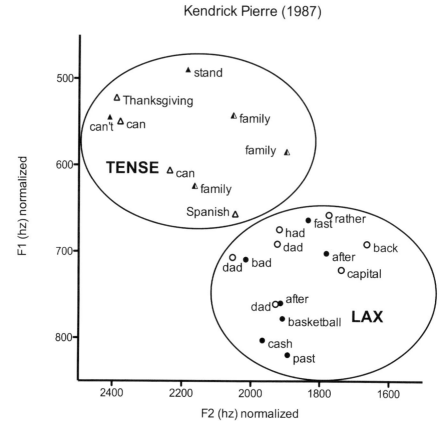

Figure 3.6: Kendrick Pierre's nasal short-A system (TELSUR-G Normalized) triangles=pre-nasal position, circles=pre-oral position. Filled=traditional NYCE tense, empty=traditional NYCE lax[8]

Becker and her colleagues also found a progression from intact NYCE systems predominating among older White speakers to transitional ones among the middle aged ones to some form of nasal system among younger speakers, i.e., those born after the 1970s. Becker (2010: 198) concludes that the complex NYCE short-A "system is being lost in this sample," a sign of deregionalization of this feature.

---

8 Labov (2010) describes *dad* as tense and indeed it could be according to the rules to be discussed above. That said, no speaker in the BQ-16 had tense *dad,* which could be because it was learned as *daddy* and then shortened since short-A is lax in open syllable position.

Becker's cautious wording limiting the claim to "this sample" implies her awareness that this finding may not reflect the state of short-A in the city as a whole. When Labov gathered his data in the early 1960s, the LES could be plausibly thought of as representative of the dialect region. Since then the demographics of that area, like much of Manhattan, have been altered enormously as described in Chapter 2. Although Coggshall and Becker (2010) examined short-A in other boroughs among White and Black speakers with similar findings, their outer borough participants include only three White speakers born after 1980. Furthermore, all three were from Brooklyn, the borough after Manhattan with greatest influx of transplants.

Therefore, just as the White loss of r-lessness was far less among some of the BQ-16 White participants than those in Becker's study on the LES, so it may be the case that the NYCE short-A split remains more robust in areas with less population shift. Actually, demographics could be expected to have even greater impact on a complex feature like the short-A split than a simple one like (r). It is generally the case that children speak more like their peers than their parents, but Payne (1980) showed that this was not the case for short-A for children who moved at an early age to Philadelphia. It was difficult for these children, who initially acquired their parents' short-A system, to acquire the local one. Becker (2010) Coggshall and Becker (2010), Becker and Wong (2009) examined long rooted New Yorkers, but the younger ones were likely surrounded as children by peers with transplant parents, which could easily have disrupted their maintenance of the system.

To investigate this possibility, I undertook a study of three generations of four White family groups from more demographically stable parts of the dialect region using a read-aloud task that targeted a variety of short-A contexts (Newman 2011). The results showed that no participant had a nasal system, but neither did any have an intact traditional NYCE one. The addition of a velar nasal (e.g., *hang*) context to the tensing class was universal in the youngest generation, but a variety of mixed systems that included elements of the nasal and traditional NYCE systems were more common.

Table 3.3: Short-A type scores of BQ-16 participants

East Asians		Blacks		Latinos		Whites	
Mandie John	3	Rashid Lewis	3	Delia Figueres	2	Carl Pisapia	0
Chang John	2	Kendrick Pierre	3	Colton Vega	3	Laura Feldman	1
Clara Chin	3	Diondre Davis	2	Missy Ibáñez	2	Andy Sullivan	0
		Darryl Hanson	3	Johan Aranda	3	Janet Krebbs	1
						Sharon Rosen	2

The BQ-16 provide further data on the state of the NYCE Short-A, and Table 3.3 shows their results. An intact system receives 0; a NYCE system plus velar nasals, 1; a mixed system, 2; and a nasal one, 3.

Two of the five young Whites show intact systems, unlike the younger participants in Newman (2011), Becker (2010) and Coggshall and Becker (2010), and two others have the intact plus velar nasal pattern. Figure 3.7 illustrates Carl Pisapia's intact short-A system. The filled-in symbols – indicating traditional BATH – dominate the tense area be they triangles for nasal contexts or circles for oral ones. Empty symbols predominate in the lax group, with one *passed* out of place. Carl varies for *family*, a word that varies in the intact NYCE system (Cohen 1970):

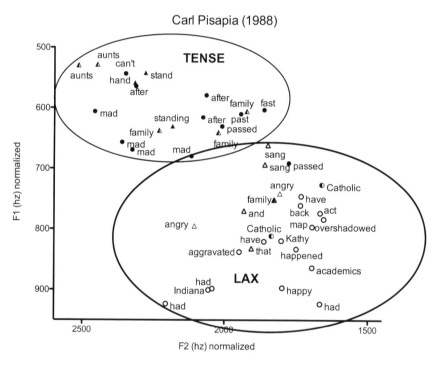

Figure 3.7: Carl Pisapia's short-A system (TELSUR-G Normalized) triangles=pre-nasal position, circles=pre-oral position. Filled=traditional NYCE tense, empty=traditional NYCE lax

Of the non-Whites, Chang, Diondre, and Missy – the oldest speakers – have mixed systems as does the much younger Delia. As can be seen in Figure 3.8, all Chang's unambiguously tense tokens are nasal, and all but one nasal token is tense. However, words that would otherwise be tense in an intact NYCE system tend to be tenser than those that would be lax. Also, there is no clear separation into two clusters, but instead some tokens fall between what seem to be the unambiguously tense and lax sets.

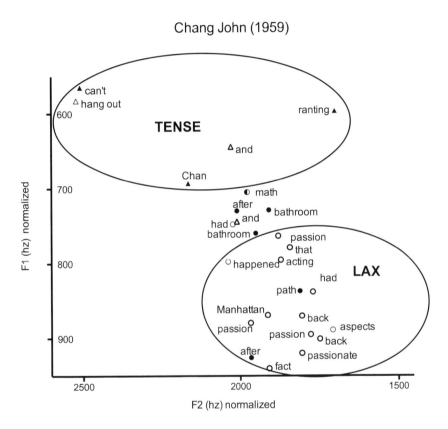

Figure 3.8: Chang John's short-A system (TELSUR-G Normalized) triangles=pre-nasal position, circles=pre-oral position. Filled=traditional NYCE tense, empty=traditional NYCE lax

The data from Newman (2011) and the BQ-16 do not refute the trend found by Becker and her colleagues that the short-A system is simplifying and may be becoming less common among White New Yorkers. However, they suggest that this decline may be happening much more slowly outside the areas they surveyed. Still it should be pointed out that Durian (2012) makes a convincing case that split short-A systems were once far more common across much of the Eastern United States and have evolved into nasal or continuous systems. New York, like the Mid-Atlantic might simply be lagging in this process of simplification.

3.3.2 The low-back system: "Send a Salami to Your Boy in the Army"

Although Labov et al. (2006) use short-A as their primary vowel diagnostic of NYCE, the raised pronunciation of THOUGHT – up to [ʊ³] 'ooh-uh' – is surely more salient for most Americans. This vowel appears in many words such as *paw, talk, caught,* but the raised pronunciation of *coffee* as [kʊ³fi] 'koo-uhffee' has become a particular NYCE stereotype. Why then did Labov et al. (2006) not use THOUGHT as a diagnostic of NYCE instead of the short-A split? One reason is that the raised pronunciation of THOUGHT is actually shared with the Mid-Atlantic region as far south as Baltimore. Also, THOUGHT forms part of a larger subsystem of vowels including LOT and PALM that share, at least historically, the lower back corner of the vowel space. Systemic patterns, be they short-A or this low back subsystem, serve to define dialects, not the pronunciation of a single phoneme. Actually, an alternative definition could rely on the fact that New York preserves the three historic low-back vowels, which merge in different combinations in other varieties as illustrated in Figure 3.9. The diagram is only phonological showing which word classes exist and says nothing about the vowels are actually pronounced, which will be discussed shortly.

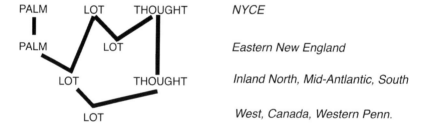

PALM   LOT   THOUGHT   *NYCE*

PALM   LOT   *Eastern New England*

LOT   THOUGHT   *Inland North, Mid-Antlantic, South*

LOT   *West, Canada, Western Penn.*

Figure 3.9: Low Back vowel word class configurations (simplified from Labov et al. 2006: 173)

Eastern New England is characterized by preserving PALM while merging of LOT and THOUGHT, called the *cot-caught* merger because those two words are homonyms where it takes place. The combined vowel is referred to as LOT here after the class that contributes the most words, and it is pronounced as [ɔ], 'aw,' whereas PALM is [ɑː] 'ah,' as in the stereotype phrase, "Pahk the cah in Hahvahd yahd." One New Yorker with this dialect is Michael Bloomberg, mayor from 2002 to 2013 but born and raised in Massachusetts. Interestingly, a *New York Times* article (Roberts 2006) reports that the mayor adapted a bit to the New York speech patterns, including raising his THOUGHT although the impression will be considerably undermined by the continued merger with LOT. Curiously, his successor,

Bill DeBlasio was also mainly raised in the Boston area, but he does not show as many Eastern New England features and lacks the cot-caught merger.

The Inland North, the Mid Atlantic and the South all have two-vowel systems with a PALM-LOT merger – with the merged class referred to as LOT after the larger source – and separate THOUGHT. Yet within this phonological commonality, the varieties show three very different phonetic outcomes. The Inland North LOT fronts to [a], similar to the Spanish vowel in *papa* (meaning *potato* or *pope*), and this pronunciation provides another clue to Dennis Franz's Chicago origins. For example, his Lt. Sipowicz pronounces *cop* and *calm* as [kʰap] and [kʰãm] respectively, instead of the NYCE [kʰɑp] and [kʰe̞ːm]. Franz's renditions cannot be phonetically respelled, but it approximates 'kap.'

The Inland North THOUGHT is also different from its NYCE rendition ending up phonetically identical to the NYCE LOT, i.e., [ɑ], 'ah.' So Franz said *officer* and *caught* as [ɑfəsɚ] and [kʰɑt] ('ahfisser' and 'caht'), instead of the more authentic [ʊəfəsə] and [kʰʊət] ('oo-uhfissa' and 'koo-uht'). This phonetic resemblance can lead to misunderstanding, such as a case I witnessed at a family wedding. A cousin from Detroit – another Inland North city – pronounced the name *Dawn* as [dãn] '(dahn)', exactly as many New Yorkers would say *Don*. As a result my family members were surprised to be presented to a woman. Had someone named *Don* been at the wedding, the Detroiters would have said his name just as Franz would, [dãn], which could conceivably have created more havoc by getting confused with *Dan*. I imagine that some misidentifications could have been worked into NYPD episodes, but alas such opportunities were lost through the show's dialect illiteracy.

The Mid-Atlantic combined LOT and PALM appear with similar values to NYCE LOT, and when New Yorkers merge these vowels, the result is similar to that found just to the south of the city. Southern dialects by contrast have a quite distinct THOUGHT that is at least in many places similar to the standard MOUTH (Labov et al. 2006: 254–256). Although African American New Yorkers have some other Southern vowel features, they use the NYCE realization of THOUGHT, as will be discussed later in this section.

Finally, in most of Canada, the Western US, and Western Pennsylvania, LOT, PALM, and THOUGHT merge into a single phoneme, also resulting in a *cot-caught* merger, with the resulting phoneme varying between [ɑ] 'ah' and [ɔ] 'aw.' The full merger provides another way to confuse the names *Don* and *Dawn* since they like *cot* and *caught* end up as homonyms. Because this system dominates California, it is frequently heard in movies. The dialectal infamy that can result when an actor with this system plays a New Yorker is exemplified by Tobey Maguire in his role of the Queens teenager, Peter Parker, who becomes Spiderman. It appears with great power comes no local authenticity.

Nevertheless, Johnson (2010) seems (at first at least) to provide a possible defense of Maguire and the directors who cast him in that role. Johnson asked adolescents in various parts of the Northeast whether they pronounced seven potential minimal pairs like *caught* and *cot* and *Dawn* and *Don* as the same or different. He found that only about one-third of his New York participants reported all seven pairs to be distinct. However, about two-thirds did so for at least five of the seven and only nine percent found them to be all the same, meaning that few ultimately reported the complete merger. Still, the implication is that some New Yorkers do have that "California style" merger. Yet any such defense of Maguire – not that Johnson was proposing one – falls apart when looking more deeply at this subset. Peter Parker is clearly a White working-class New Yorker, but Johnson observes the tendency for the ones reporting full mergers to be second-generation immigrants. This observation reflects a pattern that I have noticed teaching at Queens College. It seems anecdotally that the *cot-caught* merger is relatively more common among my second generation and generation 1.5 South Asians, who are frequently from the parts of Queens Johnson sampled. A merger for this population makes sense because South Asian languages and Indian English generally have no distinction between these vowels (Dan Silverman, personal communication). Yet it is far from the case that all South Asian New Yorkers have the *cot-caught* merger; I have had students of this background who preserve the classic NYCE THOUGHT. The social correlates of this distribution in the South Asian community would be an interesting subject for further research.

THOUGHT is examined by Labov in SSENYC as the variable (oh), which parallels its tense back partner (aeh), here called BATH. Whereas Italians raise BATH more than Jews, Labov finds the opposite for THOUGHT. He also finds that raising is increasing over time, just like BATH, as a change from below. Labov, et al. (2006), who use acoustic analysis to examine vowels across North America, establish a threshold for what they consider a raised THOUGHT as below 700 hz for the first formant (i.e., above that line on the vowel chart since, confusingly, the lower the frequency the higher it appears on the chart). All their White New York area participants produce raised variants by that criterion. Wong (2007, 2009), Coggshall and Becker (2010), and Becker (2010) find that raised THOUGHT, unlike the short-A split, is well represented among Asians, Latinos, and Blacks.

This situation may not last, at least among Asians and Whites. Wong (2007, 2012) notices lowering of THOUGHT among those Chinese Americans in her study with a tendency to orient to their own ethnic group socially. In a larger study, however, she finds an extensive trend for lowering among younger Chinese Americans (Wong 2012) generally. Becker (2010) and Coggshall and Becker (2009) also find a lowering of THOUGHT among young Whites on the LES and Brooklyn. Olivo (2013) also finds some lowering, particularly among younger women using wordlist data on Long Island but finds no ethnic variation. Finally, Becker (2011) finds that attitudes towards raised THOUGHT were not positive among a wide variety of New Yorkers, auguring a further decline, although likely quite a slow one. Nevertheless, THOUGHT clearly remains distinct from LOT for the vast majority of New Yorkers.

There is an additional complication, which was discovered after the elaboration of the vowel inventories that are the source for Table 3.2 and Figure 3.3. In SSENYC, Labov discusses NORTH, the pre-/r/ vowel in words like *lore, four,* and *fourth,* as merged with THOUGHT in its r-less pronunciation; *lore* is therefore homonymous with *law*. However, in the first acoustic study of some of the same participants Labov, Yaeger, and Steiner (1972: V2 2–9) report being surprised to find slight differences, with r-less NORTH typically slightly backer and/or higher than THOUGHT. These differences occur despite the speakers' belief that they are pronouncing them identically. This discovery gives rise to the concept of *near merger*, when a sound remains slightly distinct in production but not in awareness (Labov 1994, Labov, Karen, & Miller, 1991).

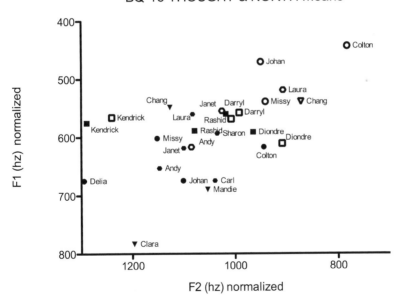

Figure 3.10: BQ-16 means of THOUGHT and NORTH. THOUGHT = filled-in NORTH = empty. Latinos = circles, Blacks = squares, Asians = triangles, Whites = hexagons

The BQ-16 provide a useful panorama of New Yorkers' THOUGHT and NORTH vowels that can support or complicate previous findings. Figure 3.10 provides the mean THOUGHT for all BQ-16s and the mean NORTH for those with r-less variants.

All five White participants have high THOUGHT and so diverge from the mainly Manhattan data of Becker (2010) and Coggshall & Becker (2010); only Carl Pisapia (who is also r-ful but has an intact short-A split) approaches Labov et al,'s (2006) lower threshold of 700 hz. for a non-raised variant. By contrast, Wong's (2012) finding about younger Chinese Americans' lowering THOUGHT does receive corroboration. Clara Chin is the only participant who fails to surpass 700 hz. Mandy John approaches it whereas her father Chang John has a much higher THOUGHT.

Probably the most interesting data visible in Figure 13.10 involve the near merger of THOUGHT and NORTH, found originally in Labov et al. (1972). The Asian, White, and Latino participants with r-less pronunciations have NORTH higher and/or backer than THOUGHT, sometimes considerably so, as in the case of Colton Vega. The Black participants have little to no difference.[9] As with (r), a superficial similarity of the Blacks to other speakers gives way to a subtler and probably unnoticeable systematic difference upon closer examination.

The second (or possibly third if we consider NORTH as a differentiated vowel) element in the NYCE low-back system is PALM. Labov refers to this vowel as (ah), which reflects its origins in the small set of descendants of Middle English long-A in words such as *father* and *calm*. This small class of words subsequently absorbed a few later borrowings like *salami*. The number of PALM words increases before /r/ in words like *guard, car,* and *army* when /r/ is not pronounced giving rise to the WWII era rhyming slogan, "Send a Salami to your Boy in the Army," still visible on the walls of Katz's Deli on Houston Street that I used in the title to this subsection. Finally, Labov, et al. (2006: 236) following on from investigations in Cohen (1970) note a shift in some words from the historical short-O class. Most descendants of short-O are lax and have come down to us as LOT, but Labov et al. (2006) report that when their morphemes end in voiced sounds they often become tense and join PALM. Labov et al. give *despondent, odd,* and *Don,* from one New Yorker in their sample as examples. At the same time, they observe that "lexical assignments to [PALM] appear to differ from one speaker to another" (Labov, et. al. 2006: 236).

One of the few researchers to look at this vowel in NYCE is Kaye (2012), although he did not conduct a study of New Yorkers' production but performed a purely phonological analysis based on his own intuitions as a native speaker of

---

9 Labov et al. (2006) show that the FORCE-NORTH merger (often called the *hoarse-horse* merger due to the fact that these two words become homonyms) is complete among Whites, but not for 2 of the three African American New Yorkers surveyed. This was not found for the BQ-16 Blacks.

NYCE. Kaye like Labov, et al. (2006) observes that some short-O words migrated to PALM in NYCE, but the rule he provides is slightly different: i.e., before voiced sounds in closed syllables, as in *god, bob, bomb,* and *doll*. Like short-A words that tense to BATH, these words remains PALM even when the syllable becomes open due to the addition of a suffix beginning with a vowel:

> "Plot" has a different stem vowel from the verb stem "plod." It should come as no surprise then, that the participial forms "plotting" and "plodding" are not homophones in spite of the flapping. They have different lexical vowels and so there is no reason for them to merge. (Kaye 2012: 337)

Part of the reason to think of PALM and THOUGHT as part of a subsystem rather than as simply independent vowels is that they interact. Labov discusses them as engaging in what he calls the New York City Chain Shift (Labov 1995: 203) as illustrated in Figure 3.11.

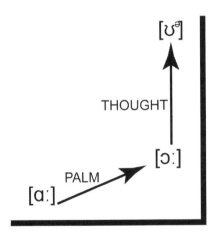

Figure 3.11: NYC Chain shift of as described by Labov (1995: 203)

A chain shift involves the movement of two or more vowels in tandem, i.e., chained together as it were. As shown in Figure 3.11, as THOUGHT moves towards [uᵊ], PALM, which starts at [ɑː] – similar to LOT but longer – and moves up and back towards the position THOUGHT abandoned. Recall, however that not all New Yorkers have a separate PALM; some follow the more common North American pattern and merge it with LOT.

For most New Yorkers LOT is lax and stable, phonetically [ɑ], but one caveat involves Latinos. Some Latino New Yorkers front a merged PALM and LOT towards

[a], the quality of the Spanish vowel in *papa*. An illustration arose once in my fieldwork at UAA, when a Dominican New Yorker pronounced the PALM word *water* as [warə]. At this point another Latino student laughed, and when I asked him why, he told me, "He sounds so Spanish." This comment reflects an association of this pronunciation with non-native speakers, although I have certainly heard it among those who were born in New York too, like the Dominican American cited above. Nevertheless, there was little evidence of it in the BQ-16. Of the Latinos, Missy had the most fronted LOT, but it was less so than the Haitian American Kendrick and the African American Rashid.

For PALM, all the participants except for Clara Chin and Mandie John show some evidence of the existence of a separate vowel class. However, at times there appears to be a declining number of words in that class; for example, for Laura, *god* is in the LOT class and Andy tends to mix the two sets, with PALM words only tending to be backer and higher. Janet Krebbs, by contrast, has robust three vowel low-back system as shown in Figure 3.12.

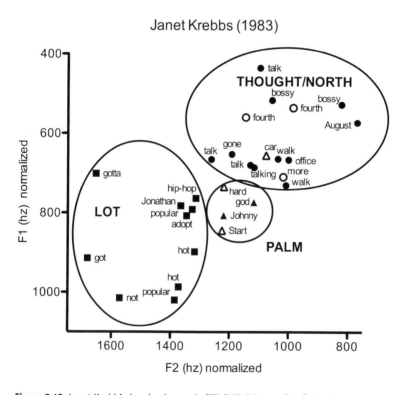

Figure 3.12: Janet Krebb's low back vowels (TELSUR-G Normalized): circles = THOUGHT, NORTH, triangles = PALM, squares = LOT, Filled = no etymological /r/, empty = etymological /t/

Note that *Johnny* (derived from the closed syllable *John*) and *god* are placed in the PALM group but the first syllable of *Jonathan* has LOT as per Kaye's (2012) rule about open syllables remaining LOT.

Figure 3.13 shows Rashid Lewis's low back system, which like all the Black participants has a distinct PALM class. *Moms* contains the conditions described by Kaye (2012) for the shift to PALM, and its showing up in the PALM class suggests that the same rules apply, but *concerts* varies slightly from Kaye's tensing condition since it is not word final although the vowel is in a closed syllable. The proper name *Don* remains low as would be expected following Kaye's rules because it is clipped from *Donald*, in which the short-O is in an open syllable. However, Labov et al. (2006) have *Don* in the PALM class for their speaker. *On* is very high and joins the THOUGHT group, which reflects a common southern pattern (Thomas 2001).

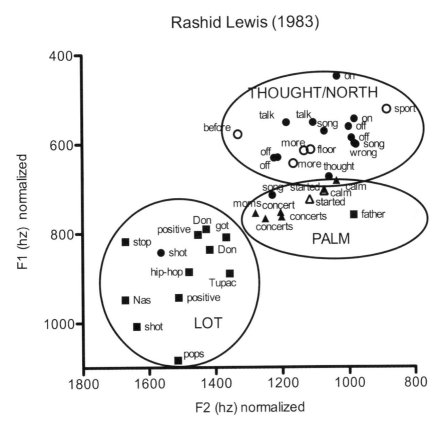

Figure 3.13: Rashid Lewis's low back vowels normed using TELSUR-G: circles = THOUGHT, NORTH, triangles = PALM, squares = LOT, Filled = no etymological /r/, empty = etymological /t/

A race-based difference in assignment to words to the low back classes is mentioned by Edwards (2004) who notes the lexical set called CLOTH – another group
of short-O words that in NYCE is merged into THOUGHT – is LOT for African Americans. Edwards also reports THOUGHT as having an upglide following the southern
pattern rather than the raising and inglide typical of NYCE. Nevertheless, Rashid
and the other Black participants do not separate CLOTH, and they raise THOUGHT
similar to other New Yorkers, as do Coggshall and Becker (2010) and Becker's
(2010) Black participants. Edwards also describes AAE PALM as fronted to [æ],
which is quite different from the pattern seen in Figure 3.13.

Figure 3.14 shows Colton's four-vowel system, which is representative of the
other Latinos, save for various permutations in lexical assignment. Missy Ibáñez
has *god* in the LOT group and *talk* in the PALM group, and Dalia puts *thought* in the
PALM group. This is clearly an area for more research.

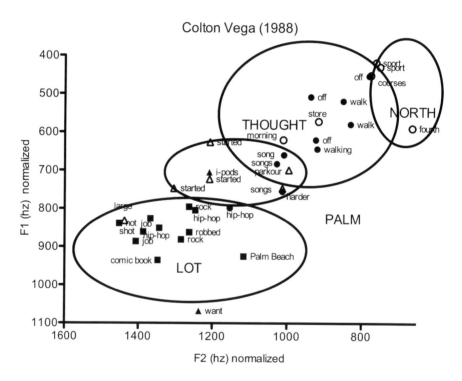

Figure 3.14: Colton Vega's low back vowels normed using TELSUR-G: circles = THOUGHT, NORTH,
triangles = PALM, squares = LOT, Filled = no etymological /r/, empty = etymological /t/

To summarize, it is possible to distinguish four different low-back vowel systems among New Yorkers each with a different number of vowels:

–   <u>Four:</u> LOT, PALM, THOUGHT, and NORTH, with the last two in near merger characteristic of some White, Asian and the Latino participants.
–   <u>Three:</u> LOT, PALM, and THOUGHT (which has absorbed NORTH) characteristic of the Black participants.
–   <u>Two:</u> LOT (which has absorbed PALM) and THOUGHT (which has absorbed NORTH) here characteristic only of the two younger East Asian participants, Mandie, and Clara
–   <u>One:</u> LOT (which now stands for all low back vowels), although this completely deregionalized pattern remains rare and limited to second-generation immigrants, probably mostly South Asians.

3.3.3 Two Diphthongs or Three?

In standard accounts of American English the diphthongs PRICE and MOUTH start with the same central low vowel [a] as nucleus and are distinguished by their glides: towards [ɪ] and [ʊ] respectively, thus *pie* and *pow* are [pʰaɪ] and [pʰaʊ].

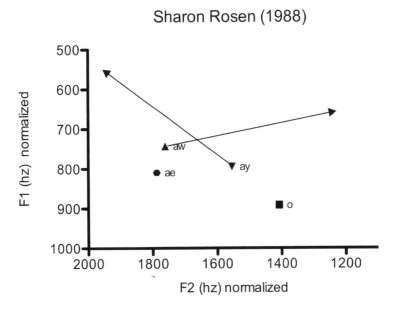

Figure 3.15: Sharon Rosen's mean nucleus and glides for PRICE and MOUTH (TELSUR Normalized)

Labov in SSENYC and Labov, et al. (2006: 235) following earlier dialectologists such as Hubbell (1950) and Bronstein (1962) report a change in this pattern in NYCE. The nucleus of PRICE shifts back so *pie* becomes [pʰɑ¹] 'pah-y' while that of MOUTH moves towards the front leaving *pow* as [pʰæᵁ] 'pa-w.'

Because this change increases the distance of nucleus to glide target, it is called *nucleus-glide differentiation*. In a vowel chart the backing of one nucleus and the fronting of the other leads the trajectories of the two glides to cross. This crossing pattern can be seen Sharon Rosen's mean PRICE and MOUTH in Figure 3.15. Yet although Sharon's mean MOUTH nucleus is clearly well fronted and so quite near TRAP, her PRICE mean nucleus is central and therefore distant from LOT. The crossing is actually created only by the fronting of MOUTH not the backing of PRICE.

Kaye (2012) suggests that Hubbell, Bronstein, and Labov's account is incomplete in a way that provides clues to the source of Sharon's lack of symmetry. Although Kaye agrees that MOUTH behaves as they describe, he limits the backing of the nucleus of PRICE to certain phonetic contexts. These consist of the same environments that trigger the reassignment of short-o words from LOT to PALM plus open syllables, an environment in which short-O never appears. So on Kaye's account, words like *prize, pry, pie,* and *despise* have longer durations and become backed in the way Labov describes as [ɑ¹] but words like *price, ripe,* and *cider* remain [a¹]. Following Thomas (2010) – who was referring to a different process involving similar environments – I refer to the backer diphthong with the keyword PRIZE. It is worth noting that Labov, et al. (2006: 237) observe this process taking place in Philadelphia.

Kaye's account is theoretical and based on his intuitions as a native New Yorker although Thomas's (2001) lone White New York speaker (an older woman) shows this PRICE/PRIZE distribution. I am aware of no other empirical data. Fortunately, the BQ-16 can begin to provide some evidence. First, Sharon shows no sign of Kaye's suggested split or Labov's backing of PRICE/PRIZE, but she does so in an unusual way: not backing PRIZE at all, and the other four White participants show this distinction. Figure 3.16 shows the nuclei of Andy Sullivan's PRICE and PRIZE with his mean LOT given for reference. Note that *high school* follows the PRICE, which fits my own intuition, although *high*, on its own, is in my PRIZE class. Unfortunately, *high* did not appear in Andy's interview outside that compound.[10]

---

10 Thomas Kettig (personal communication), a sociolinguist from Jackson Heights like me but generation younger reports that for him *high school* is also PRIZE.

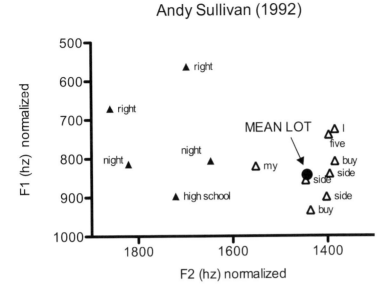

Figure 3.16: Andy Sullivan's PRICE vs PRIZE nuclei (TELSUR Normalized): empty triangles PRIZE, filled triangles PRICE.

This split appears limited to White New Yorkers, although as Sharon Rosen's data shows not all of them. Still, to go out on a limb, I would say this backing of PRIZE and fronting of MOUTH – forms a major cue to a White ethnic NYCE. Certainly, of the BQ-16, none of the non-Whites show it. Significantly, the split creates minimal pairs such as *rider* and *writer* and *wider* and *whiter*. The first member of these pairs preserves the backer nucleus and longer duration of PRIZE; the second maintains the more central vowel quality and shorter duration of PRICE.

Nevertheless, all four Latinos give some evidence of a very closely related though unexpected phenomenon, so-called Canadian raising, i.e., the heightening of the nucleus of PRICE and MOUTH before voiceless consonants. This process is not limited to Canada, although its realization in the word *about*, 'aboot' has become a Canadian stereotype. An example is seen with Johan Aranda, who shows a tendency for following voiceless stops to raise PRICE nuclei and leave PRIZE nuclei low. MOUTH however is not affected, as it would be in Canada and probably most other Canadian-raising regions. In Figure 3.17, potentially raising environments – before voiceless consonants – are indicated by filled triangles and non-raising ones – all other environments – are empty triangles. The triangles point up for PRICE/PRIZE and down for MOUTH. Another feature of Johan's diphthongs shared with the other Latinos are just how spread out the nuclei are horizontally. In fact, the tendency here is one of nucleus glide shortening, with PRICE more front and MOUTH more back, a feature also associated with Canada by Labov, et al. (2006):

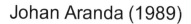

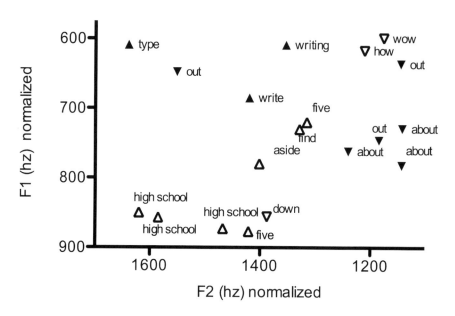

Figure 3.17: Johan Aranda's PRICE, PRIZE, MOUTH nuclei: upward pointing triangles PRICE/PRIZE, downward triangles MOUTH, empty for following voiceless contexts; filled for other contexts.

Curiously, a mirror image of Johan's pattern can be found for Missy Ibáñez who raises primarily MOUTH nuclei with voiceless following consonants. The other two Latinos show more sporadic raising of both.

The phenomenon discussed by Thomas (2010) referred to earlier in which he used the keyword PRIZE is the reduction of the glide producing a monophthong [ɑː] ('ah'). PRICE words do not show that process in many varieties of American English, including most varieties of AAE. For speakers who have this PRICE/PRIZE differentiation, *wide* is [wɑːd] ('wahd'), *why* is [wɑː] ('wah'), but *white* is [waˈt], i.e., still with a diphthong. Only in the Deep South, do White and Black speakers say 'waht' for *white*. Despite the notoriety of this feature, among the four Black speakers in the BQ-16, only two, Kendrick and Rashid, showed it in their interviews, and of the Latinos, Colton and Missy did as well.

3.3.4 Back and Front Upgliding Vowels

Labov et al. (2006: 235) describe the NYCE upgliding vowels FLEECE, FACE, GOAT and GOOSE as indicative of "the conservative character" of NYCE. This statement mostly refers to the behavior of the back vowels GOAT and GOOSE, which unlike other varieties such as the Mid-Atlantic dialect, remain quite far back in the vowel space. Only GOOSE becomes fronted and only after the coronal consonants – those involving the front of the tongue including /t/, /d/, /s/, /n/, /l/, /r/, /ʃ/, /θ/, /ð/, and /ʒ/ – and these usually retain a back glide. Almost all White varieties of North American English show some degree of fronting in this context. In other words, NYCE participates but lags in a process that is widespread across other varieties.

In the popular mind extremely fronted pronunciations are most associated with California, for example in the pronunciation of the iconic GOOSE word, *dude*, as [dyd], although since /d/ is a coronal context, NYCE also fronts that word somewhat. Only words like *boo, coop, move, ghoul*, and so on are not fronted in New York but are in the West. So Tobey Maguire's fronting of these vowels helps mark him as a southern Californian instead of the native of Queens he was playing in the *Spiderman* movies.

The BQ-16 can be divided into two profiles in terms of GOOSE fronting: Fronting in coronal contexts prevails among Whites and Asians, whereas for Latinos and African Americans there is no or very limited fronting in any context. This state of affairs concurs with Thomas's (2001) findings for African American throughout the US, although Fought (2003, 2006) reports that some sectors of the Latino community in California are beginning to front too.

Labov et al. (2006) add that NYCE has the nucleus of the tense upgliding vowels FACE, GOAT, and GOOSE in non-coronal contexts quite near the corresponding lax monophthongs DRESS, STRUT, and FOOT respectively. The only divergence from this closeness with a lax pair is FLEECE, which is considerably higher than KIT, its equivalent. However, Olivo (2013) examines these vowels among Long Islanders. She finds that in *free* position, when they end the syllable as in *bee, seedy, bay, baby, beau, soda, boo*, and *booty* they are somewhat lower than in checked position *checked* position, when they are followed by a consonant that ends the syllable, as in *beat, bate, boat*, and *boot*. Interestingly, Labov, et al. (2006: 237) find the same result in Philadelphia, where they describe the lowering as a new and vigorous change in progress, with increasing lowering of the vowels in free position. However, Olivo finds a slightly different course of events in Long Island. For GOAT and especially FACE, the distance between the free and checked positions is increasing, but for GOOSE and especially FLEECE it is decreasing. Also, a wider distance appears most common in more traditional White Long

Islanders with other dense NYCE features. The difference was largely absent from non-Whites. Citing an unpublished paper (Olivo and Koops 2013), Olivo (2013: 17) states the following:

> We posited that the high vowel [allophonic] splits are demonstrative of the "traditional" or "classic" NYCE and the splits in the mid vowels are demonstrative of a millennial variety of NYCE at least as it is spoken on Long Island.

Of the BQ-16 only Andy showed any sign of an allophonic distribution of free and checked FLEECE, and none showed any of FACE. The number of tokens examined in these cases was too low to come to a firm conclusion, but if these trends are confirmed, it would be about the only purely geographic distinction found in NYCE so far.

3.3.5 Other conditioned patterns

The lowering described by Olivo (2013), the fronting of GOOSE before coronal consonants is called a conditioned change because it only takes place in specific phonological contexts. Another type of pattern conditioned by phonological context is called *neutralization*, which consists of two phonemes merging only in certain environments. One common neutralization in AAE is where KIT and DRESS merge before nasal consonants, called the *pin-pen* merger since these two words become homonyms. Edwards (2004) claims this neutralization is limited to southern AAE along with southern White varieties, and Coggshall and Becker (2010) agree that it is absent in NYCE AAE. However, two of the three African American participants in Labov, et al. (2006: 299) have this merger. Also, its presence is assumed in the amusing scatological rhyme by the Nuyorican underground rap artist, J-Vega – "I been spin/nin' the shit like a toilet since ten." Of the BQ-16, Rashid Lewis showed the greatest tendency to have a *pin-pen* merger. Figure 3.18 is a vowel chart that shows some overlap of his pin/pen vowels along with a general tendency to maintain the two the basic distinction.

Coggshall and Becker also report the absence of another common southern neutralization, this one of lax-tense differences such FACE and DRESS and KIT and FLEECE before /l/. In dialects in which this neutralization takes place, *hill* and *heel* and *jail* and *jell* become homonyms. Despite that report, this neutralization is quite common among both Latinos and AAE speakers in New York. All three African American participants in Labov et al. (2006: 299) have it, and it occurs variably among all the Black participants in the BQ-16 along with Missy and Colton.

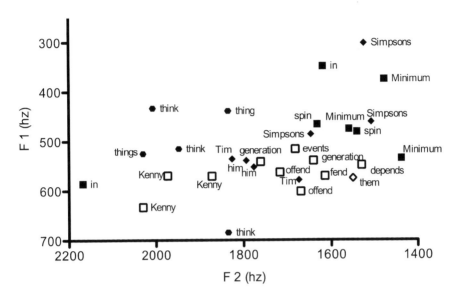

Figure 3.18: Rashid Lewis's pin/pen vowels. Diamonds=following /m/, hexagons following /ŋ/, and squares following /n/. Filled shapes are /ɪ/ and empty shapes are /ɛ/

Another neutralization occurs in most varieties of North American English before /r/. This is the well-known cases in which various combinations of *merry, Mary, marry,* and *Murray* become homonyms. NYCE unusually preserves all four distinctions. The final issue also involves pre-/r/ vowels, although it is not a neutralization. Traditionally, NYCE preserves an older pattern in North American English by which words such as *orange, Oregon, Florida, authority, minority, coral, moral, historic,* and so on are pronounced with the same vowel as *star,* pronounced r-fully; so *orange* for example is [ɑɹəndʒ] ('ahrange'). However, it is clear that younger White speakers are switching to the more common North American NORTH pattern word by word. Older New Yorkers often say *moral* as [mɑɹl̩] 'mahral' and *coral* as [kʰɑɹl̩] 'cahral', but I have [mɔɹl̩] and [kʰɔɹl̩] as do most Americans. Although I vary with *minority, historic,* and *authority,* I retain the older pronunciation the rest of the words including *Florida, Oregon,* and *orange.* Younger people often rarely retain that vowel with the words I show variation with, and some have deregionalized this feature entirely.

3.4 Consonants

3.4.1 Dis and dat: (dh) and (th)

Earlier in this chapter the phrase '*toidy-toid and toid*' was discussed with reference to the r- less vowel [3ɪ], which was described by Labov in SSENYC as coming
to represent NYCE in the popular imagination. But another motive for the iconic
status of this phrase is the [t̪] 't' variant of Labov's variable (th). As mentioned in
Chapter 1, (th) and its pair (dh) – the first sound in *that* – actually function along
a vernacular to standard continuum in many English dialects.

These pronunciations are described phonetically as dental stops [t̪] for (th)
and [d̪] for (dh). The sound is created by the tongue blocking (i.e, stopping) the air
being exhaled at the teeth and then releasing it suddenly. The opposing standard
variants – [θ] and [ð] for (th) and (dh) respectively are described phonetically
as *dental fricatives*. The term fricative refers to the fact the sound heard is the
friction created when tongue forces air through a tight space at the teeth rather
than blocking it entirely before letting it explode out as with the stop. There is
also a third variant called an *affricate* transcribed as [tθ] and [dð], which falls in
between. This consists of a very short stop followed by a longer frication. Actually, most hearers do not notice any difference between the affricate and fricative,
but the stop is quite salient, and thus leads to stereotypes like '*toidy-toid and toid*'
and '*dis and dat*' for *this and that*.

In SSENYC Labov (233) writes, "The great majority of New Yorkers use some
stops and affricates in their everyday speech for the variables (th) and (dh)." For
White speakers (dh) and (th) behave similarly in terms of how social class and
attention to speech correlate with rates of stopping. However, Labov et al. (1968)
note that for Blacks the two variables behave differently. First, in AAE (th) and
(dh) stops appear primarily in onsets (i.e., syllable beginnings), such as *thirty*
and *this*. In codas (i.e., syllable closings) such as in *breathe* and *tooth* and to some
extent medially (i.e., between vowels) as in *brother* and *Kathy* another variant is
common: labiodental fricatives yielding [bɹiv] and [tʰuf] ('breev' and 'toof') and
[bɹʌvə] and [kʰæfi] ('bruhva' and 'Kaffi') respectively. Those, labiodental variants appear nationwide in AAE (Edwards 2004, Thomas 2007, Thomas & Wassink
2010, but the [f] variant for (th) is more common than the [v] variant for (dh). Silverman (1968) notes that the labiodental forms appear frequently among Puerto
Rican New Yorkers too. Although the Puerto Rican member of the BQ-16 Colton
Vega did not present them, Missy Ibáñez – a Dominican American – did and at
high rates, although only for (th).

Even in onsets, where the labiodentals do not appear, Blacks and Whites
differ in rates and patterns of th- and dh-stopping as the appearance of dental

stops is called. In Labov, et al. (1968a) and SSENYC rates are determined through a scale whereby each fricative was assigned 1, each affricate 2, and each stop 3. Then using the formula *mean score minus 1 times 100,* an index was assigned to participants. A categorical standard fricative user would get 0; a speaker with only affricates would get 100; and a pure stop user would get 200. SSENYC provides mean indexes by social class for the mostly White participants on the LES. Labov, et al. (1968a) provide the equivalents for the predominantly Black lower SES boys in Harlem. In that study, the boys were divided into four peer groups plus some who did not participate in the main youth peer culture and were called *lames* as described in Chapter 2. Labov et al. (1968) also provide a comparison group of lower SES White boys from Inwood, which lies at the northern tip of

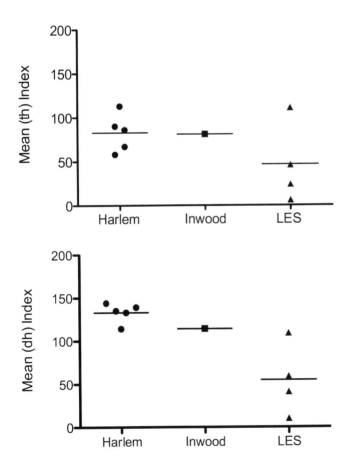

Figure 3.19: Average interview style (th) above and (dh) below indexes from Labov, et al. (1968a: 94) and SSENYC. Line = grand mean

Manhattan. Figure 3.19 graphically summarizes of all these data. Each point under *Harlem* represents the mean for one of the peer groups, which are equivalent socioeconomically. Each point under *LES* stands for the mean of one of the social classes of speakers under 40 years old, which of course vary in SES. There is only one point for *Inwood*, because only one peer group – of similar SES to the Harlem groups – was examined there. The lines show the grand means (i.e., the means of the means) for each community.

In the lower graphic for (dh), the low SES Harlem and Inwood peer groups show similarly high (dh) indexes as expected. The pattern is confirmed in the LES groups where the triangles represent predominantly White samples of different SES ranks, which – although not labeled in the chart – follow the expected order. The lowest SES LES group is comparable socioeconomically and linguistically with the Inwood and Harlem groups and has a similar index.

In the (th) chart above, the White groups on the LES mirror the (dh) chart, although the Inwood group is a bit lower than expected. The major difference lies with the Black groups, which, despite being interchangeable socioeconomically, show random variation. Consequently, Labov et al. (1968a) concluded that for AAE speakers variation in (dh) is more consistent than (th). So (dh) and (th) show yet another case of surface similarities in the use of variables across the Black-White divide that conceal systematic variation.

Unlike with the other variables, Labov in SSENYC claims that there is no evidence for linguistic change in progress for (dh) and (th), but no later studies have confirmed or refuted this prediction in the years since. Therefore, the BQ-16 can begin this task, and their data are shown in Figures 3.20 for (th) above and (dh) below broken down by race.

The BQ-16 data are supported by acoustic analyses unlike the exclusively auditory judgments available in the 1960s, and Labov's data represent group scores whereas the BQ-16 are individuals. Yet with those cautions accepted, the BQ-16 data suggest that Labov was probably right to posit little on-going change for the White group, except possibly the lowest SES, here represented by Janet. There does appear to be change in the form of a major reduction in the use of affricate and above all stop forms of (dh) among African Americans. Rashid is comparable socially to the gang members in Labov et al. (1968), but he shows a remarkably diminished (dh) score of 28 compared to them. By contrast, his (th) scores, like those of the other Blacks, are quite high. It is certainly possible that he is an outlier with respect to others of his background. Nevertheless, he made categorical use of the vernacular AAE coda/medial variant [f] for (th) and one use of the less common [v] for (dh).

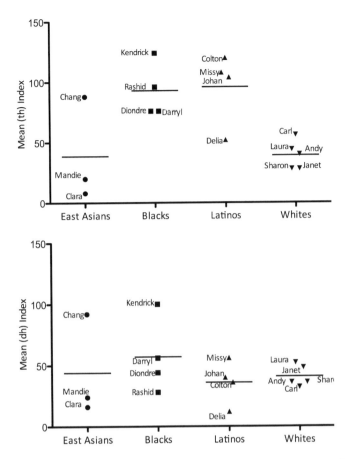

Figure 3.20: BQ-16 Indexes for (th) above and (dh) below. Lines are grand mean

The highest indexes belong to Kendrick Pierre, which is initially surprising because he is in college and his social class origins are higher than Rashid's; Kendrick's father was a teacher in Haiti, who became an electrician in New York. Rashid reported receiving little to no economic support from his father, and said his mother was dependent now on his income. However there is an explanation ready at hand Kendrick's higher rate of stopping in the influence of Haitian Creole – which has no dental fricatives – as a substrate. A similar interpretation can be constructed for Darryl, who has the second highest index. Darryl is an upwardly mobile Jamaican American and so brings forward a potential Jamaican Creole substrate – again Jamaican has no dental fricatives. Interestingly, Newlin-Lukowicz (2013) reports similar high rates of stopping among second generation

Polish New Yorkers, and finds internal evidence for a substrate origin for this feature and for its use as an ethnic marker.

Mandie John and Clara Chin have the lowest (dh) and (th) indexes, whereas Chang John has a quite high one. Chang is the oldest Asian American, and he is also mostly non-rhotic, raises THOUGHT, and shows some influence of the NYCE short-A system. The Latinos show even less correlation between the two variables than the Black members of the BQ-16 since the stop variant is far more common with (th) than (dh). This result is exactly what would be expected from substrate influence. The stop variant of (th) – [t̪] – matches the Spanish /t/ in its articulation whereas the fricative variant [θ] does not exist in Latin American Spanish. By contrast, the fricative form [ð] of (dh) resembles a dental approximant Spanish allophone of /d/ (Hualde 2005).

In sum, (dh) and (th) show a different patterns for each of the racialized groups. Whereas the Whites show relatively little change, the neat association of at least (dh) with SES in the Black group may have gone by the wayside. Also immigration seems likely to have brought in substrate effects from at least Haitian Creole, Jamaican Creole, Polish, Spanish – and probably other languages – that increase th- and dh-stopping in ways that seem to defy traditional SES stratification. This is therefore an interesting variable to explored in future research.

3.4.2 Other Racially Differentiated Consonants

Only a few other consonants have been examined by variationists in New York. One is /l/. In coda position – i.e., after a vowel – as in *coal* and *cold* – /l/ varies between a consonantal [ɫ] and pronounced as a vowel like [ʊ] or [w] rendering 'co-oo' or 'co-ood' or elided entirely. Similarly, syllabic /l/ – i.e., when /l/ constitutes the entirety of the syllable as relaxed rapid pronunciations of *battle* and *dazzle* – the consonant can be the consonant [ɫ] and the vocalized form [ʊ], leading to 'badoo' and 'dazzoo' in phonetic respelling. This process is common in American English, particularly in AAE (Thomas 2007).

Labov et al. (1968a) found high rates the vocalization in their Harlem study particularly after unrounded vowels (all but /o/, /u/, or /ʊ/) leading to [pæʊ] '*pa-oo*' for *pal* or [piʊ] 'pee-oo' for *peel*. After rounded vowels elision was common leading to [boᵘ] for 'bo' for *bowl* (homophonous with *beau*), and [kʰuː] 'coo' for *cool*. In Slomanson and Newman (2004) we found similar results for AAE speakers, who showed near categorical vocalized or elided /l/ codas (we did not distinguish between them). We also found that Latinos in peer cultures such as Hip-Hop, which is affiliated culturally with African Americans, vocalize nearly 78 % of their coda /l/s, and those with largely Latino-peer cultural orientations follow with 71 %. However, other Latinos, who orient more to White-associated peer cultures such as rock and nerd vocalize /l/s at rates similar to White New Yorkers, about 40 % of the time. Incidentally, this is the first study to note vocalization at all among White New Yorkers.

In onsets or between vowels, /l/ is never vocalized in NYCE. There is, nevertheless, variation in its realization between whether the tongue arches towards the back in what is called a *dark*-l [ɫ] or more towards the palate in a *light* or *clear*-l [l]. Although it is often claimed that in English, /l/ is clear in onsets and dark (or vocalized) in codas, Yavas (2011) argues that in most American English onset /l/ tends to be dark. Actually, his observation is preceded by Hubbell (1950) with respect to New Yorkers, and the NYCE /l/ may be darker than many American English varieties. In Slomanson and Newman (2004) and Newman (2010) we found high rates of dark /l/s in onsets in all groups except among Latinos, who tend to use clear /l/s. This is another candidate for substrate effects given the fact that /l/ is clear in Spanish. In fact, when I have asked Latino participants what cues they use to determine if someone speaks Latino English, they often produce a clear variant of /l/, often giving the word *like* as an illustration. The clear-l pronunciation in that word may be becoming a stereotype, although the clear variant is not restricted lexically. Unsurprisingly, given its presence in Spanish, Santa Ana (1996: 73–74) also observes this feature in Chicano English.

In Newman (2010) I examined three other New York Latino English consonantal variables of substrate Spanish origin. Two involve weaker /b/s and /d/s between vowels. These two cases involve the application in English of what is called the Spanish *spirantization* rule. According to this phonological rule, voiced stops /b/, /d/ and /g/ are realized as approximants – i.e., sounds made when the articulators are separated wide enough that there is little to no friction – or they are elided completely (Hualde 2005). This rule applies in different ways in different Spanish dialects, but it most consistent in the environment I examined, i.e., between vowels. As mentioned earlier, the Spanish spirant /d/ is similar to the English [ð] as in *the*. So in the Spanish word *estudio* is pronounced either [estuðjo] 'estutheeo' if the approximant is used or [estujo] 'estueeo' if it is elided. For native speakers of NYLE, the common Spanish learner pronunciation of adding the so-called epethetic *e* before s+consonant (as in the stereotype '*I espeek Espanish*') *never* occurs. However, the spirantization rule can be applied, yielding '[stuðjo] 'stutheeo' or [stujo] 'stueeo.' Spirantization even occurs across word boundaries as in Spanish, as in *candy bar* being pronounced [kʰændiβaɹ], 'candy var' but with the two lips almost touching rather than the top teeth and bottom lip as in the English [v].

In syllable final position, [d] and [t] tend to be elided in Spanish, so the capital of Spain is often pronounced [maðri] 'Mathree' (although [maðrið] '*Mathrith*' is possible) in that language, and a similar effect can be found in NYLE. In Newman (2010) I found that Latino participants' rate of deletion varied between almost 0 % – which matched rates of Whites – and 80 %. This process also appears in AAE (Thomas 2007), but it is far less frequent. I am not aware of research on this phenomenon on other forms of Latino English.

Another Spanish substrate variable discussed in the literature for Chicanos (see Santa Ana & Bayley 2004) is the pronunciation of /d/, /n/, and /t/ with the tongue tip on or near the teeth rather than the blade (or top on or near the alveolar ridge), as is usual in most varieties of English. This pronunciation appears common in NYLE too, although there is no research on it yet. Interestingly, unlike elsewhere in the English-speaking world in New York it is not unique to Latinos. On the contrary, it is related to a distinctive characteristic of White NYCE discussed by Hubbell (1950), which he calls a *dentalized* pronunciation of these three sounds plus /s/ and /z/:

> In the less cultivated speech of the city [there exist] several rather striking phonetic differences. The most important of these is the articulation of [t] (and of the other alveolar consonants) with the tongue-point in contact with the inner surfaces of the upper or, more commonly, the lower teeth. The stop is not a true dental, however, for the primary closure is made between the blade of the tongue and the alveolar ridge. (Hubbell 1950: 25)

Hubbell heads off any idea that this pronunciation is a result of substrate from either Yiddish or Italian, which like Spanish have true dental /t/, /d/, and /n/ (Herzog, et al. 1992:40, Jacobs 2005:109). Despite those disavowals, it is hard to reject a substrate hypothesis, in part because he reports that dentalization increased exactly when the second generation of Italian and Ashkenazi Jewish immigrants came of age. Furthermore, to my ears, current White NYCE versions sound dental, and self-reports by many though not all students in my classes reveal that most feel no touch of the tongue on the alveolar ridge when they pronounce them.

The difference between the dental(ized) and alveolar pronunciations is hard to describe impressionistically and impossible to transcribe via phonetic respellings. In IPA they are indicated by tooth-shaped diacritics placed below the letter – [t̪], [d̪], and [n̪] – versus their plain alveolar cousins – [t], [d], and [n]. Interestingly, good examples can be heard from many New York area politicians, such as the late former Mayor Ed Koch, John Liu (the Taiwanese American former city comptroller), and Governor Andrew Cuomo. Senator Bernie Sanders of Vermont, a New York native, also uses it as do several of the BQ-16 including Laura, Andy, Chang, and all the Latinos.

Dental articulations are most striking when released before a pause. Most of the time, Americans tend to barely release stops in these positions, but New Yorkers, particularly White New Yorkers, often release them strongly. Steinmetz (1981), Benor (2008, 2009, 2010), Fader (2007), and Levon (2006) consider released final stops to be a marker of Jewishness. They do not mention place of articulation, but released *dental* /t/s and /d/s are actually widespread in New York among non-Jews and Jews alike.

There may also be race-based differences in onset /r/s, i.e., those at or near the beginning of syllables. In Newman and Wu (2011) we noted that most of our Asian speakers appeared to pronounce /r/ with the tongue higher in the mouth than non-Asians,[11] although I am aware no other research along these lines. Finally, Hubbell (1950) claims that in New York onset /r/ tends to be produced by a bunching of the tongue, unlike the retroflex (i.e., bent back) tongue shape he believes to be more common elsewhere in the US. It is unclear how he came to this conclusion because it was only later that technology was able to show such differences with security. Whatever differences exist between the bunched and retroflex articulations have only recently begun to be examined acoustically (Thomas 2011), and in any case they are difficult to perceive (Twist, et al. 2007).

Table 3.4: NYCE features from Hubbell (1950)

Phoneme	Examples	Hubbell	Further Comments
Final /t/ before syllabic sonorants	*metal, better, button* ('me'l, be'r, bu'n')	Glottal stops. The use before syllabic /l/ is "one of the chief shibboleths of New Yorkese" Hubbell (1950: 32).	This is common in some American and other varieties of English (see Eddington & Channer 2010). Perhaps the NYCE usage predates other reports.
/ʒ/	*Jacques, beige*	Tendency to use affricate pronunciation.	Many New Yorkers never say French borrowings with the original fricative pronunciation.
/hj/	*Human, huge* ('Uman,' 'Uge')	Voiced pronunciation /j/	Very common particularly among Whites but probably diminishing.
/ju/ after alvoelars	*due, new,* ('doo,' 'noo')	Lost occasionally in *regular* and *particular* but not *mute, view* or *beauty*. Variable in *pubic, gubernatorial,* and *percolate,* In *new, tube,* and *duty,* with /j/ preserved in upper SES speech.	Loss of /j/ seems more advanced. Absence is categorical in upper middle class, but BQ-16 show some cases of /j/ in *new* although never in the city name.
/wh/	*What, where*	Merged with /w/, except among upper classes, merging *witch* and *which*.	The original voiceless [ʍ] mainly appears in hypercorrection.

11 Technical note: this is based on measures of F1.

3.4.3 Hubbell's inventory

Hubbell (1950) conducted his research under misplaced notions of dialect authenticity, which caused him to eliminate second generation New Yorkers. As a result he provides a limited range of NYCE. Nevertheless, he delivers a remarkably complete phonetic inventory, which includes pretty virtually phoneme in the NYCE he examined. His book, therefore, is required reading for anyone working on this dialect. Table 3.4 reproduces a few features that he lists that have particularly local aspects and have not already been discussed in this chapter along with my brief observations.

3.4.4 Consonant clusters

Another group of NYCE phonological features that has received sociolinguistic attention involves combinations of consonants. The most studied of these is loss of /d/ and /t/ after other consonants as in *lived*, *talked*, *end* or *bent*, although this phenomenon, called *consonant cluster simplification* (CCS), can also occur with other clusters such as /ks/ or /sk/ as in *box* or *desk* respectively. CCS has received considerable research attention because it occurs in all forms of English although at different rates. It is particularly frequent in AAE (Edwards 2004, Thomas 2007, Thomas & Wassink 2010), and such clusters do not exist in Spanish codas leading to substrate effects in Hispanized Englishes (Wolfram 1974).

Labov, et al. (1968a) discuss CCS in detail and find very high rates among the Harlem boys they studied, but subsequent research on AAE does not reveal any differences specific to NYCE. Wolfram (1974) examined teenage boys from East Harlem, a heavily Puerto Rican community with considerable presence of African Americans. He found that while simplification rates with /t/ and /d/ were higher for both Puerto Ricans and Blacks than for Whites, Puerto Rican boys with African American friends had the highest rates of all. A different form of simplification occurs in plurals like *desks* and *tests*. Although no cases occurred in the BQ-16 corpus, it is not unusual to hear vernacular speaking Blacks and Latinos insert a vowel before the final /s/ producing [dɛskɪs] and [tɛstɪs] ('deskis' and 'testis'). This feature is highly stigmatized.

There is also an interesting phenomenon involving consonant clusters in onsets particularly with Whites, although I find anecdotally that it is not limited to that group. This is what is called *S-retraction*: the pronunciation of /s/ in /str/ clusters as [ʃ]. So *street* and *stray* sound like [ʃtɹit] 'shtreet' and [ʃtreɪ] 'shtray'. S-retraction is common in a number of English dialects (e.g., Baker, Archangeli, & Mielke 2011) and is widespread in NYCE. Finally, there is a stereotype of White

NYCE that involves the addition of a stop creating a cluster where none is found in Standard English. This is the so-called intrusive-G in words like *long, king, singer*, in which a released /g/ is pronounced so *singer* has the same final syllable as *finger*. There is even a stereotype in the pronunciation, 'Lawn-Guy Land' for Long Island; in fact, some New Yorkers believe it is found mainly "on the Island" although there is no evidence for such a claim. This is also a stigmatized pronunciation, and Jochnowitz (1968) mentions it is as categorical among his child Lubavitcher Hasidic Jewish participants.

3.5 Suprasegmental Factors

The term suprasegmentals refers to features that range over various sounds, such as stress, intonation, speech rhythm, and voice quality. Until recently these aspects of speech have not received much research attention in variationist sociolinguistics, although their importance has long been understood. Tannen (1981: 137), for instance, lists several such features as components of what she calls *New York Jewish conversational style*. They include faster speech rate, wide pitch and amplitude shifts, and specific voice quality. However, Tannen never obtained any measures to substantiate her assertion. It is also unclear to what extent she believes that this style extends to non-Jewish New Yorkers.

Recently, there has been a surge in interest in suprasegmentals supported by new tools developed by phoneticians that facilitate their measurement. One that has been examined using these tools is rhythm, which has long been known to vary between languages. Some languages like Chinese and Spanish tend towards relatively even syllable durations and so sound more staccato and are referred to as *syllable timed*. Other languages like English – at least most varieties of English – and German have less evenly timed syllables and are referred to as *stressed timed*, on the hypothesis these languages have relatively even periods between stressed syllables.

Grabe and Low (2002) measure this difference by comparing the similarity of adjacent vowel lengths in samples of speech of various languages. Rather than two classes, they find rhythmic differences are laid out on a continuum. British English, one of the varieties they measured, indeed has relatively heterogeneous vowel lengths, but it is not the most extreme in their sample, an honor that belongs to Thai. The most homogeneous lengths (and so greatest syllable-timing) are found in Mandarin Chinese closely followed by Spanish. Grabe and Low also examined Singapore English, which is considerably influenced by Chinese and, not surprisingly, it falls between Mandarin and British English. This issue is relevant for NYCE because of the many Chinese Americans and Latinos in the dialect region. Thomas and Carter (2006) studied Latinos in the South on syllable timing and found it to be almost categorical. In Newman (2010), however, I found that only one quarter of Latino New Yorkers in the sample were clearly more syllable timed than non-Latinos. Another of my studies (Newman & Wu 2011) found similar results for one Latino out of two and two of four Chinese Americans.

That study also showed racial differences in another suprasegmental feature *voice quality*. In English we often vary our voice production to add emphasis or emotion, much as we might do with intonation. Of particular note on this score is *creaky voice* (also called *vocal fry*), which is produced in part by tightening the vocal cords as we speak to produce a kind of popping sound, like something frying. If the vocal cords are loosened instead of tensed, the result is breathy voice, so-called because of its whispery sound. Between the two we find modal voicing, our normal output, but this normality also can vary, involving a touch less or more tension in the vocal cords. There is probably much individual variation, but there is also dialectal variation. In Newman and Wu (2011) we found that six out of eight of our Asian American New Yorkers had slightly less vocal cord tension than the non-Asians as measured acoustically. Moreover, it was precisely these individuals who were most frequently identifiable as Asians by our judges.

3.6 Conclusion

NYCE is largely distinguished from other regional forms of American English by its phonology and phonetics, and the different forms of NYCE that depend on class or ethnicity are in good part distinguished from each other in the same way. However, recent studies based mainly in Manhattan show a process of deregionalization, i.e., a loss of distinctive NYCE pronunciations particularly among Whites and Asians particularly for vowels. The BQ-16 suggest that this tendency may be much less rapid in more peripheral communities.

The BQ-16 data also suggest a hypothesis regarding the nature of racialization especially when compared with findings from earlier studies such as SSENYC and Labov, et al. (1968a, b). This hypothesis involves a general question regarding whether or not racial minorities are converging or diverging from local Whites (see Coggshall & Becker 2010 for an exploration of this question involving NYCE). The data discussed above suggest that although there is greater use of variants common to all racialized groups, these groups and particularly the Blacks still betray less noticeable but distinctive systems of organization. If future research confirms this pattern of superficial convergence and subtle but systematic difference, it could yield a new and better understanding of the intersection of co-territorial ethnic identities and dialect.

4 Morphology and Syntax

4.1 Background

One day while teaching at the Urban Arts Academy, I had a particularly sparse collection of homework and began a typical teacher rant: "You have to do your homework. How can you expect to learn and pass this course if you don't do your homework?" My meaning seemed clear enough, but my ninth graders looked befuddled. A few looked around the room, and one finally asked me, "Who do you mean?" Fortunately, my background in linguistics suggested a source for the confusion. I alternate *you guys* and bare *you* in second person plural (2PP) address, but my ninth graders appeared to require plural marking to understand plural meaning in a second person pronoun. They interpreted my *you* as my calling out a single member of a plurally homework-deficient class.

A likely reason for our discordant systems is the racial differences between most of my students and me. The Black and Latino students – the whole class except for two or three White students – spoke forms of NYCE that were at least influenced by AAE. Consequently, they used a 2PP form based on *you all* – usually pronounced with the /l/ vocalized as [juɑʷ] ('you-ahw') and [juæ] ('you-a'), not the stereotypical southern [jɑɬ], ('y'all,'). According to Trudgill and Chambers (1991: 8), in systems with 2PP pronouns like this one, bare *"you* is singular only."[1]

I begin with this anecdote because it illustrates the predominant racial split involving morphology – the structure of words – and syntax – the structure of phrases and sentences – in NYCE and other varieties in North American English as well. There are some morphosyntactic differences that play out among regions,– the primarily White difference between *y'all* and *you guys* being the most prominent – but they tend to be few (Trudgill and Chambers 1991). Only Newfoundland and Labrador English (Clarke 2010) and Appalachian English (Wolfram 1991) present consistent robust regional differentiation on these levels. However, internal racially rooted morphosyntactic differences within regions can be significant, and as this case shows, occasionally lead to miscommunication. Apart from 2PP pronouns, AAE presents a number of morphosyntactic differences from Standard English and local White vernaculars, and the AAE forms are often the most stigmatized (Spears 2001).

It is worth noting also that robust morphosyntactic particularities of a dialect will invariably be accompanied by phonological differentiation, but phonological variation need not entail many morphosyntactic idiosyncrasies. This asym-

---

1 Separate singular and plural 2P forms are also characteristic of Spanish

metry explains why regional varieties like NYCE often get referred to by the term *accent*, but AAE is invariably referred to as a *dialect*. Morphosyntactic variation appears to be in some ways more profound systemically and socially than variation that is primarily phonological, and as Spears observes, AAE phonology is mostly far less stigmatized than morphosyntactic distinctions.

The next section describes a few aspects of morphosyntactic variation that relate to NYCE regionally, and the one after explores the internal variation associated with the three ethnically or racially defined groups for which data are available: African Americans, Latinos, and Jews.

4.2 Regional NYCE features

4.2.1 Morphology

Trudgill and Chambers (1991b) lament the paucity of sociolinguistic studies on morphology and syntax, and since their study appeared, the situation has not improved with regard to NYCE. The only systematic morphological study is over half a century old: Atwood's (1953) survey of verb forms across the eastern states based on data actually collected two decades earlier for the *Linguistic Atlas of the United States and Canada*. Despite its age, Atwood does show an interesting result: Notwithstanding New Yorkers' reputation for speaking badly, the verb forms used by the New York informants during the 1930s were apparently more standard than those reported in most other Eastern locales.

For instance, there were a number of common non-standard simple past forms found among Atlas informants in the city, but they invariably were common elsewhere too. Examples include *hung* as in the capital punishment, *dove* for *dived*, and *dreamt* [drɛmpt] – which of course is standard in British English – for the normal American *dreamed*. All these forms are still used in my experience; in fact I use them myself. Like most New Yorkers I know I also use *snuck* in place of standard *sneaked*, a form not mentioned by Atwood; but *snuck* also appears quite widespread. Other Eastern regions, by contrast, reported a wider array of non-standard verb past tenses. Those include *clumb* for *climbed, catched* for *caught, come* for *came,* all of which were widespread but missing among the New York informants. Atwood (1953: 38) interprets these data as a result of more rapid evolution in New York and nearby areas:

> In general, the older forms tend to become uncommon or disappear first in the New York City area (including n[orthern] N[ew] J[ersey] and the lower Hudson Valley), in parts of e[astern] P[ennsylvani]a, and in the more urbanized areas of s[outhern] N[ew] Eng[land].

Atwood also finds irregular participial forms such as *bit* for *bitten*, *broke* for *broken*, and *drove* for *driven* existing only outside the New York region. He does mention two exceptional local verb forms including pronunciation of *won't* as [wunt] ('woont') and *daren't* (from *dare not*) as /dæsənt/ ('dassunt'). I cannot recall hearing either growing up in the 1960s. The negative of *dare* – an important word among children   was strictly *don't dare*.

An important point to consider in Atwood's findings is that the New York informants were all White. This racial homogeneity follows from the Atlas methodology of sampling only natives of the area under investigation. Puerto Ricans had yet to arrive, and most African Americans in New York were relatively recent arrivals. African Americans were interviewed in the South, but unfortunately there appear to have been no pre-Great-Migration African American informants in what was then a much Whiter city.

In traditional dialect surveys like the Atlas fieldworkers interview informants individually. Technology now allows for the rapid collection of much larger data-sets, and since morphosyntax can be expressed in written form, it would seem particularly apt for internet surveys. Yet the full possibilities of this method have yet to be realized. One exception is Vaux and Golder's (2003) on-line survey of 122 English usages in the US. Unfortunately, the survey contains only two morphological items, and one, a preference for *dragged* versus *drug* as past tense for *to drag* showed no specificity to NYCE. However, the other was the 2PP pronoun usage, and that did. That question is shown below with the nation-wide results:

What word(s) do you use to address a group of two or more people?

a. you all (12.63%)	d. you guys (42.53%)	g. you (24.82%)
b. yous, youse (0.67%)	e. you 'uns (0.20%)	h. other (4.62%)
c. you lot (0.18%)	f. yins (0.37%)	i. y'all (13.99%)

Only a single choice was allowed, which distorts the results since many individuals surely use more than one form. Still the answers provide interesting information regarding the distribution of lesser-used forms. Nationally (b), *yous, youse* is quite rare, but the accompanying map, reproduced as Figure 4.1 shows that it is heavily concentrated in New York and vicinity:

Vaux and Golder do not give as a choice, a NYCE stereotype that combines *youse* with *you guys* to make *youse guys*. In my experience *youse*, though not *youse guys* – which I cannot recall hearing outside a dialect performance context – is found with a certain frequency. The pronunciation is frequently reduced to [jɪz]. Anecdotally, one particularly prolific user I have run into is our tax preparer Chris, yielding statements like, "Youse are getting more back from the feds this year." Although *youse* is stigmatized, this usage by an educated speaker – Chris has advanced

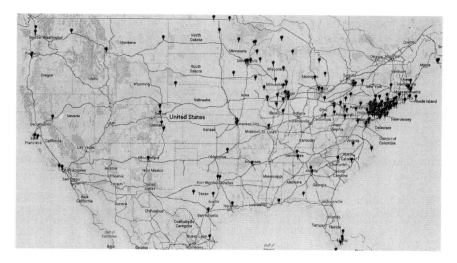

Figure 4.1: use of yous/youse as reported in Vaux and Golder (2003) Map generated by Emily Tucker Prud'hommeaux:[2]

degrees – makes clear that it is not just a lower class form. My feeling is that Chris would be unlikely to use this form in a business meeting, and that his use of it with my husband and me indexes familiarity and friendliness. Nevertheless, *youse* is a minority variant, and Chris also employs *you guys,* which is widely used throughout the US according to Vaux and Golder (2003). The other main forms in Vaux and Golder are *you all* and its phonological reduction to *y'all. Y'all* is stereotypically southern, but based on a telephone survey, Tillery, Winkle, and Bailey (2000) report its rapid spread outside that region although they show little presence in the New York area. Nevertheless, as is already clear, *you all* based forms are common among New Yorkers whose English is AAE or influenced by AAE, albeit with the pronunciation as described at the beginning of this chapter.

4.2.2 Syntax

Vaux and Golder (2003) ask eight questions relating to syntax, but only one shows any regional specificity for the New York area,[3] the preference for *on line* in place

---

2 Although *youse* rarely appears in the US outside the New York region, it is found in Ireland, Scotland, parts of England, and Newfoundland (Clarke 2010).

3 They include four items on different uses of *anymore* plus "Would you say 'Are you coming with?' … to mean "Are you coming with us?" "Would you say 'where are you at?' …, and "Can you use more than one modal at a time? (e.g., 'I might could do that').

of *in line*, for standing as in, "I on line stood in the cold for two hours before they opened the doors." (Vaux and Golder 2003). It seems likely that most non-standard structures used by New Yorkers are the same as those in other vernacular varieties of American English. Examples range from those that barely elicit notice like *do you got?* or use of *a*-pronounced as schwa – before nouns starting with vowels (e.g., *'a apple'*) to stigmatized constructions such as negative concord (e.g., *I didn't buy none*). Nevertheless, anecdotally there are two non-standard structures that I suspect, admittedly speculatively, may be more common in New York than most other locales, although they are clearly not limited to the New York area (Butters 1974, 1976, McCloskey 2006). One involves the extension of interrogative constructions (i.e., subject-auxiliary inversion) to indirect questions as in the following example from Chang John, the older Chinese American in the BQ-16. Interestingly, Chang "corrects" from the standard pattern to the non-standard one.

> Chang: I wrote paper complaining about why I had ... why did I have to take these liberal arts subjects.

Hardly peculiar to this dataset, I have heard this construction from New Yorkers of many backgrounds. Chang, in fact, is a lawyer. Other non-standard structures that appear commonly in NYCE are counterfactuals. In Standard English these take the form of an irrealis for present situations (Huddleston & Pullum 2001) or past perfect for past ones in the *if-clause* and a conditional or past conditional in the conditional (i.e. *then*) clause as in:

> *If I were a billionaire, I would donate $50,000,000 to Queens College.*

> *If I had been a billionaire, I would have donated $50,000,000 to Queens College.*

Probably more common throughout the English speaking world is the use of *was* in the place of *were* as the irrealis:

> *If I was a billionaire, I would donate $50,000,000 to Queens College.*

For many New Yorkers, however, another reformulation appears in which the *if* clause in both examples also contains *would*:

> *If I would be a billionaire, I would donate $50,000,000 to Queens College* or

> *If I would have been a billionaire, I would have donated $50,000,000 to Queens College.*

Although there is no survey or corpus research evidence with regard to these structures at least in NYCE, they are discussed by Fader (2007: 9), who gives the following example from her ethnographic fieldwork on Hasidic Jews in Brooklyn: "If I would be an anthropologist, I would look like Ayala." Fader suggests that this construction is peculiar to that community. However, I suspect it is actually the most common way to express counterfactuals in NYCE; I have certainly heard it all my life including, again, from well-educated professionals.

4.3 Internal Ethnic-based Variation

4.3.1 African American English

You-all 2PP pronouns were brought to New York from the South in the Great Migration along with other AAE constructions. A problematic 2PP form developed more recently, although exactly how or where it was coined may never be known, and it is unlikely to be exclusive to NYCE. This form might be referred to as the *n-word you* and is probably best rendered *you-all-niggaz*, although the *all* is reduced sometimes to the point of elision i.e., as *ya-niggaz*. It is associated with Hip-Hop and is common in rap lyrics as in this example from Darryl Hanson's Latino friend *Tropics*:

> Tropics: 'cause **'ya-niggaz'** [jə'nɪgəz] can't see/ that when I host a show, it blows off this meter shit

I have also heard it in conversations among young people, not always Black, as is the case for the word *nigga*, which is discussed outside the pronominal format in Chapter 6. More traditional AAE core structures also widely heard in New York include the following described variously in Labov et al. (1968a), Wolfram (1969, 2007), Baugh (1999), Rickford and Rickford (2000). I leave out common forms like multiple negation and *ain't* that are generally shared across non-standard varieties:
- copula deletion ("She happy"),
- third person sing. – s deletion, particularly common in negatives ("He go," it "don't")
- invariant *be* ("She be happy all the time."),
- remote past *been* ("The baby been born."),
- completive *done* ("I done been through it all."),
- simple past with *had* ("We had ate it.")
- past *to be* leveling to *was* ("We was rhyming together.")

- non-inversion in aux-V questions ("I can go to the bathroom?")
- double comparatives. ("I learned more better sometimes")

Most of these forms are found at widely varying rates among Latino New Yorkers; the example for remote past *been* above is from a Dominican American at UAA. They are also used to varying degrees by others who identify with inner-city minority culture and particularly with Hip-Hop. This is even true of some Whites (Cutler 2008, 2010) and other racialized groups such as Middle Easterners and South Asians including Indo-Caribbeans. By contrast, individuals of all races who do not identify much with urban minority culture typically avoid AAE structures and forms. One example is Evan, the African American hacker discussed in Chapter 2, and I have noticed that many Latino gay men and boys also rarely use these forms. At UAA, for instance, there were four Puerto Rican gay boys – including John who was quoted in Chapter 2 with his friend Janet – and one of Black West Indian origin, I will call Niall. The three Puerto Ricans I interviewed did not use any AAE syntactic forms, although one used considerable AAE phonology, but Niall did use such forms. Niall was involved in the gay Christopher Street pier scene, which was composed of mainly lower SES Black and Latino youth who hang out on or near the docks in the West Village area. He was also a member of a voguing house, an urban gay subculture featured in the 1990 film documentary *Paris is Burning*.

Cases like those outlined in the last paragraph suggest that the idea of a division into ethnic-based dialects could perhaps be better analyzed as stance vis-à-vis different urban vernacular identities. Yet this kind of post-racial construction of ethnic variation does not seem adequate either. AAE forms have spread most intensively and systematically into other Black communities and least into White and East Asian groups. Niall not only identified with cultural manifestations rooted in the lower SES urban minority experience, he was also a Black West Indian. His identity as second generation urban Black New Yorker is about all he shares with Kendrick Pierre, the Haitian American, and Darryl Hanson, the Jamaican American, of the BQ-16. Yet they also used many core AAE traits listed above along with, like Niall, AAE phonology. As mentioned in Chapter 2, Ibrahim (1999, 2001, 2004) argues that young African immigrants construct of their racial identity as Black – an identity that may be absent in their home countries.

The centrality of racial identity needs to be considered in understanding Kendrick and Darryl's use non-standard AAE morphosyntactic forms. Kendrick was a successful and ambitious college student when interviewed, and Darryl went to a prestigious state university and was self-consciously intellectual. Their use of AAE grammar was not an impediment to their progress into the professional classes nor should it have been. On this point, it is worth emphasizing that Diondre Davis – a middle class African American in the BQ-16 – also used some of these forms in her interview. Despite the stigma attached to them, AAE morphosyntactic structures need to be understood as indexes of integration into and identification with the larger urban Black or urban minority mainstream, not as failure to master Standard English. The ability to style shift and dialect shift many Black New Yorkers possess is a mark of their recognition that each person has multiple social identities including professional and class identities in addition to racial ones. These issues and the broader public response to them are analyzed by Alim and Smitherman (2012) with particular reference to Barack Obama's language use.

4.3.2 Spanish calques: No longer devil-owned

As discussed in the previous section some Latino New Yorkers use morphosyntactic forms that originated in AAE, but others do not or do so sparingly. There are, however, syntactic constructions that specifically characterize New York Latino English (NYLE). Some are *calques* – also called *loan translations* – from Spanish. These are when English words are used in structures or with meanings that match Spanish equivalents. An interesting example was produced by Humberto, a native New Yorker with a Puerto Rican father and Salvadorian mother, who was interviewed with his friend Cristóbal for Newman (2010). This is his response to a question about what constitutes good graffiti:

> Humberto: It's just stuff that you're raised on, and it's like this phrase, "you want to be famous." Like Korn-1, he's famous. Everybody knows who Korn-1 is. Or Nato, everybody knows –
>
> Cristóbal: – Yeah, Nato –
>
> Humberto: – Oh my god, he's famous. He has fame. That's what niggas [=guys] say, "He has fame." And you write your shit and try to get famous and shit like that.

Humberto's last turn juxtaposes two synonymous verb phrases, "has fame" with "is famous." Both are grammatical English, but a search of the Corpus of Contemporary American English (COCA) provides 615 hits for "is famous" – including with the contraction – compared to only nine for "has fame." Moreover, of these nine, seven involve the irrelevant auxiliary use of *have* as in "What kind of impact has fame had on your marriage." Clearly "he has fame," although it is grammatical, is not frequent. It is, however, a literal translation of the common Spanish phrase, *tiene fama*.

Not all forms characteristic of NYLE are traceable to Spanish calques, and those forms are assumed to be derived ultimately from second language learning errors that become incorporated into native English. Table 4.1 provides examples of both types of structures from Johan Aranda, who was the most prolific producer of them in the BQ-16:

Table 4.1: Johan Aranda's Latino English Syntax Features with Glosses

	Johan's Phrase	Non-Spanish Influenced Equivalent	Spanish Equivalent
1	There was no point **of** it	There was no point to it	No tenía sentido hacerlo
2	**On** midtown	In Midtown	En Midtown
3	That school is **nothing** about no art	That school had nothing to do with art	Esa escuela no tiene nada que ver con el arte
4	Some of them **call 'em like that**	Some people call them that	Algunos los llaman así
5	**How they are**	What they're like	Como son
6	But **as well he listens** to	But he listens to Spanish rock as well	Pero también escucha Rock en español
7	Obeying **to** their rules	Obeying their rules	Obedecer (a) sus reglas
8	People that **they** come from things that are alike	People that come from things that are alike	La gente que viene de cosas que son parecidas.

In example (1) "There was no point of it" the preposition *of* in place of *to* diverges from other varieties of English. Since there is no obvious source in Spanish for the anomalous preposition, the source lies ultimately in second language learning, a supposition that is supported by the tendency for prepositions to be confused by learners. The source of (2) "**On** midtown" requires no conjecture. The Spanish preposition *en* translates as either *on* or *in* indistinctly, and the substitution of one for the other is often made by second language learners of Spanish background. In (3) "That school is **nothing** about no art" the use of *nothing* seems to reflect its usual Spanish equivalent *nada*, although the rest of the construction is not at all Spanish-like except for the negative concord, which of course is also found in nonstandard English. For (4) "Some of them call 'em **like** that" the Spanish translation is *Algunos lo llaman así*, where *así* can be directly translated as *like that*. *Like that* turned out to be a common discourse marker (i.e., a word or phrase used to organize information) in interviews with Latinos as in this example from a UAA student called Edwin, who was born in New York:

Edwin: Yeah, the ones that are into Hip-Hop, I can relate to them cause, I like Hip-Hop or the ones that are into Techno, I can relate to them cause, I like Techno, **like that**.

The source of example (5) **"How they are"** is complicated. In Spanish the distinction between *how are they* and *what are they like* is accomplished by using different verbs – *cómo están* in the first case and *cómo son* in the second. But in general *están* and *son* both get translated as *(they) are*. As a result, this construction is quite common in second language learners of Spanish background. Example (6) "but **as well he listens** to Spanish rock" uses normal Spanish word order. The source of (7) *to* in "Obeying **to** their rules" is the Spanish preposition *a*, which is variably associated with the verb *obedecer*, the equivalent of *obey*. Example (8) "People that **they** come from things that are alike" adds what is called a *resumptive pronoun* to the relative clause. Spanish does not have resumptive pronouns, but Szmrecsanyi and Kortmann (2009) state that they appear frequently in second language English. I have noticed them in other NYLE speakers.

Despite the fact that at least three of these constructions (4, 5 and 8) were attested in other Latino speakers, Johan's particularly heavy usage raises the question of whether he should be classified as a native speaker of English or just a proficient second language learner. He reported coming to New York at the age of three and said that his older sister began speaking English to him soon after. He must have begun to speak English more heavily in elementary school, where from his description he probably attended a self-contained ESL class for most of his early grades. It is possible that Johan's description of his early life contains inaccuracies although I have no reason to doubt him beyond the general fuzziness of early memories. Still, the outlines of his story do not so much settle the question of his native speaker status as call into question any clear division between native and non-native speakers. The issue certainly cannot be reduced to age of arrival. Unlike Johan, Missy Ibáñez was born in New York, but she recalled first encountering English in kindergarten when she began ESL and bilingual education. She may have had less early English input than Johan.

Skepticism regarding sharp native/nonnative divisions in looking at *language contact* phenomena – the technical term for the kind of constructions listed in Table 4.1 – is supported by Sharma and Sankaran's (2011) study of South Asian immigrants in London. These researchers show that the conversion of what were originally second language traits into first language sociolinguistic variants takes three generations. Their view concords with Mufwene's (2008) "Ecological Model" of language contact. Mufwene argues for the key role in the transmission of contact phenomena of members of the immigrant community, such as Johan's sister, who speak to young children in incompletely acquired English. For instance, Johan's sister might have said, *in* for *on*, and her error becomes Johan's primary first language input.

Mufwene's term *ecological* expresses a comparison of language to organisms. As he sees it, gene-like chunks of information such as conflating *on* and *in* with origin in one language (like Spanish) can become integrated into another (like English) in contact situations. Just as the mixing of genes produces a complex and unpredictable variety of traits, so the results of language contact can be quite unexpected. No better example of this complexity can be found than in an interaction I had with a UAA student I will call Chris when I was teaching there. It occurred before my work as a researcher began, and Chris was not my student, so I have no idea about his background beyond that he was Latino and the fact that he "presented" as a native speaker of English. Chris was working as an intern making photocopies for teachers, and one day, when he was having a great deal of difficulty with paper jamming, he lamented to me, "This machine is owned by the devil." I found the idea of the photocopier being the property of Satan (and perhaps only leased to the Board of Education) amusing, considering what many of my colleagues felt about the Board. Yet about a week or so later, the machine was fixed and was churning out copies like a champ, and I commented on the improvement. Chris responded, "Yeah, it's no longer devil-owned."

It was only later that I realized what was happening linguistically. The Spanish word *poseer* can be translated indistinctly as *possessed* or *owned*. What Chris meant by *owned by the devil* was what would be normally translated as *possessed by the devil*; so Chris's phrase was a Spanish calque. But notice the phrase, *no longer devil owned*. Syntactically, nothing could be more alien to Spanish than that kind of participial phrase; the word-for-word translation *diablo poseído* is uninterpretable. Yet in English if *possessed* were used – i.e., *no longer devil possessed* – the result is also ungrammatical. For example, we cannot say that a formerly family firm is *no longer family possessed*, but we can say it is *no longer family owned*. So, just as *family owned* is grammatical, so is *devil owned*. Chris had unwittingly created a new structure with elements of both languages that has no exact parallel in either.

4.3.3 Goyim can't say that: Jewish English

Once at a linguistics talk, Ellen Prince – a late and much lamented University of Pennsylvania linguist of Brooklyn roots – gave as an example, "A Cadillac, he bought!" She then announced "That's Yinglish. Goyim can't say that." To the uninitiated, Prince meant that the sentence was grammatical only in Yiddish-contact English. In truth, although I am Jewish, I would not say it either, although

I have heard such expressions from friends and family members more grammatically in touch with their roots. This structure is called *topicalization,* and it involves the shift to the beginning of the sentence for emphasis of a noun phrase (NP) direct object (Feinstein 1980). Most varieties of English can topicalize only definite NPs. So for most English speakers **The** *Cadillac, he bought* is grammatical, but **A** *Cadillac, he bought* is not. Topicalized indefinites are, unsurprisingly, perfectly grammatical in Yiddish.

Yinglish appears to be an exception to the generalization that morphological and syntactic distinctions follow racial divisions. However, it is important not to make too much of any peculiarities. As Benor (2009: 238) cautions, "since most American Jews are of European origin and are seen as white, most speak varieties of English similar to non-Jewish European Americans." Yet the wide circulation of terms like Yinglish, Jewish English, and Yeshivish (from *yeshiva*, i.e., Orthodox Jewish school) presupposes the existence of salient identifiable ethnodialectal traits.

My lack of these traits fits the pattern by which the quantity of Yiddish-contact features tends to track Jews' degree of ethno-religious identification. Jews who grew up in more intensely religious families and/or with more ethnically homogeneous social networks tend to have more of these distinct linguistic features. Jews who develop more intense links later in life also tend to adopt them (Benor 2012). The list below orders Jewish groups along with associated sociolinguistic research from top to bottom from least entho-religiously identified as Jewish:

- Hasidic (Jochnowitz 1968, Steinmetz 1981, Fader 2007, Benor 2009)
- Modern Orthodox (Steinmetz 1981, Benor 2009, 2012),
- Conservative (Benor 2009),
- Reconstructionist (Benor 2009), and
- Reform (Levon 2006, Benor 2009).
- Secular (Tannen 1981, Schiffrin 1984)

Fader (2007) observes that a distinctively Jewish way of speaking serves quite consciously as a tool for maintaining separateness from mainstream American society for the Hasidic groups she studied. Yet some degree of distinctiveness has been found throughout the spectrum of Jewish identities, although for the secular Jews these involve only discourse and politeness norms (discussed in Chapter 5) and lexicon (discussed in Chapter 6). Not all this research was done in New York; Benor studied Jews in California, and Levon did so in Philadelphia. Yet Steinmetz (1981: 3) argues, "the center of American Orthodoxy is, as it has always been, New York City and its environs," and much the same can be said for the other denominations and even secular Jewish identities. As Benor (2011) observes that

Jewish communities sometimes preserve some NYCE features as they spread out from the mother city.[4]

The name Yinglish implies that most ethnolinguistically marked Jewish features involve the influence of Yiddish, although liturgical languages such as Biblical Hebrew and Aramaic have some influence on the more religious. There are no reports of influence of the other diaspora Jewish languages present in New York such as Judeo-Spanish or Bukharian (a Jewish form of Persian spoken by Jews from Central Asia). Besides topicalizations, there are a number of Yiddish calques in Yinglish. Steinmetz (1981: 9) gives *make* and *say* in *make Shabbos* (prepare Sabbath) or *say Kaddish* instead of *recite Kaddish,* the traditional mourner's prayer. Benor (2009: 257) provides more general Yiddish transfer such as present tense for present perfect: e.g., "I know someone who**'s** already frum [=religious] for 20 years" instead of *who's been.* Another example she gives is the post-verbal placement of adverbial phrases as in "You'll be stuck studying all day Torah." One stereotype is the use of *from* instead of *about* with *know*, as in this *New York Times* profile of a non-Jewish expert in Yiddish theatre written by non-Jewish reporter: "What did he know from Yiddish? Growing up in Kansas City, Mo., he was an altar boy at St. Andrew's Episcopal Church" (Kilgannon 2012). In addition, Fader (2007) and Benor (2009: 257) mention an extension of the use of *by* as in "Are you eating by Rabbi Fischer" instead of *at Rabbi Fischer's.*

4.4 Summary: Contact and Future Research

It might appear from the first section of the chapter that there is really little of interest in the morphology and syntax of NYCE due the considerable deregionalization discussed in the early part of this chapter. However, the extensive language contact discussed involving Spanish and Yiddish in the following two sections are probably just the tip of the iceberg. In a city in which over sixty percent of the population is first or second generation of immigrants, there is clearly a great deal of language contact taking place. Given the current interest in using language contact to understand the language faculty itself, the city and region provide a potential data goldmine, but one that has gone so far largely unexploited.

---

4 This observation should not be universalized. My parents, their friends, and my relatives who grew up in Detroit have all the major features of that city. My grandmother, who was born and raised in Arkansas, where my great-grandparents had what was called a "Jew store," had Ozark features.

5 Discourse Factors

5.1 Background

In a scene set in Iowa in the 1983 Oscar award winning movie *Terms of Endearment,* the heroine Emma Horton (played by Debra Winger) finds herself at the cashier's in a store without enough money. One by one she gives back items while the cashier mechanically announces the new total, which never makes it down to the amount she has. Fortunately, she is rescued by Sam Burns, a banker played by John Lithgow, who happens to be there. After she accepts his offer to lend her the money for her groceries, he tells off the cashier:

> Sam: You're a very rude young woman. I know Douglas from the Rotary, and I can't believe he'd want you treating customers so badly.
>
> Cashier: I don't think I was treating her badly.
>
> Sam: Then you must be from New York.

This snippet of dialog associates New Yorkers with rudeness, set against high Iowa standards of polite behavior valued by the boss, a member of the "all American" Rotary Club. Actually, New York is one of those places with such a reputation for rudeness that visitors often expect to be treated poorly. I cannot remember the number of times that people have told me how surprised they were at being treated kindly in my hometown. It is not that rudeness does not exist New York, of course, but it is hardly a particular characteristic of New Yorkers. So where does our bad reputation come from?

Part of the answer is related to the topic of this chapter *discourse*, i.e., the way that meaning is organized in language above the level of the sentence. Discourse is composed of linguistic practices, i.e., the multifarious ways people use language rather than the details of the phonology, morphology, syntax, and lexicon out of which language is constructed. The connection with politeness follows from fact that what might be considered appropriate or even required linguistic behavior in one culture can be seen as rude or even taboo in another.

Conversations are a major linguistic site for these culturally determined expectations and evaluations. Cultures can vary quite radically in what topics are judged legitimate for different types of conversation and how conversations are expected to be organized. A pioneering study of this dynamic by the sociolinguist Deborah Tannen explored the conversational norms that differ between New Yorkers, specifically Jewish New Yorkers, and (non-Jewish) "out of towners." Her study is examined in the next section. Another set of discourse genres that appear in pioneering work involving New York by Labov et al. (1968b) are associated with African Americans. They are explored in the following section. The section after that examines bilingual discourse practices, which are naturally common in communities with many immigrants like New York. The primary focus there is on Latinos, and again it is based on seminal research, in this case by Zentella and Urciuoli, who explored these phenomena with respect to Puerto Ricans.

5.2 New York Jewish Conversational Style

Comedians can be very perceptive about cultural conflicts in communication. A classic example appears in another famous movie, Woody Allen's 1977 *Annie Hall*. This movie chronicles the relationship between a New York Jewish comedian called Alvy Singer, played by Allen, and Annie, a White Protestant from Wisconsin played by Diane Keaton. In one hilarious scene (search on YouTube for "Annie Hall Easter dinner") stereotypes of both groups explode in glorious exaggeration. It begins with the Hall family Easter Dinner with Alvy as guest. The Halls engage in a series of conversations that are so banal that Alvy disconnects and enters his own fevered imagination. He imagines Annie's creepily silent grandmother visualizing him stereotypically in full Hasidic garb, and more contemptuously than enviously describes the Halls as "so healthy" and "so American." This characterization leads him to a memory of an equivalent dinner with his own family, who all talk over each other and argue cacophonously. The contrast with the Halls could not be greater. Whereas *Terms of Endearment* evaluates New Yorkers negatively, Allen clearly prefers Alvy's New York family to the Halls. Unlike "God's frozen chosen" from Wisconsin, Alvy's family is alive, vibrant, and honest about their feelings and beliefs. The Hasidic image held by the grandmother implies that Allen, or at least Alvy, sees the Halls' Midwestern manners as a façade potentially concealing malevolence and bigotry.

The communicative contrasts that lie behind the caricatures have been the subject of important sociolinguistic research. This work was performed by the founder of the study of conversational style, Deborah Tannen (1981, 1984), who curiously enough used a real holiday dinner conversation as fodder. Tannen's focus was a Thanksgiving attended by three New York Jews, two Californians and an English woman; Tannen was one of the New Yorkers. Tannen observes that the New Yorkers all had positive memories of the dinner and the conversation, but the non-New Yorkers felt left out. She then analyzed the interactions and noticed the tendency of the New Yorkers to dominate the conversations:

> Whereas the tapes contained many examples of interchanges between two or three of the
> New Yorkers, [they] had no example of talk among non-New Yorkers in which the New
> Yorkers did not participate. (Tannen 1981: 135)

Tannen provides three sources for the New Yorkers' conversational dominance.
First, the New Yorkers engaged in short or non-existent pauses between turns
if not outright overlaps with one another whereas the non-New Yorkers waited
for noticeable pauses as a signal that they could start to talk. Tannen also finds
that the New Yorkers also had faster pacing, greater expressiveness, and a greater
tendency to engage in personal topics in conversation than the non-New Yorkers.
Thus, the New Yorkers also tended to control the conversation thematically.
Finally, the New Yorkers also engaged in more narrative creating extended discourse, yielding less time for others to speak. Tannen concludes that these differences follow from discordant although tacit rules for conversation. For example,
when one New Yorker spoke while another was still talking, that overlap was
interpreted as a sign of engagement in what the first person was saying. By contrast, the non-New Yorkers interpreted the same behavior as an attempt to gain
the floor:

> [New Yorkers have] a conversational economy in which it is not the business of the listener
> to make room for another speaker to speak. Rather it is the business of the listener to show
> enthusiasm; the speaker in this system can be counted on to find room to speak. (Tannen
> 1981: 142)

These different assumptions are linked to different balances cultures place
between what Brown and Levinson (1978) call *positive politeness* and *negative
politeness*. In my experience, these terms can cause endless confusion among
students, which is a shame because the concepts are extraordinarily useful in
understanding how problems arise in cross-cultural communication. Positive
politeness is not presence of politeness. It is a kind of politeness that consists in
the expression of friendliness, affection, or kindness, in sum approval of a person
and what they are doing. By the same token, negative politeness is not absence of
politeness. It is expression of due respect and consideration for another's wishes
and needs. It is easy to see how these concepts apply in Tannen's interpretation
of the conflict:

> I would like to suggest that the conversational style of the New Yorkers at the Thanksgiv-
> ing dinner can be seen as conventionalized strategies serving the need for involvement,
> whereas the non-New York participants expected strategies serving the need for indepen-
> dence. (Tannen 1981: 137)

If a person comes from a culture in which negative politeness is highly valued, the de-emphasis on it can be interpreted as incivility. Tannen concludes that what she calls "high engagement" style is typical of not just of New York Jews but New Yorkers generally. I certainly have noticed similar styles among Italian Americans, Irish Americans, Latinos from the Caribbean, African Americans, and Eastern Europeans. These groups together form a large proportion of New York's population and so set the cultural parameters of the city.

It should be pointed out that Allen's portrayal of the Halls presents the other side of the coin. What is perceived as *too much* concern with negative politeness can seem like insincerity and consequently unreliability, thus the paranoia about the grandmother. Generally, negative politeness strategies involve indirect communication whereas many New Yorkers and others from more positive-politeness oriented backgrounds expect greater transparency. So it can be hard for us to read the intentions of interlocutors from cultures that tend to, as we see it, beat around the bush. At the same time, the lack of positive politeness can give rise to negative impressions. This is a particular issue for White transplants, who not only often come from these more-negative politeness oriented backgrounds but are typically financially and socially privileged. Members of this group can be seen as arrogant if they do not interact socially with neighbors and shopkeepers in ways New Yorkers are used to. What they might see is a polite lack of imposition on strangers and distant acquaintances can be read as asserting superiority and condescension.

In addition, negative politeness oriented cultural norms tend to discourage face-threatening topics because there is an effort to make sure no one is put on the spot or challenged. For those from cultures less invested in maintaining group harmony, the resulting conversations can seem dull. This is certainly not in issue for the Singers, whose dinner conversation consists largely of arguments. Yet when the issue is settled, smiles return; it is more like a game than a quarrel. This is similar to my experience with arguments within family and friends, New Yorkers and Jews from elsewhere. If the topic is not personally threatening, taking opposing positions can be treated as a sport. This position is supported in a study of Ashkenazi Jews by Schiffrin (1984) in Philadelphia. She finds that what she calls "sociable argument" functioned for her participants as a way of strengthening not fraying bonds.

> Sociable argument displays the tolerance of conflict through the playful enactment of such conflict-tolerance made possible by the taken-for-granted level of intimacy of the relationship. Whereas serious argument would be negatively evaluated and avoided in my presence, then, sociable argument would be positively evaluated and encouraged precisely because of its ratificatory meaning. (Schiffrin 1984: 331)

Even serious argument could have its positive side among Schiffrin's participants since she reports that "thrashing it out" was valued as a way of settling
serious disputes between family members. Again, I think that many other immigrant groups and minorities in New York – e.g., Caribbean Latinos and southern
Europeans – have a similar approach to disagreement, but these groups form a
smaller proportions of the populations in most other parts of the country.

Of course the arguments in *Annie Hall* were exaggerated because Woody Allen
was trafficking in stereotypes for humorous effects. A stereotype invariably sub-
sumes individual identity into a group as if that group formed a cultural monolith.
I certainly know Jewish New Yorkers who do not follow the behaviors that Tannen
describes. However, such norms are better seen not as governing individual behavior directly but dictating how criticism and approval of behaviors are likely to be
received and justified in a community. A quiet New York Jew (or Italian or Puerto
Rican) who never disputes their interlocutor might not be criticized. However,
these characteristics do not tend to elicit much approval either. Instead, such a
person might be described as timid. By contrast, being assertive in conversation
is more likely to be accepted. So cultural norms like these are really about relative
degrees of consensus in a community; they should not be overstated, but they are
not inexistent either. Obviously, most encounters between New Yorkers and individuals from societies with higher valuations of negative politeness or lower ones
of positive politeness play out perfectly smoothly. Nevertheless, Woody Allen por-
trays and Tannen and Schiffrin describe experiences that many can identify with.

5.3 Research on African American Communicative Genres

Although Labov is best known for founding the field of variationist sociolinguistics, another area of his research involves literacy in inner-city communities.
The first project in this direction was Labov et al.'s (1968a, b) Harlem study of
teenage and preteen boys that provided much of the AAE data in Chapter 3. Part
of that research highlights the extraordinary oral skills of those boys, in marked
contrast to their high rates of school failure and often-serious difficulties with
reading. The full study was not published commercially, although various findings have appeared elsewhere (mostly in Labov 1972b). One particularly well-
known chapter of that book "The Logic of Non-Standard English" is a brilliant
takedown of the claims of limited verbal abilities of inner-city youth. In it Labov
provides a quote from a gang member Larry discussing the existence of God,
designed to refute then-common claims of cognitive and linguistic deficits of
inner-city youths. Larry's argument is delivered in non-standard English, but the
reasoning itself was thoughtful, impressive, and abstract. A short excerpt is given

below. LH is Larry. KC is the interviewer. The original sound file associated with excerpt is available at (http://www.acls.org/publications/audio/labov/page2.aspx?id=4462):

LH: But you don't really know if it's a God or not. Nobody really knows that.

KC: That's true.

LH: Nobody.

KC: That's true. That's true. But, just saying that there is a God. What color is he? White or black?

LH: ... He be white, man.

KC: Why?

LH: Why? I'll tell you why. 'Cause it – the average whitey out here got everything, you dig it? An' the nigger ain't got shit, you know, you understand? So um, for then, for then, or that to happen, you know it ain't no black god that's doin' that bullshit ...

KC: Yeah, I got to go for that, boy!

LH: Dig it, that's square business, man! (Labov 2009)

If that lesson should be forgotten, the excerpt from my interview with Rashid Lewis in which he described himself as a "prisoner of the ghetto" on page 46 shows a sophisticated abstract reasoning in similarly expressive if not poetic language. Recall that Rashid's answer was in response to a question I had about whether he felt that the situation between the races had improved compared to the stories he had heard from older family and friends. I think my motivation for the question was based in my own childhood memories during the time Labov and his colleagues were conducting their Harlem study. I had a single Black classmate in fifth grade, and none earlier. My first encounter with large numbers of African Americans took place in sixth grade when I went to middle school. My initial impression was that they were aggressive and a bit scary, in large part, I can see now, because of the great deal of hard-hitting verbal play that went on between them. Given these kinds of differences and the fact that Latinos, Whites, and Blacks mostly came from different elementary schools, each group sat separately in the lunchroom as if that was the natural order of things.

Outside the lunchroom, I can remember talking to Latino kids but not Black ones. The way it worked in sixth grade, if my memory is correct, was that Latinos communicated with both Blacks and Whites although friendships remained within each group. Blacks and Whites had no real contact at all. I cannot remember a single Black classmate from sixth grade. In seventh grade, a tracking system took effect that separated all but the "low-performing" White kids into the advanced tracks where we were joined by only a few "high-performing" Blacks but few if any Latinos. It was not until high school that racial boundaries lowered enough for us to get to know each other as individuals across the color lines, including, curiously, some of my Black classmates from middle school.

I include these personal reflections because they match Labov, et al.'s (1968a: 3) report of the segregation in New York at the time from the other side of the color bar: "There are no non-Puerto Rican white members of the adolescent groups studied, and the members do not have white friends (or think it is possible to have white friends)." What Whites were missing out on was a remarkably rich verbal culture, which I saw only foggily from a distance and through the filter of my own fears. Labov, et al (1968b) describe the following oral genres:

- *Louding:* "a series of loud, negative remarks about someone's behavior (usually in the third person) in the presence of others" (Labov, et al 1968b: 14) that often culminate in physical fights and function as peer mediated discipline.
- *Songs:* sometimes-obligatory singing sessions independent of an ability to hold a tune.
- *Toasts* (aka Jokes): a "body of oral epic poetry" with "many complex metrical arrangements" (Labov, et al 1968b: 55). These are often first person narratives by antiheros telling exploits of street life using stock characters such as pimps and "ho's."
- *Ritual Insults* (aka the *dozens, signifying, sounding,* and more recently *snaps*): insults that often take the form of rhymed couplets. Labov et al (1968b: 77) provide the example, "I hate to talk about your mother, she's a good old soul. She got a ten-ton pussy and a rubber asshole." This is a very old African American tradition and well studied by a number of folklorists over the years. Labov et al. report that the tradition had evolved in the direction of improvisation by the 1960s.
- *Rifting or riffing:* "a style of speech – an elevated, high flown delivery...The occult knowledge that is delivered in this way is described as 'heavy'...[and] is learned by rote; adepts are examined in a speech event known as 'putting someone on the square,' or 'being on the square'; they are asked a series of difficult questions before an audience, and must deliver the right answers to maintain their claim to know" (Labov, et al 1968b: 136). This knowledge was particularly associated with various Muslim or quasi-Muslim groups at the time such as the Nation of Islam and the Five Percent Nation (aka the Nation of Gods and Earths). Both groups were associated with Black nationalism

during the 1960s and have common roots, with the Five Percenters formed by dissidents from the Nation of Islam.

These genres are not presented by Labov et al. as expressly New York forms. However, it is impossible to look at the songs, toasts, ritual insults, and rifting, and not see how ten years later they came together in Hip-Hop, and that is, in its origins, a truly New York story.

Hip-hop began in the 1970s in the Bronx at the height of the time when that borough was burning (see Chapter 2), and a number of Hip-Hop genres that were forming at that time are traceable to the ones Labov, et al. (1968b) observe in Harlem. These include rap battles, in which two MCs hurl rhymed insults at each other. As with its predecessor described above, in battles a common theme involves insulting the opponent's mother typically in sexual ways. Another common MC genre, the *cipha*, grows out of Five Percenter practices, as do a number of Hip-Hop expressions and forms. Battles, ciphas, and precomposed songs called *writtens* also feature elements of toasts including narrations with first person protagonists and various stock characters (see Newman 2001, 2005). Hip-Hop has since gone on to become a worldwide phenomenon, and there is no doubt that it is one of the major cultural and linguistic contributions of New York to the world.

5.4 Bilingual Repertoires: Language Contact in New York

Once while doing research at UAA, I was chatting to Wilson, a Nuyorican student, in the photography studio when a friend of his walked in. Wilson then turned to me and said, "sorry, we speak Spanglish." The word, *Spanglish* is used in various ways in New York, and it was only the context that made clear what Wilson meant. One common meaning – which Wilson did not mean – is the borrowing of English words into the local variety of Spanish for example, *bildin* for "building" (Otheguy 2011: 506) instead of *edificio*, the term used in Spanish elsewhere. Other contact effects described as *Spanglish* that Wilson did not mean involve calques of English grammar and/or idiomatic expressions into Spanish (see Chapter 4 and Otheguy 2011).

Instead what Wilson was telling me was that he habitually codeswitched with his friend and was going to do so now; the conversation would not be entirely in English or Spanish but both. He assumed that this would exclude me because he did not know I spoke Spanish, and so he wanted to politely warn me about this. Codeswitching occurs in many bilingual settings, but it has various forms, and the particular patterns can differ widely. New York Latinos often switch within sentences, as it is put in a classic and memorably titled article on the subject, "Sometimes I start a sentence in English y termino en español" (Poplack 1980). Urciuoli (1996) sees codeswitching in the New York Puerto Rican community as an emergent and context dependent amalgamation of the two languages:

> Whether or not people regard English and Spanish as rigidly separate depends on the dynamics of the situation. Sometimes the social functions of language – the ways people use language, for example, scolding, teasing, gossiping – can be done in either code or both, code-switched. There is no clear sense of code boundary. At other times, one code may specifically heighten the function by making the scolding more pointed, the play funnier, the gossip more biting. In these cases, a sense of distinction between English and Spanish becomes important. (Urciuoli 1996: 76)

Zentella (1997) argues that codeswitching along with the other forms of hybridization mentioned above should not be confused with the creation of a new language called Spanglish. She, along with Urciuoli, is particularly careful to refute any implication that these phenomena involve a decline in linguistic abilities. As she says, "The pejorative connotations of [Spanglish] reflect negative evaluations of the linguistic and/or intellectual abilities of those who codeswitch." She continues by saying that such concerns initially led her to reject the term. However, she later says that her position,

> has been modified by the recognition that more NYPRs [New York Puerto Ricans] are referring to "Spanglish" as a positive way of identifying their switching... [M]embers of the second and third generations of NYPRs are rehabilitating "Spanglish," along with their unembarrassed adoption of "Nuyorican" as an identity label. (Zentella 1997: 82)

Zentella's rehabilitation of the word *Spanglish* is contested by Otheguy and Stern (2011) who worry that the word cannot be disentangled from its negative connotations and because they feel that it is scientifically vacuous. Both sides agree, however, that stigma attached to Spanish-English contact effects, including but not limited to code switching, is entirely based on prejudice against the New York Latino community. Ultimately, Zentella's dispute with Otheguy and Stern is over the validity of the term *Spanglish* not the legitimacy of the practices it represents. Like all linguists, they see language contact phenomena as natural and expected in bilingual societies. They also recognize that the ability to codeswitch requires significant levels of proficiency in both languages. Unfortunately, this is a message that bears repeating. The idea of linguistic defectiveness of New York Spanish-English bilinguals is widespread and sometimes held by Latinos themselves. In a way parallel to the loss of prestige of NYCE itself – which as Bonfiglio points out also arose from racial prejudice against immigrants – the prejudices against the Latino community get turned against their speech habits. Those prejudices then get absorbed by members of that community as linguistic self-hatred.

If any doubts still exist that it is not really the linguistic hybridity itself that is the source of the lack of prestige, further evidence can be found in the very different treatment given to the Yiddish-English contact phenomena referred to as *Yinglish* (see Chapter 4).[1] *Yinglish* is not understood pejoratively, although Fader (2007) documents cases of Yiddish-English codeswitching along similar lines to that seen among Latinos. Instead, Yiddish contact phenomena are often cultivated as a cultural icon of old-world immigrant roots and/or as a desired separation of its speakers from secular or *goyishe* society by the very religious.

There has been other work on linguistic hybridity in New York. Schieffelin (1994) provides data on codeswitching as a way of aiding language acquisition in a Haitian New York family. Angermeyer (2005) shows how codeswitching, complete with shifts in alphabets, occur in signs and ads posted by Russian New Yorkers. Ultimately all these studies show that the embrace of linguistic hybridity marks a healthy approach to language. Such an embrace entails a vision of identity that refuses to accept the linguistic and cultural insecurities that cause some to condemn bilingualism, bilingual practices, and bilingual people. As such, it is congruent with a New York trait that goes back to its earliest days in which plural identity is seen as New York identity.

5.5 Further Research

The three discourse phenomena examined here embody the multicultural nature of the city, but this outline is pale reflection because it summarizes only the research that has been done not all there is to be done. In a research class called Voices in New York, which I have taught in the past few years with the linguistic anthropologist Miki Makihara, our students have begun work on a variety of interesting topics in pragmatics and discourse. A few of these include:
– Language socialization in Afghan families,
– Codeswitching among Japanese and Brazilian New Yorkers,
– The system for adapting English words into Polish among immigrants who speak that language.
– Communication across ethnic lines in a largely Pakistani limo service
– Construction of ethnic identity in South Asian and White rap artists.
– The trilingual practices of MCs in the Bukharian Jewish community.

---

1 Actually, *Yinglish* involves borrowing of Hebrew in addition to Yiddish lexicon (Steinmetz 1981).

As single semester undergraduate research projects, the conclusions of these studies must be regarded as tentative. However, they provide examples of the many topics that can form the next wave of studies on NYCE discourse.

6 Lexicon (the vocabulary of a person, language, or branch of knowledge)

6.1 Background

New York Governor Andrew Cuomo once dismissed objections to a proposed convention center by claiming that the project would "cost the State of New York bubkes" (Kaplan 2012). For those confused by what he meant, the fifth edition of the on-line *American Heritage Dictionary* defines *bubkes* as "A worthless amount; little or nothing." Miriam Webster adds the etymology as from, "Yiddish (probably short for *kozebubkes*, literally, goat droppings)." Interestingly, the reporter did not bother to define the word; he presumably assumed that *Times* readers would understand.

Yiddishisms like *bubkes* have taken on an iconic role in NYCE, and surely there are not too many places that an Italian American politician could use a word like *bubkes* to a general audience and expect to be understood. Yet the governor's usage actually is actually one case of a wider phenomenon characteristic of language contact. As discussed in the previous three chapters, immigrant bilingualism often leads to a variety of hybrid linguistic phenomena including lexical borrowing. Borrowed words can end up used by descendants of immigrants who may no longer be fully bilingual and spread beyond the original community. Furthermore, in a place like New York that revels in its diversity, such words can become emblematic of local identity itself. The particularly central role of Yiddishisms reflects the close association of New York City identity with Ashkenazi Jews and their culture.

However, the NYCE lexicon has many sources, not just Jews or even immigrants generally. Allen (1993: 4) estimates that "perhaps two thousand words and phrases" have emerged over the years in the city's linguistic cauldron. The processes of coining, borrowing, filtering, and disseminating of new words continue to this day. At the same time, the larger economy, media culture, and interregional migration tend to impose national terms locally and to extend coinages and borrowings that emerge in New York to other regions.

The contributions of immigrant languages are presented in the next section, followed by an exploration of traditional local vocabulary of other origins. This is followed by a discussion of the impact on the NYCE lexicon of a sociolinguistic division that should be by now more than familiar: race. The final section discusses these factors from the perspective of the encounter between local peculiarities, deregionalization, and non-regional social differences.

6.2 Immigrant Contributions

6.2.1 Yiddishisms

Cuomo's use of *bubkes* seems designed to make a point in a folksy way and so show that he was a *mensch* – a good guy – and not least a New Yorker. However, the governor was actually stepping into a linguistic minefield for politicians from which not even the Jewish (although originally Bostonian) former mayor Michael Bloomberg had been able to return unscathed. Bloomberg's trouble involved running afoul of the city's Yiddish *mavens*, who are quick to point out any divergence for authentic Yiddish grammar. According the *New York Times*, the mayor described the State Senate's move to adjourn without voting on his control of schools as "meshugeneh'" (Roberts 2009). He meant to describe the decision as *crazy*, but *meshugeneh* in Yiddish is a noun meaning *crazy person*; the adjective, as the mavens pointed out, is *meshuga*. The mayor so-called "solecism" was echoed by then State Senator, Hiram Monserrate in a counterattack: "We believe it would be meshugeneh not to include parents in the education of our children." Unlike the mayor, Monserrate might have been given linguistic pass on the grounds of his *goyishe* (i.e., non-Jewish) background had he not gone on to call Bloomberg a *yenta*. That term was described by the *Times* reporter's Yiddish consultant, Michael Wex as meaning "a female motor mouth." So Monserrate moved from understandable lack of fidelity to Yiddish grammar to unpardonable sexism.

Nevertheless, these two politicians' Yiddish predicaments pale in comparison to the linguistic *klutziness* of former US Senator Alfonse D'Amato. During that senator's 1998 failed reelection bid, he referred to his Jewish opponent Chuck Schumer as a *putzhead*. A Yiddish speaker or just someone more familiar with the language could have told D'Amato that *putz* is a vulgar word for *penis*. Calling an opponent a *dickhead* is not something a politician would want to be caught doing, and Schumer's campaign milked the incident for all it was worth. D'Amato might have been confused because of the term *putzing around* has come to mean just wasting time doing useless things. Also *putz* is not the most common Yiddish word for the male sexual organ that gets applied to people. A better-known one is *schmuck*, although this term is really only used idiomatically essentially with the meaning of *asshole*. At times even this figurative sense falls away. A number of the Latinos at UAA would sometimes say, "What the schmuck!" as a humorous euphemism for "What the fuck." There are of course many less offensive Yiddish words commonly used in NYCE. Some the best known are listed below with definitions quoted verbatim from the *American Heritage Dictionary* on line, with my comments in square brackets [].

- *Chutzpah*: (n) Utter nerve; effrontery:
- *Glitsch*: (n) A minor malfunction, mishap, or technical problem; a snag: a computer glitch; a navigational glitch; a glitch in the negotiations. [very widespread now due to its use in technology]
- *Kibbitz*: (v) To chat; converse
- *Mazel-tov*: (exclamation) Used to express congratulations or best wishes
- *Mensch*: (n) A person having admirable characteristics, such as fortitude and firmness of purpose [but unpretentiously]
- *Mishigas*: (n) [craziness, abstract noun related to *mishuga*]
- *Oy vey*: (exclamation) [said as expression of despair]
- *Schlemiel*: (n) [loser, person who always screws up]
- *Schlep*: (v) To carry clumsily or with difficulty; lug... To move slowly or laboriously. (n) An arduous journey
- *Schlock*: (n) Something, such as merchandise or literature, that is inferior or shoddy. (adj) Of inferior quality; cheap or shoddy
- *Schmooze*: (v) To converse casually, [sometimes though not necessarily] in order to gain an advantage or make a social connection. [engage in small talk]
- *Spiel*: (n) A lengthy or extravagant speech or argument usually intended to persuade. (v) To talk or say (something) at length or extravagantly.
- *Tush*: (n) The buttocks. [The more exclusively Yiddish *tuchas* appears restricted to Jews.]

Some of these words have expanded to US English generally through their use by Jewish media personalities, although many retain their association with New York since they remain more widely by Jews and non-Jews alike in the region. Yet it would be wrong to believe that they are universally employed by New Yorkers. When I taught at UAA I asked my students out of curiosity how many Yiddishisms they knew, and beyond, *schmuck*, there was little familiarity. However, while New Yorkers from a non-Jewish background may not learn these terms growing up, as they move through diverse work places, they are still liable to pick them up. This acquisition can involve expressions as well as simple words. In the 1970s I waited tables at a New York restaurant, and once while looking for an order that was right in front of my nose, a Puerto Rican cook held it up and said, "What do you think this is, chopped liver?" I expect that he picked up this expression working with Jews, chopped liver being the Ashkenazi answer to foie gras. In a diverse city like New York these kinds of interactions ultimately enrich the common language as individuals pick up colorful expressions brought by colleagues of different origins.

6.2.2 Lexical contributions from other languages

In New York, as elsewhere, borrowings from immigrant languages have often entered wider circulation as references to cultural items and practices that immigrants bring. Italian and southern Italian dialects are consequently overrepresented in food terminology due to the wide appeal of Italian cuisine. Of course, a wide array of food-related Italianisms have become familiar worldwide, but even some reasonably widespread ones have taken on a New York flavor due immigrants' particular regional dialects. *Calzone,* for example, is a widely known turnover shaped savory pastry with a variety of fillings, but New Yorkers often follow a southern Italian dialect phonological rule and drop the final /e/ but with an English /z/ resulting in /kælzon/ ('kalzone'). In other parts of the US, I have heard the last vowel pronounced as /e/ ('ay') or /i/ ('ee'). Similarly, *calamari* can lose its final vowel, and for some Italian American New Yorkers, the /l/ becomes /d/, yielding /kæləmæd/.[1]

Other words associated with Italian Americans were developed in New York. The local practice of referring to a whole pizza as a *pie* is a calque of the meaning of the Italian original, and in local usage a round pizza pie with thin crust is either *regular* or more pretentiously *Neapolitan.* By contrast a square pizza pie with a thick crust is *Sicilian.* Note that *pizza places* are not quite the same as *pizzerias.* Pizza places sell by the slice, have counter service, and permit the customer to stand or sit down and eat; pizzerias are more traditional restaurants that sell only whole pies invariably ordered from and delivered by a server. A "no slices" sign in the window often lets potential customers know of the establishment's pizzeria status.

Another classic New York word, mentioned in Chapter 2, is also associated with pizza places, *hero* sandwiches. The origin of this name is presumably in local marketing: some now-forgotten deli or pizza place that claimed that its sandwiches were so large they were heroic or possibly it would take a hero to finish one. *Hero* thus takes its place as the New York equivalent of the Philadelphia *hoagie,* the New England *grinder,* and the Southern *po'boy.* All these colorful local terms are under threat from national chains trying to homogenize the sandwich eaters of America into calling them *subs.* The New York use of *hero* may have impacted another sandwich from farther east in the Mediterranean: the Greek pita and meat sandwich called *gyro.* In some areas of the country a more authentically Greek pronunciation is preserved: /jiro/ ('yee-roh'). However, in New York

---

1 I owe this observation to the CUNY linguist Christina Tortora, who in fact took me to a Staten Island pizza place, where the server obliged us unbidden by referring to calamari using this pronunciation.

the spelling pronunciation /dʒaɪro/ (jie-roh') is normal. The Greek pronunciation would be too close to the name of the Italian sandwich.

Italian-Americans have also made some less savory contributions to the NYCE lexicon using sources in Italian, southern Italian dialects, English, and a mix. With the advent of *Jersey Shore*, for example, the words *guido* and *guidette* spread across the US, from the Italian boy's name that is cognate with *Guy*. Both terms – *guido* for a male and *guidette* for a female – were used for years in the metro area to refer to members of the working class Italian American youth culture made nationally famous on that show. Italian organized crime is also associated with New York, of course. Although words like *mafia*, *don*, and *Cosa Nostra* are known and used worldwide, the term used for a member in New York is *wiseguy*, which is evidently not an Italian lexeme. There is also a whole jargon associated with the mafia, from *made members*, who have been initiated, to the *consigliere*, who advises the *don*. All these terms are familiar to the broader public via popular culture and news reports. Of course, it is wrong to limit the Italian American contribution to NYCE to such stereotypical domains. There are plenty of other Italian-isms in NYCE, although most have remained within the community. The short list below with the original definitions is taken from Jim Lampos's *Brooklynisms* webpage http://www.lampos.com/brooklyn.htm again with definitions as provided:

- *Cugutza*: Hard head.
- *Filgia de butana*: Daughter of an unsavory woman.
- *Madone*: Something like saying "Oh my God." Literally: "Madonna"
- *Scoumbaish*: When you cook, make sure you have enough for everyone. Don't scoumbaish.
- *Shem*: A jerk, or a stupid person. Short for the Italian word pronounced 'Shemanooda.'

The languages of other immigrant groups have also contributed food vocabulary such as the already mentioned Greek example of *gyro*. A more recent case involves food trucks that sell spicy sliced kebab-style meat with rice and/or gyro sand-wiches and often other Middle Eastern dishes such as falafel or hummus. Similar product arrays can be found all over the world using terms from Greek, Turkish, or Arabic. However, when sold from these mobile kitchens in New York, the entire menu is referred to as *halal food*, or sometimes just *halal*, as in "I'm gonna get a halal." The source is the signs on the trucks that assure observant Muslims that their food is prepared following Islamic dietary laws; yet the term has been taken up by non-Muslim New Yorkers to mean just those items on the trucks' menus.

Where food can be bought is also distinct in New York. In most of the US small stores that sell basic groceries are referred to as a *convenience stores*. However, that term is rarely used in New York, although I have seen it on signs. Instead one type of small grocery is called a *bodega*, which comes from Puerto Rican Spanish. *Bodegas* originally only referred to stores that sell Latin American products as well as general staples, but they can also refer to similar stores run by Egyptians among other immigrant groups. Bigger stores with large produce selections are referred to as *Korean stores, Korean delis,* or *Korean fruit stores.* They offer East Asian products, and in Manhattan there are typically prepared foods, salad bars, and flowers. As the name indicates, the markets are invariably owned by Koreans, although it appears that their numbers are diminishing.

Along with Korean stores, there are, of course a variety of explicitly ethnically labeled institutions, such as *Jewish deli(catessen)*, which tend to be called a *New York* (style) *delis* elsewhere. Whereas a plain *deli* will usually have few if any tables and no waiter service, *Jewish delis* are more often than not a kind of restaurant. When Jewish religious dietary rules are followed, they can be called *kosher delis.* By contrast, non-table service Jewish food stores without meat and an emphasis on smoked fish and dairy products are referred to as *appetizing stores.* These stores often sell bagels, but many bagel *mavens* claim that those sold directly from *bagel factories* (stores that boil and then bake the bagels on site) are better. There are also *Greek diners* (which are almost all diners), and to get away from the food theme New York has *Russian baths*, where you can bathe communally and get beaten with birch branches.

Bodega is in general circulation, but Spanish has contributed other words that are still mainly restricted to the Latino community, including beyond New York. One example is *papichulo* or, less frequently, *mamichula*, a term for hot guy or gal, in particular one who is self-conscious about appearance. Similar to *wiseguy*, an English expression has been adapted for a similar meaning: *pretty boy* and (again less commonly) *pretty girl.* In many varieties of English, the term *pretty boy* contains homophobic implications of effeminacy or possibly just a preppy look. However, as it was used in UAA, the term was essentially identical to *papichulo*, and it had positive connotations. A different gendered pair *cholo/ chola* (for males and females respectively) is a slur for indigenous people in parts of South America, but refers to someone in an urban thug subculture in many parts of the Latino US diaspora including New York. A recent and perhaps still localized import is reported by Crocker (2014) in a study of a Manhattan restaurant. This word is *carnal* an address term from Mexican Spanish, where it implies a fraternal type friendship. Crocker says it spread from Mexican workers speaking in Spanish and English to the entire staff.

Finally, Latino English words can reflect the Spanish uses of an originally English word that was borrowed into Spanish where it acquired a slightly different meaning. For example, in a video by a New York on the *Moral Courage* YouTube

Channel a teenager named Kevin Santiago narrates confronting another boy who bullied a seventh grader.[2] Kevin reports telling the bully, "What you did to that man wasn't cool." In non-Latino English, it is unlikely that a 12 to 13 year old would be referred to as a *man,* but in many varieties of Latin American Spanish, the word *man* has become a slang term meaning *guy.* Kevin just reimports the word into English with the Spanish sense. This kind of usage – like machines that are no longer devil-owned – exemplifies the often unintentional creativity characteristic of human language and is what makes linguistic hybridity so interesting!

6.3 Words Original to NYCE

Besides the *exogenous* words (i.e., those with origin outside English) discussed above, other NYCE words that have developed through endogenous processes, although in some cases the origins seem mysterious and the meanings counter-intuitive. It is hard to see how *regular coffee* came to mean *coffee with milk,* for example, or how a mix of chocolate syrup, milk, and soda came to be called an *egg cream* given the absence of egg and cream. A more recent case seems to be sweet fruit flavored alcoholic drinks often sold in bodegas that are referred to as *nutcrackers* or *nutties*; the origin of that term is unknown to me.

Traditional dialectologists who have examined the NYCE lexicon have focused however not on these relatively recent coinages or the immigrant language borrowings discussed in the last section but much older terms mainly of English and Dutch origin. The two major studies of this kind (Kurath 1949 and Carver 1987) are word geographies, i.e., lexical inventories that differentiate regions. Both are derived from larger projects: Kurath's from the Linguistic Atlas of the United States and Canada (LAUSC) and Carver's from the *Dictionary of American Regional English* (DARE). The LAUSC data – the same used for Atwood's (1953) study of verb forms in Chapter 4 – were obtained during the 1930s, whereas the DARE data were collected during the 1960s, and those thirty years show major deregionalization. Carver (1987: 39) notes that at the time of the LAUSC data collection virtually half the distinctive elements of NYCE and the Hudson Valley were "Anglicized remnants of the Dutch vocabulary." Many of these (e.g., *olicook* and *rolliche* for *donut* and *little roll* respectively) were gone by the 1960s. Other Dutch-origin words, such as *cruller* (an éclair shaped donut) and *stoop* (for stairs to an above street level house entrance) remained in use, as the do today, but they

---

2 The video available at http://www.youtube.com/watch?v=TstO_xRejHg or http://www.irshad-manji.com/mctv (last accessed January 25, 2014) provides an excellent sample of NYLE speech in addition to an inspiring story.

had spread well beyond the region. Other words given in the DARE database are broadly geographically restricted to the northeast, east, or sometimes both coasts (see Vaux and Golder 2003 for survey data). These include the following from Carver (1987: 39):

- *Brook:* a small stream
- *Clapboard:* wood slats used to cover the exterior of buildings
- *Cobblestone*: small smooth or rounded stones [typically as bumpy pavement on streets].
- *Guinea:* [a slur for] a person of Italian heritage
- *Route such and such:* a numbered and lettered rural road [e.g., *Route 17*, actually not necessarily rural] as opposed to the California variant *the 17*.
- *Scallion:* green onion
- *Soda:* carbonated soft drink

Interestingly, the Dutch word *kill* like *brook* also means *stream,* but it is now restricted to names of particular waterways, such as Kill Van Kull, which separates Staten Island from New Jersey. The lexeme can actually be found incorporated into place names up the Hudson Valley and at least as far west as Tremperskill in Andes, NY in the Catskill Mountains.[3]

In contrast to word geographies, which focus on traditional lexicon, Allen (1993) produced a monograph on New York slang mostly until 1950. This work is remarkable in its comprehensiveness and the connections the author makes between slang and sociological developments. I remember some words he mentions from my childhood such as *spaldeen* (a pink rubber ball made by the Spalding company) and the use of *farmer* to refer to anyone from out of town.

Many items Allen cites were coined in New York and later spread elsewhere. One is *Tin Pan Alley* (Allen 1993: 63), which originally referred to a street with where music publishers were concentrated, although the actual place changed over time. Other cities later developed their own Tin Pan Alleys. Other more common words coined in New York include, *traffic jam* and *rush hour,* which of course spread so widely that the New York association is effectively lost. The term *subway* was also a New Yorkism according to Allen and was later shared with many other cities including Philadelphia, Newark, Toronto, and, interestingly, Glasgow where it may have, of course, developed independently. Nevertheless, as Allen (1993: 96) points out the traditional name for the PATH (Port Authority Trans Hudson) trains to New Jersey – still used when I was a child – was the *Hudson Tubes*. *Tube,* of course,

---

3 See http://highcountrynews.tumblr.com/image/19961443376 for a distribution of stream names around the US. The western limit may be contiguous or nearly so with eastern limit of the Inland North vowel system (see Chapter 3).

is more associated with London's system, which predates New York's. Another of Allen's underground examples remains local: *straphanger*, used to refer to subway riders who held onto straps hanging from the ceiling of the cars when standing. The straps have long since been replaced by metal bars, and the term is really only used in news reports and by organizations like *The Straphangers Campaign*, which lobbies for better mass transit. Another bit of mostly lost subway nomenclature is the use of the original operating company names: IRT (from the Interborough Rapid Transit) for the numbered trains, and BMT (Brooklyn-Manhattan Transit) and IND (Independent) for the lettered ones. Allen does not mention this, but the use of *train* in preference to *line* for a single route is a NYCE characteristic and can function as a shibboleth. Anyone who says the *E-line* or (God forbid!) *the blue line* (for the E-train's color on the map) is immediately identifiable as an out-of-towner. A New Yorker will usually say the *E-train* and may not even know the relevant color or will at least have to think about it visualizing a subway map.[4] The term *line* applies by contrast to the route the tracks follow and so can include a group of trains that share the same route for part of their journey such as the *8th Avenue Line*,[5] which includes the *A*, C and *E*, trains. An alternative term for the joint portion is naturally *ACE*, although other lines like 6th Avenue with its B, D, F, and M or Broadway's N, Q, and R are not so acronym friendly. Only if there one train on a portion or the entirety of a route, is a New Yorker likely to refer to "the L line" or "the 7 line."

The use of subway routes as markers of neighborhoods has become common in Hip-Hop and R&B, as in Jennifer Lopez's 1999 debut album, *On the 6*, a reference to her Bronx neighborhood served by the 6-train. New Yorkers actually have a remarkable number of ways to refer to where they live, and these designations are not stable. Allen reports a number of neighborhood names that spread elsewhere. One is the *Tenderloin*, the once unofficial red light district, originally coinciding with west midtown (Allen 1993: 179). Zacks (2012) attributes the name to a late 19th century police captain, who upon being transferred to that area from one with less opportunity for bribes said, "All my life I've been living on rump steak. Now, I'm gonna eat tenderloin." Now, the name mainly is used for a neighborhood near downtown San Francisco. The lower part of the original New York Tenderloin was split into Chelsea and Hell's Kitchen; the upper part joined the Upper West Side, and the original name faded away.

---

4 This preference has an interesting effect on NYC Spanish. In the Buenos Aires subway (el Subte), where letters are used, people say "la E," to refer to lines for example, and in Madrid and Barcelona, where numbers are used, it possible to hear "la 1" based on the feminine gender of *la línea*. Most Spanish speakers in New York, however, say "el E" or "el 1" based on the masculine gender of *el tren*.

5 *Route*, by the way, varies in its pronunciation in NYCE between /rut/ ('root') and /raᵘt/ ('rout').

On that point, real estate agents are notorious for altering the nomenclature of neighborhoods to suit their marketing strategies. In some cases, like the *East Village*, the prestige of neighboring *Greenwich Village* was borrowed to overcome the poor reputation of the LES out of which The East Village was carved (Becker 2010). In other neighborhoods, a damaging name like *Hell's Kitchen* was simply changed, in this case taking advantage of the local *DeWitt Clinton Park* to produce *Clinton,* although the older term retains its devotees. Other invented names are slightly tongue-in-cheek. SoHo officially refers to South of Houston Street (pronounced /haʊstn̩ / 'house-ton') but simultaneously nods to the London neighborhood. *Tribeca* stands for *Triangle below Canal,* but it is actually a quadrangle. *Carroll Gardens, Cobble Hill* and *Boerum Hill* are also real estate inventions, but they have gained local legitimacy. Their success is probably due to the fact that they refer to parts of what was once known as *South Brooklyn,* a designation that suffered from the fact that it referred to a relatively northerly section of the borough of Brooklyn.

Other place names persist through the centuries. Dutch vocabulary remains present today almost entirely in geographic designations such as the *kill* place names mentioned earlier. The region is also full of Dutch-English hybrids like *New Dorp, Sandy Hook* in New Jersey and *Red Hook* in Brooklyn; *dorp* means *village,* and *hoek* means *corner* (see Kurath 1949, Romaine 2001). *Staten Island* also was named in honor of their High Mightinesses, the Dutch governing council, usually translated into English as the *States General,* and even Broadway descends from Brede Wegh (Dillard 1989: 29). Sometimes just Dutch spelling and pronunciation were Anglicized as in *Brooklyn, Flushing,* and *Harlem* from *Breukelen,*[6] *Vlissingen,* and *Haarlem* respectively. *Spuyten Duyvil* the entrance from the Hudson to the Harlem rivers separating the Bronx from Manhattan is clearly Dutch, but it has unsettled etymology. The New York City Department of Parks and Recreation (2000) suggests it might come from *Devils Whirlpool.* However, they also give the charmingly dubious version I learned at school, which was popularized by Washington Irving in his *Knickerbocker's History of New York.* Incidentally, the relevant passage begins with a notorious literary phrase:

> It was a dark and stormy night when the good Antony arrived at the creek (sagely denominated Haerlem river) which separates the island of Manna-hata from the mainland. The wind was high, the elements were in an uproar, and no Charon could be found to ferry the adventurous sounder of brass across the water. For a short time he vapored like an impa-

---

6 Incidentally, the CUNY syntactian of Dutch origins Marcel Den Dinken pointed out to me that in the Netherlands, Breukelen is in the province of Utrecht, but the New Utrecht was incorporated into the Borough of Brooklyn. The heart of the former town is now in Bensonhurst.

tient ghost upon the brink, and then, bethinking himself of the urgency of his errand, took a hearty embrace of his stone bottle, swore most valorously that he would swim across in spite of the devil (spyt den duyvel), and daringly plunged into the stream. Luckless Antony scarce had he buffeted half-way over when he was observed to struggle violently, as if battling with the spirit of the waters. Instinctively he put his trumpet to his mouth, and giving a vehement blast sank for ever to the bottom. (Irving 1809, Book 7, Chapter 10)

Other New York coinages have altered meanings over time. Allen (1993: 81) reports *rubbernecking* originally referred to the behavior of a "gawking tourist." Now it refers to drivers' slowing down to see an accident on a highway. Allen (1993: 451) also mentions *drag*, which he says originated in British cant (i.e., slang used by marginalized groups), but which entered US English through NYCE. *Drag* originally meant *street*, and this sense can still be seen in *main drag* as the principal street in an area or town or as in *drag race*. It is easy to see how that meaning gave rise to *drag queen*. Then, since a drag queen is defined by what she wears, *drag* has come to be used for any identity-giving outfit. I have, for example, heard people referring to an ultra-orthodox Jew as wearing *full Hasidic drag*.

A few of the many other slang items Allen mentions are listed below along with his comments, with my comments as before in square brackets:

- *Joint* can refer to almost any place [restaurant, bar, coffee shop, disco] with only slight pejoration (p. 146).
- *[Bum's rush]* was initiated ... not as a means of expelling drunks but of repelling daring daylight raids by fleet-footed indigents on the free lunch counters (p. 168).
- *Shopping-bag ladies* is now sometimes shortened to *bag ladies*, which in New York causes a confusion with *bag women*, or runners for the numbers racket; both terms are probably of New York origin. Shopping bag ladies are not new to city streets and were noted in descriptions of New York early in this century. Even then they tended to carry all their possessions in large bags filled to bursting and to wear many layers of clothing (pp. 196–197).
- *Slum* tells an unusually revealing story of American urban development, social change, and accompanying ideologies. The semantic changes in *slum* and its partial eclipse by the word *ghetto* in public discourse is an illustration, first, of the relation of class to ethnicity and race and, second, of their recent drawing apart in response to the reality of urban poverty (p. 230).

The last entry is one of the few in Allen's book that refers to relatively recent lexical developments. To get a more general account of contemporary words and usages, it is necessary to turn to the Internet. The most complete on-line source for New Yorkisms was created by word sleuth extraordinaire and former NYC traffic court judge Barry Popik. Popik's website (http://www.barrypopik.com) contains a large and growing selection of words, expressions, and sayings used in many areas of city life. A few with examples are listed below to give a sense of what is located there. My comments are in again in [square brackets]:

- Banking/Finance/Insurance: *"A rolling loan gathers no loss"* (banking adage)
- Buildings/Housing/Public Spaces: *Garden Apartments:* [Apartments in buildings around a shared private garden space, classically in Jackson Heights]
- Names/Phrases: *Going All City* (Graffiti Slang) means putting your graffiti on trains in every borough
- Music/Dance/Theatre: *"Don't quit your day job"* (show business adage)
- Neighborhoods: *Yupper West Side* [blend of Yuppie and Upper West Side]
- Newspapers/Media: *Columny* (calumny from a columnist)
- Nicknames/Slogans: *City That Never Sleeps*
- Schools: [Popik notes an important distinction: SUNY (State University of New York) is pronounced /suni/ ('sue-knee'), but *CUNY* (City University of New York) is pronounced /kjuni/ ('Q-knee').

Popik gives a category all its own to the city's nickname, *The Big Apple:*

> "The Big Apple" was the catchphrase of New York *Morning Telegraph* track writer John J. Fitz Gerald in the 1920s. He admitted this twice and it was the name of three of his columns. He picked up the term from African-American ("dusky" he called them) stable hands at the Fair Grounds racetrack in New Orleans, probably on January 14, 1920.

> Fitz Gerald's first New York *Morning Telegraph* "Around the Big Apple" column, on February 18, 1924, proudly declared:

> *The Big Apple. The dream of every lad that ever threw a leg over a thoroughbred and the goal of all horsemen. There's only one Big Apple. That's New York. ...*

> "The Big Apple" was revived in the 1970s by Charles Gillett, president of the New York Convention and Visitors Bureau.

> The origins of "the Big Apple" were solved in the 1990s by Gerald Cohen and Barry Popik. A "Big Apple Corner" street sign was dedicated in 1997 at West 54th Street and Broadway, where Fitz Gerald last lived. (Popik 2004)

Jim Lampos's Brooklynisms page (http://www.lampos.com/brooklyn.htm) was mentioned in reference to Italianisms in the previous section. A few non-Italian examples Lampos provides are listed below with their definitions. Again, my interventions are in square brackets:

- *Boss*: What your local deli or bodega guy calls you when he doesn't know your name. It's a term of good will. He might even call you "Big Boss," which is even better. You don't want to be called "Pal" or "Buddy," since they usually have sarcastic overtones. If he calls you "Chief," you're really in trouble.
- *Carfare*: A subway token, or money for the subway. A holdover from the days when streetcars were the primary form of public transit. [Today there are no more tokens]
- *Ring a Leevio/Ringolievio:* A children's street game [actually a form of team hide-and-seek related to *manhunt*].
- *Salugi/Saloogi:* A game of "keep away" that kids play, whereby one kid's hat is stolen, and other kids continually taunt him by throwing it past him or over his head to someone else. Usually the same kid is picked on all the time. It is a widely-held theory that mayor Rudy Giuliani was often the victim of salugi. [In my experience it was a book bag that would get stolen, and the game was announced by the shout "Salugi!" My friends and I rotated victims in an egalitarian manner.]
- *Skel*: A junkie, street-person, or lowlife. (Two retired NYPD officers wrote us to say that "skel" was commonly used by cops on the Brooklyn beat in the early 1960's. The term had entered general usage by the 80's.)
- *Sliding Pon*: A regular playground slide. Also called a sliding pond. We have no idea why. [In my experience only *sliding pond*]
- *Stick Ball: Baseball played with a broom handle and a 'Spaldeen'*

There are of course more items – too many to list here – on these and other sites. Those interested should follow the links, find their favorites, other terms, and/or suggest updates.

There are other words that, while common in much of the English-speaking world, show local peculiarities. A New Yorker is capable of using the phrase *the city* as a synonym for New York even when they are in another smaller city; the same is true of *out-of-town* and *out-of-towner*. However, upon return to the New York area, *the city* only refers to Manhattan. A few mostly older Brooklynites reserve the term *New York*, for that borough, a remnant of the days of Brooklyn's independence. Everywhere outside Manhattan, by contrast, is referred to as the *Outer Boroughs* even by those who live there. Further out, *Long Island* or just *the Island* generally refers only to Nassau and Suffolk Counties, a testimony to the greater cultural importance of the city line over topography. As a result, Long Island City, a neighborhood in Queens by the East River, is not actually in Long Island. Also, New Jersey often loses its *New*, which can injure the sensibilities of *Jerseyites*, despite the standard references to the *Jersey Shore* and of course *Jersey City*. The border of *upstate* is somewhat vague, although for me it begins wherever the suburbs end (see Chapter 2). Residents of upstate are mostly ignored, but on occasion have been referred to contemptuously as *Apple Knockers*. Finally, *Upstate* can serve as a metonym for the prisons too many city residents, mostly of working class or low income minority background, are kept in.

6.4 Racial Factors

6.4.1 Racial Variation

In Chapter 3, I showed that *on* is pronounced with the THOUGHT vowel, 'awn' for at least some Blacks but LOT, 'ahn' for most others. It is worth noting that this difference passes largely unnoticed. By contrast, a highly salient difference in pronunciation involves the word *aunt*. For most Blacks and Latinos New Yorkers, this word receives a back vowel either PALM or LOT, (i.e., 'ahnt') whereas for most Whites and Asians, it is front as TRAP, (i.e., homophonous with *ant*).

Another word, *ask* is pronounced by some Blacks and Latinos as /æks/ '*ax*', although this is less frequent than the backed version of *aunt*. Atwood (1953) reports that this pronunciation was found only below the Mason-Dixon line, and it was clearly brought to New York by the Great Migration. Although I have heard of claims of White New Yorkers that pronounce it in this way too, I have only actually encountered one who did so. *Ax* is highly stigmatized, although metatheses (i.e., reversals) of the /k/ and /s/ go back to Old English. In fact, no better illustration of the social roots of linguistic prejudice can be found than the condemnation of this pronunciation. The back pronunciation of *aunt*, on the other hand, is not stigmatized possibly because it is also common in Britain and Eastern New England.

Word meaning can also be divided racially. One case is *punk*, which in the Latino and African American communities usually means *weak person*, at least among the young. The original AAE meaning was receptive male partner in anal sex, although in my experience at UAA students were unaware of that origin, and they used the word a lot! By contrast, among most Whites and probably Asians, *punk* has a primary meaning of juvenile delinquent. Age is also a factor since the delinquent sense predominates among older Whites; at UAA, the White students were fully aware of and used *punk* in the *weak person* sense. Of course, *punk* has also developed a reference to musical style and peer culture originally drawn from the White sense, and this meaning was known to all at UAA, as it is elsewhere among New Yorkers. In other cases, a term might exist among Black and Latino New Yorkers but be relatively absent among Whites. This was the case of *herb*, with the /h/ pronounced, i.e., as the name. A herb is someone dominated by another, and a favorite line of the teens, "You my herb " was typically an invitation for a mock fight.

6.4.2 The N-word

Once during some group work with ninth graders at UAA, an African American boy, Dave, called me over and pointed to Matt, a White classmate in his group and said, "he called me a Nigger." Dave had a reputation for unreliability, and Matt's best friend was Kareem, a Black classmate who was calmly sitting next to him as the third member of the group. Although I had ample reason for skepticism, the situation had to be sorted out. So I asked Kareem if there was a racial incident, and he laughed and said no, upon which Dave also began to laugh in a way that indicated to me that his accusation was not meant seriously.

Rahman (2012) in a study of the use of this word by African American comedians, discusses various levels of complexity in the use and meaning of this word, undoubtedly the most problematic one in the English language. First, she points to a lexical split between *nigger* and *nigga*. Only the r-ful form is unambiguously the slur, whereas the r-less one is an in-group ethnic identifier, i.e., a synonym for *Black guy*. Rahman (2012: 138) puts it as follows: "African Americans are consciously aware of the significance of the schwa ending in the AAE form *nigga*." She argues that the use of *nigga* has a specific function in terms of social meaning:

> [N]igga continues because the term has shown that it is a linguistic resource with the capacity to convey social meaning not retrievable from other ethnically colored terms; considered alone and without regard for pejorative meanings that have historically come from outside the community, the meanings that have evolved for *nigga* within the African American community actually enrich the lexicon of AAE. Use of *nigga* is generally restricted to African American males, who typically use the term to address and refer exclusively to other males ... The fundamental survival meaning of the term *nigga* allows speakers to place it into contexts that give expression to a number of attitudinal stances that highlight affective aspects of identity. (Rahman 2012: 141)

Given this discussion, it is not hard to figure out what happened in the group. Matt had used *nigga* not *nigger* to refer to Dave. Although Dave was not really earnest in his complaint, he was relying on the well-known taboo against Whites using either variant. I am not aware of any other White student at UAA using *nigga* or even of Matt using it again.

The question remains as to why Matt used the term and what it meant for the teenagers at UAA. Actually, the semantic scope and use of this word at UAA and in New York differs somewhat from that described by Rahman (2012) for her comedians and by extension the US generally. First, one reason I did not react strongly to Matt's usage was that other students had already explained as far as they were concerned *nigga* had "changed its meaning" and referred to any male, i.e., no different than *guy* or *dude,* not just Blacks. In other words, it had lost its sense not only as a slur – as Rahman observes – but also the ethnic identity reference. The following example illustrates this use from an interview by Kareem years later when I hired him as a research assistant with Darryl Hammond of the BQ-16:

> Kareem: What do you think of female rappers?

> Darryl: I think female rappers is ill [=cool]. Niggas is ill too.

Even more clearly, later in the same interview Darryl refers to, "this White nigga, Francis." On occasion, even I have been referred to by this word. This semantic shift explains how the form could be combined with *you all* or *you* into the innovative 2PP form *y'all-niggaz* as discussed in Chapter 4. If it just means *guy,* it can follow that form down the route to grammaticalization. The r-ful form nevertheless retained its meaning not just as a racial slur in the wrong hands but as a reclaimed ethnic identity label in the right ones, although without the gender specificity. One example of the latter was a girl with an African American father and Puerto Rican mother who described herself as a *Niggerican.*

Although White UAA students did not – apart from Matt – generally use *nigga,* Latinos did quite freely, as in the quote by Humberto in Chapter 4. African American sociolinguists have told me that the non-ethnic identity semantics have long existed in AAE. Nevertheless, such usage also parallels a common Caribbean Spanish slang usage of *negro/negra,* to refer to people generally of whatever phenotype, as in *mi negra* for *my girlfriend.* Thus, Spanish substrate might have reinforced an already existing AAE practice. More recently, some of African American Queens College students have told me that they have been struck by how the term has become particularly frequent among South Asians.

Yet neither the claim of innocuousness nor the elimination of ethnic identity reference was accepted by adults at UAA, paralleling a generational shift noted by Rahman (2012: 159). Even among youths, use of the n-word was largely limited to those affiliated with Hip-Hop culture, and it is contested even there. There is a substantial sector of people within Hip-Hop who oppose the use of this word, given how tied up it is with its history of racism and dehumanization, a controversy also discussed by Rahman (2012). For instance, a Hip-Hop oriented video produced in New York by an organization called "President Please" (http://www. presidentplease.com) after the 2008 election suggests that the word *president* be substituted. Although the video takes the form of a spoof news report with tongue firmly in cheek, the premise is serious.

In my own experience, it is hard to overestimate the hurt this word can cause, especially those who had lived through the civil rights struggle. An older Black college student once came up to me after the subject came up in a linguistics class discussion to say just how upset what she saw as young people's careless use of the word made her feel. The slippery nature of the semantic distinctions the teens made in justifying their own use can be seen in how easily an exchange like that between Matt and Dave could have blown up into something more complicated. I was able to calmly explain some of this to Matt at the end of the class.

6.4.3 The city divided

The ways race and class divide New York geographically as well lexically is reflected in two clippings from the word *neighborhood*: *nabe* and *hood*. *Nabe* is used for middle class and upper middle class communities, for example those in Brownstone Brooklyn. *Hood,* by contrast, refers to primarily low-income areas, such as East New York or South Jamaica. It is as if the word *neighborhood* has to be split and divided between the types of communities, such is the gulf in power, wealth, and worldview.

Hoods suffer from the general marginalization from what people in *nabes* think of mainstream as city life, and they undoubtedly get the short end of city services and the long end of policing. Yet hoods are rich in cultural creativity, and having survived being brought up in one can mark an individual positively as strong and authentic. The term *ghetto,* if anything, crystalizes some of the qualities of *hoods*. On the one hand, *ghetto* has come to be used as an adjective to describe anything shoddy, substandard, or even just messy. For example, a UAA student I hired as a research assistant said I had "the *ghettoest* office" due to the perpetual state of disorder of my desk and the shelves. It also forms part of larger expressions, such as the term "prisoner of the ghetto," which Rashid Lewis used to describe himself as a child in a quote on page 41. On the other hand, *ghetto* is not entirely a negative concept; *ghetto fabulous* refers to a form of prosperity that retains ghetto style and energy but in a nice house and with an expensive car, and, of course plenty of bling.

These uses of *ghetto* form part of a larger urban slang that originates in African American and Latino communities in New York and other cities and sometimes works its way to suburban areas. New words then emerge in urban areas to replace them. A short list that appeared in my UAA interviews, and are therefore sometimes a decade old, include POSSESIVE+*boy* for male friend as in *my boy(s), his boy(s).* Less often this appears with *girl* for female friend of a girl. Both are clipped from *homeboy/homegirl,* which originally referred to someone from the same hometown. *Ill* was used for *cool,* as Darryl did above, but I have no cases of *sick,* which is now common in pop culture with the same meaning. *Wack* was *bad,* but the more recent *rachet* had yet to appear. *Aight* was common for *all right. Bounce* was used for *leave,* and *popo* meant police. *Gangsta* sometimes meant the same as *thug,* i.e., someone who while not necessarily a gang member lived an outlaw life, but it also could mean simply *authentic* and *real; thug,* on the other hand, did not allow for this semantic shit. So, someone as *happy-go-lucky* and intellectual as Darryl described himself as *gangsta* precisely because, "I'm not a thug, and I'll tell you I'm not a thug." *Gangbanger,* for gang member, was not used, although I have heard it more recently. *Blunt* referred to a cigar filled with *weed* (i.e., marijuana). You need *cheese,* (i.e., *money*) of course to get that weed. *Pot* remained in use but mainly to refer to *potheads,* although the White UAA students used that term in preference to *weed. Mad* was and is a common intensifier – i.e., a word like *really* and *very* that indicate a stronger than normal quality of an adjective. Hopefully, this is a *mad interesting* book. In a study of a corpus of tweets Khachadurian (2013) found that *mad* remains concentrated heavily in the New York area in contrast to *wicked,* found mainly around Boston, and *hella* more widespread but apparently California based.

6.5 Glocal Words in New York and beyond

Apart from *mad,* the words mentioned above are not exclusive to New York but, form part of the international urban vernacular that Alim (2004b) calls Hip-Hop Nation language. Sociolinguists have traditionally downplayed the effects of media on dialect change with the claim that face-to-face communication is the key to transmission of variable patterns. However, the usual targets of this claim are grammar and pronunciation. It is widely recognized that lexical items are more peripheral to the linguistic system, and consequently more easily spread across dialects than grammatical forms. Hip-Hop – through songs, magazines, videos, and radio – is an important example of such a conduit. Elements that emerge first in the New York hip-hop community spread to other regions, and those coined in Chicago, Los Angeles, *the Dirty South,* and other Hip-Hop centers end up in New York as well.

This spread of lexical items can be limited, as can be seen in the case *mad,* but it is part of a long-term process. It is clear even by comparing the word geography data collected in the 1930s for LAUSC (Kurath 1949) to that collected for DARE (Carver 1987) that there was a decline in regionally specific vocabulary. One way to understand the lexical deregionalization during that period is through widening of economic horizons. When tools, clothes, food, and other products were largely created and sold locally, discussion of them largely remained local; so the terms used to describe them could also remain local. However, as items came to be sold nationally and produced far from point of sale, the names used by producers and sellers were applied across dialect borders. In other words, local dialect terms depended on locally based economic ecologies. As those ecologies diminished in importance and were increasing replaced by national and even international ones, the local terms got replaced by words with larger circulations. This is the reason that terms such *hero* are threatened by national chains. This word is dependent on mom-and-pop pizza places and independent delis. Fortunately – for more than just dialect preservation – in New York there is probably greater resistance to chains then elsewhere, particularly in the sectors of small commerce and restaurants. So *hero* endures.

Hip-Hop although an international phenomenon is not ultimately as homogenizing as might first appear in large part because of the value placed on local identity within the culture. Rap artists invariably *represent* where they are from and what they value about their communities. In part for this reason, Hip-Hop has been described not so much as globalizing as *glocal* (Robertson 1995, Pennycook & Alim 2007), which refers to its simultaneous global and local nature. Pennycook (2007: 103) expresses the idea through the Hip-Hop mantra of keeping it real:

> One of the most fascinating elements of the global/local relations in hip- hop, then, is what we might call the global spread of authenticity. Here is a perfect example of a tension between on the one hand the spread of a cultural dictate to adhere to certain principles of what it means to be authentic, and on the other, a process of localization that makes such an expression of staying true to oneself dependent on local contexts, languages, cultures, and understandings of the real.

Hip-Hop shares the ethos of valuing difference and local particularity with other recent cultural phenomena (Roudometof 2005). In New York these glocal movements include slow food, with its preference for the locally grown, microbreweries, and the growth of neighborhood newspapers even as larger ones decline. In a way, however, New York has always been a glocal city, the repurposing of Eastern European Jewish lexemes as representing New York identity is classic example of glocalness. So particular dialect terms might disappear or spread nationally but New Yorkers will find new ways to express our local identity in our words.

7 The History and Study of NYCE

NYCE is, of course, a product of the history of the dialect region, and particularly its always-diverse population. However, the forms NYCE takes are not necessarily predictable just from knowledge of those historical events and resulting changing demographics over time. For example, as the NYU linguist John Singler once pointed out to me, a substantial proportion of city's population once consisted of German Americans; yet it hard to see what if any linguistic traces they have left on NYCE. The next section explores the various contributions of different groups throughout the ages, and it shows some counterintuitive outcomes. The following section looks at dialectological research along with later sociolinguistic studies and the role of heterogeneity and linguistic stigma in the foundation of the field of variationist sociolinguistics.

7.1 Early NYCE

7.1.1 Origins

Fischer (1989) traces linguistic and cultural differences between Eastern New England, the Upper South, the Delaware Valley, and Appalachia to the various regional British origins of the settlers who initially colonized each region. Dillard (1992) and Montgomery (1996, 2001, 2004) suggest he may overstate the strength of those linguistic connections, but they agree on the principle: The different mixes of features of the settlers' regional British and Irish English dialects form the starting points of English dialect development in each area (see also Schneider 2007, Trudgill 2004). Oddly, although New York was a major center in British North America, it is skipped over in virtually all these searches for the origins of American English.

By contrast, the interest in colonial New York displayed by cultural historians could not be greater, and a common theme in these histories is that the city's cultural distinctiveness can be traced to its foundation as a Dutch rather than English colony (Goodfriend 1992, Shorto 2004, Reitano 2006). Goodfriend (1992: 4), for instance, emphasizes "the enduring legacy of Dutch colonization in New York." Shorto (2004) even wrote a best-selling history based on the idea that some defining American characteristics like free enterprise and religious and cultural pluralism are ultimately rooted more in Holland's colony than in any of Britain's. So why not also look for the roots of the distinctiveness of NYCE in the influence of the Dutch language?

Nevertheless, identification of any Dutch influence is almost as hard to find as that of the much later German immigrants. Only Pederson (2001: 267) describes NYCE as a "broadly different and complex isolate...originally most closely bound to the Hudson Valley...and its Dutch Heritage," and even he is silent on what that Dutch linguistic heritage might consist of. Actually, the only unambiguous Dutch linguistic traces appear in the place names, now lost words such as *olicook,* and formerly local ones such as *stoop* discussed in Chapter 6 (Dillard 1989). Grammar is more central to dialectal origins and character than lexicon, and there is no sign of any Dutch substrate influence on NYCE phonology or morphosyntax. Therefore, although Pederson is certainly right that the zone of Dutch colonization lines up reasonably closely (although not exactly; see Chapter 2) to still current dialect regions, there is no reason to believe that the source for this difference lies in the Dutch language. This absence is surprising because Dutch was still the majority language 40 years after English conquest (Dillard 1989, Kretzschmar, et al. 1994: 162). So just like other North American colonists' dialects outside French Canada, New Yorkers' initial phonological and morphosyntactic features were, it seems, entirely British.

The English speakers who brought those features actually began to arrive even before Peter Stuyvesant's surrender of New Amsterdam in 1664. Their specific origins – and so their original dialects – have not been traced in a comprehensive way, but some facts stand out in the historical literature. Gravesend in what is now Brooklyn – the first English-speaking town settled in the New Netherlands period – was founded by a Londoner, Lady Deborah Moody. Kretzschmar, et al. (2003) note that Quakers mainly from the English midlands settled in Flushing beginning in Dutch times too, although they add that Greenwich Village (despite the southern English name) was founded by not by the English but by Scots. After 1664, English speakers came – with a fleeting interruption when the Dutch briefly retook their old colony in 1673 – in ever-larger numbers.

The profile of those settlers was probably fairly typical of the original settlement pattern in early British North America. The largest contingent all along the Atlantic coast, except Newfoundland where the Irish and West Country English predominated (Clarke 2010), came from the southeast and midlands of England. In all these colonies there were admixtures of northern English and Scots. Later, large numbers of Scots-Irish began to arrive and spread out into the interior (Kurath 1949, Montgomery 1996, 2001) bypassing New York. The southern English heritage can be seen in the fact that the NYCE vowel system, like that of most of North America, is largely derivable from the various ones used in that region at the time of settlement.[1] The initial dialects differed only in the specific mixtures of regional origins given the differences even across small areas of England. So any investigation into the birth of NYCE would have to begin with an account of the origins of those earliest settlers.

Nevertheless, the NYCE origins story cannot be one simply be a linking of settlers to different parts of Britain. After all, they and their descendants did not always they stay where they landed. From the beginning, there was movement up and down the coast and inland. Consequently, another major factor shaping early colonial dialects was how the first settlers and the immediately succeeding generations moved. For example, one well-known early New Yorker (or more accurately Nieuwe Nederlander) was Anne Hutchinson. Hutchinson was from Lincolnshire, in the east midlands of England, and she first settled in Boston. She was then exiled because her heretical beliefs disturbed the Puritan authorities there, and after a stop in Rhode Island she ended up in the more tolerant Dutch colony with a group of followers. Eastern New Jersey and Westchester received later exiles from Massachusetts and its equally fanatical offshoots in Connecticut. As time went on, and New York became integrated into British North America, New Yorkers certainly left for other colonies and those from elsewhere arrived in the growing city. It is most likely that the distances traveled by migrants were often quite small, to the next village, perhaps, or across a river. Other times the distances could be quite large. For example, one famous early New Yorker was Alexander Hamilton, who came from the island of Nevis in the West Indies after a stop in Boston.

The effects of these early resettlements – and the reason to think most were shorter than Hamilton's – can be seen in present day dialectal transitions. Despite, Peterson's description of NYCE as an isolate, the most salient geographical characteristic of the NYCE vowel system is how it fits into patterns of features shared with neighboring dialects. The NYCE short-A split provides a good illustration. The roots may lie in the TRAP-BATH split that originated in southern England in the Early Modern English era. However, as discussed in Chapter 3, the closest relatives of the NYCE version are found close to home: from Providence to Baltimore and up to Albany (Labov, et al. 2006). Durian (2012) finds that similar systems were once far more widespread arriving as at least as far as Ohio, but again this spread follows normal westward settlement routes.

The ways English speaking colonial settlers moved, however important, is not the only potential factor shaping early NYCE. A potentially important social factor affecting the colonial city was the distrust of its diversity by those would

---

1 It should be noted that this is not the same as the one used there now, which has evolved as all English varieties have.

come to be called out-of-towners. Goodfriend (1992: 3) and Reitano (2006: 23), for instance, report a complaint by an English colonist that New York held "too great a mixture of nations and the English the least part." It is hard not see in such comments a foreshadowing of early 20th century xenophobic and racist sentiments which Bonfiglio (2002) sees as source of the stigma still attached to NYCE. What role such sentiments may have played in influencing colonial New Yorkers' linguistic behavior is, at this point, open to speculation.

7.1.2 Early Evolution of NYCE

Audio recording and observations by trained dialectologists emerge almost simultaneously towards the end of the 19th Century. Before that time determining the nature of NYCE is necessarily a kind of detective work reliant on one or both of two kinds of clues. One is reconstruction, depending on general principles of linguistic evolution, comparison with other present-day and better known past dialects, and our knowledge of population movements. This method works better for some features than others. One that it works well for is the short-A split. Similarly, the origin of r-lessness, which will be discussed later in this chapter, as discussed in Chapter 3 can be reconstructed enough to know that the earliest NYCE was r-ful. For other features, it is also necessary to examine the second kind of clues: written records. This is the situation for two other examples discussed below: the origin of th- and dh-stopping and the early use of *youse*. Writing is obviously a record of language, but it inevitably leaves a degree of uncertainty because, as Montgomery (2001: 96) points out, written texts invariably, "veil speech in one way or another." Montgomery summarizes five types of written evidence together with their respective advantages and disadvantages:

1. Observations by outsiders: These consist of reflections on speech in a region by travellers. As Montgomery (2001: 98) puts it, such observations can "suggest less about the observed than the observers' expectations," but when treated critically they can provide useful data on differences at the time.

2. Commentaries of early grammarians and lexicographers: These specialists were often acute observers, but their comments characteristically consist of condemnations. The complaints provide evidence for the existence of the condemned forms and something about their social distribution. However, if a form did not rise to the level of irritating the grammarian, it probably was not commented on.

3. Attestations: Novelists often attempt to give characters speech to indicate carefully delineated social identities. If their portrayals are accurate, they provide prima facie evidence for phonological and grammatical forms in

use by real people who fit that profile. Unfortunately, however, writers may not be concerned with or capable of accurate dialect portrayals. Moreover, in colonial times Montgomery (2001:100) reports that "literary dialect was a code to be manipulated for literary effect, mainly for parody and burlesque." Later authors might have used dialect in the same way. Montgomery does not mention them, but there are also attestations in short vignettes popular in 19th century periodicals, and they share the virtues and drawbacks of their more literary counterparts.

4. Poetic Rhymes: These sources are used for vowel quality, although Montgomery warns that the variable spellings used at the time can be an obstacle to interpretation, and so rhymes need to be treated as cautiously as other sources.

5. Original records and manuscripts: These consist of letters and public documents, which are best when written by less educated speakers who rely more on their pronunciation than spelling conventions. Montgomery considers them indispensible for revealing variation, but they have the disadvantage of requiring considerable delving into sometimes-obscure archives.

A convincing depiction of the history of NYCE would require data from as many of these five types of materials as possible. Allen (1993), whose examination of slang was discussed in the previous chapter, is the largest such effort, although Bailey (2012) provides some additional data. Both rely primarily on observations by outsiders and literary attestations, although Bailey makes some use of grammarians' commentaries. Both authors' reports generally begin with the mid to late 19th Century when this kind of material becomes abundant. Allen, since he is examining slang, is only focused on the lexicon, and Bailey pays much attention to the lexicon too. Very little research explores early grammar, including phonology. So, just as when I presented some tentative new data in earlier chapters, the historical discussion that follows of the three NYCE features is presented *programmatically,* i.e., in the spirit of encouraging new research. There are quite a few potential thesis and dissertation topics awaiting interested researchers!

As mentioned above, determining the source of r-lessness, relies in good part on reconstruction based on later states of the language and historical conditions. For example, known written attestations from the mid nineteenth century – to be shown shortly – confirm r-less pronunciations. So, how do we know the earliest New Yorkers were r-ful? The answer lies in the fact that r-lessness first appears in the much more abundant records in England towards the end of the 18th century (Labov 1994). This date is, of course, well after English speakers came in large numbers to New York; so those early arrivals were almost certainly r-ful as well. Two hypotheses have been put forward for how r-lessness emerged.

One, offered by Labov (1994: 90, n 11) relies on a change from above (i.e., from above the level of consciousness). His proposal is that r-lessness was adopted by New Yorkers "under the influence of the [then] new London prestige form, just as citizens of Boston, Richmond, Savannah, and Charleston did." This is an exact replica – though in reverse – to the current process by which New York is becoming r-ful, now under the influence from American standard r-ful forms. Although Labov himself does not go into details, the obvious challenge for this hypothesis is to account for why r-lessness is limited to just those areas in North America if it the pronunciation was spreading out from London generally. It is particularly significant that Philadelphia, the most important American city in the colonial era and a major Atlantic port, has always been r-ful. Nevertheless, Kurath (1949: 7) provides a ready explanation for that city's resistance to the spread of London models:

> From the earliest time Philadelphia must have displayed a greater social independence of England than the other seaports. It had no royal governor and fewer English officials to provide intimate contacts with fashionable London society. Although some prominent merchant families joined the Anglican church in the decades preceding the Revolution, the Quakers retained their dominance socially as well as politically. It is noteworthy that Loyalists were less numerous here than in the other seaports when the colonies declared their independence.

Incidentally, the predominant r-fulness of the bulk of North America follows easily from this perspective. One source is tendency of much midlands interior settlement to go through Philadelphia, and the interior itself generally would be even less subject to London influence. The Scots-Irish may also have played a role in maintaining r-fulness; the dialect of Ulster remains r-ful to this day (Montgomery 2001, 2006).

The alternative account is by Bonfiglio (2002) who sees NYCE r-lessness as a continuation of a weakening of /r/ that had already begun in southern England before colonization but had not yet gone on to completion at time of settlement. In other words, early English colonists in New York along with Boston, Richmond, Savannah, and Charleston may have been rhotic, but most usually pronounced their /r/s in a manner that was already en route to vocalization. As time went on, /r/ vanished on both sides of the Atlantic via continued parallel evolution.

Again however, this explanation must overcome the exceptional behavior of the rest of North America given the fact that the highest proportions of colonists were from southern England in those places too. However, Fischer (1989) and Montgomery (1995, 2001) report that Philadelphia received a relatively larger minority of northern and north-midland dialect speakers than other areas, along with non-English early immigrants. These speakers' /r/s had less tendency to weaken. Montgomery (2004: 311) citing Kurath (1928) provides support for this position since Kurath notes the higher proportion of southern English migration to eastern New England and the southern coast than elsewhere as a cause of r-lessness there. It is certainly possible, of course, that both motives played some role.

The disagreement over the cause of NYCE r-lessness is about mechanism, imitation versus continuing evolution, not the source, which lies is in 17th Century southern England under either hypothesis. The origin of /θ/-/ð/ stopping as in 'tink' and 'dis' for *think* and *this* is a quite different case because the source itself is not clear. To turn to the detective analogy, there are too many suspects. The phonemes /θ/-/ð/ appear as stops in many dialects of English as well as Dutch. Stopping might, therefore, have been characteristic of NYCE from the beginning. However, stop pronunciations are also characteristic of English learners of German, Irish, Yiddish, and Italian language origin. So it might also have arrived with 19th century immigrants who spoke those languages.

A decision between these two potential sources can be made by dating the emergence of the feature in the written record. According to what we might call Colonial Origin Hypothesis, stopping would be of English and/or Dutch origin, perhaps reinforced by colonial-era Germans and French Protestants, who arrived in substantial numbers early on. This hypothesis would be supported if it could be found in the record as a native feature before the arrival of Italian, Jewish, later German, and Irish immigrants beginning in the mid 19th Century. By contrast according to the Immigrant Origin Hypothesis, stopping would be expected to only appear in the written record in the non-native English of the first generation of one or more of these immigrant groups. Then, about 25 years later, would it appear as a native feature associated with the second generation.

Because of the much later date in question than that concerning r-lessness, there are materials available that depict the speech of New Yorkers at exactly the right time. Some of the most easily available include the works of Horatio Alger. Alger is justly famous for the archetype of the poor teenage or preteen boy who makes good, and he apparently had considerable contact with youths of the type he wrote about, both native born and immigrants (Hoyt 1974). Even better, his works are heavy on dialog, and his characters are presented as speaking non-standard forms. For example, his first major success, a 1868 novel called *Ragged Dick; or, Street Life in New York with the Boot Blacks* has the following example of the title character's speech; significant non-standard features are in **boldface**:

"This coat once belonged to General Washington," said Dick, comically. "He wore it all through the Revolution, and it got **torn some**, 'cause he **fit** so hard. When he did he told his **widder** to give it to some smart young **feller** that **hadn't got none** of his own; so she gave it to me. But if you'd like it, sir, to remember General Washington by, I'll let you have it **reasonable**" (Alger 1868: 4).

Just in the first 20 pages Dick also produces the following non-standard forms again as indicated in boldface:

- **"they was"** (p. 5)
- "He wouldn't dare speak to such a young swell as **I be** now. **Ain't** it rich? (p. 13)
- **"He don't** know me" (p. 14)
- "I **knowed** a young man" (p. 15)
- "I once blacked his boots by a **partic'lar** appointment" (p. 16)
- "I **can't go the white hat**. It **ain't** becomin' to my style of beauty. (p. 16)
- "My **servants is** so dishonest that I wouldn't like to trust **'em** with a silver pitcher." (p. 17)
- "When I come into my fortune, I'll take my meals there **reg'lar**." (p. 19)
- "That must have been a **valooble** lamp." (p. 19)
- "A man of **fortun** (p. 19)"
- "I can read the little words pretty well, but the big words **is** what **stick** me." (p. 20)

Many of the non-standard forms shown above are supraregional or even just characteristic of relaxed styles of English generally. The spellings with <r> of *feller* and *widder* (*fellow* and *widow*) are indicative or r-lessness because the *er* represents a schwa (Bailey 2012) as it does in contemporary British phonetic respellings. Some non-standard verb forms do not appear in modern NYCE, such as *fit* as past of *fight*. Yet this form could quite plausibly have been characteristic of NYCE at the time Alger was writing. Atwood (1953) reports it as present in much of the northeast including the Hudson Valley among older speakers as late as the 1930s and suggests that older nonstandard form first disappeared in urban areas like New York. A similar case is, "He wouldn't dare speak to such a young swell as **I be** now." This is not the *habitual be* of contemporary AAE. It is called finite *be* and is described by Atwood as of English origin and present elsewhere in the northeast. Another vernacular form admitting the same analysis can be found in different novel *Phil the Fiddler or, The Story of a Young Street Musician,* where Dick (who appears in various works) says:

> "Jest stop a minute, Tim Rafferty," said he. "I'm **a-goin'** to intervoo you for the Herald. That's what they do with all the big rascals nowadays." (Alger 1872)

Although *a-prefixation* is now largely limited to Appalachian English, it was more widespread in the past and is also originally from southern England (Montgomery 2001). So it appears that, barring other contrary evidence, we can take Alger's rendition of the vernacular *NYCE* as at least potentially realistic.

Therefore, it seems significant that /θ/ and /ð/ are consistently represented through standard spelling in Dick's and other native street boys' speech. The absence of phonetic respellings representing these phoneme in mouths of native speakers is made more noteworthy because d- and t-respellings do appear in *Phil the Fiddler* in the mouth of a non-native speaker. The title character of that novel is an Italian immigrant boy with what we would now call learner English, and he is represented as saying "Shoe fly, don't **bouder** [for bother] me." In the same book Tim Rafferty says, "I can fight him **wid** one hand." Tim's origins are obscure, but he is also represented as saying "Then he's an ould haythen, and you may tell him so, with Tim Rafferty's compliments." This last quote is clearly recognizable as a representation of Irish English, and certainly the character's name evokes Irish background. Note that Tim also has /ð/ as [ð] outside the *with* context.[2] The appearance of stopping in immigrants but not among native New Yorkers of the lowest classes is exactly what would be expected based on the Immigrant Origin Hypothesis.

Nevertheless, Montgomery's warnings still should be kept in mind. Alger's use of dialect serves an emblematic not a scientific end, and even Tim's Irish accent vanishes later, when maybe his creator forgot about or was not interested in highlighting his Irishness. Still, the impression derived from Alger is reinforced by contemporaneous attestations of stopping as representative of foreign and African American characters in vignettes in periodicals. The following citations were provided in response by George Thompson to a query I made on the American Dialect Society listserv (ads-l). They date to just before the time of Alger's writing. Thompson's own glosses are in square brackets; citations are in parentheses following the quote; and relevant words are in bold:

- [a dandy is jostled into an "old fat black woman;" she says:] Wat **de** debbel you mean by **dat**, hey; why'nt you knock agin your own color, hey? mus'nt **tink** to bang gin me wen you like; I'll give you jab side **de** head nex time you doot. (21) (By Simon Snipe. Containing An Evening at the African Theatre).
- [a mutton-pie man, with a German (Jewish?) accent:] Shentlemens, I peg your pardon, but **dish** plame crowd won't shtir a pit. (29) from Sports of New-York. (*A Trip to the Races With Two Appropriate Songs*. New York, 1823, pp. 17–32)
- [a little girl at a German's butcher's stall, with her dog] Vot you vants, Eh? *** Shoost a little liver? Vell-- *** And **dere's** a pone for **de** leetle tog. (Saturday

---

2 An explicitly Irish character also produces a similarly recognizable pattern, "Out wid ye " said she, flourishing a broom, which she had snatched up. "Is that the way you inter a dacint woman's house, ye spalpeen "

Night in The Bowery. *Christian Union (1870–1893)*; Mar 29, 1871; 3, 13; *American Periodicals* pg. 206)

No examples of phonetic respelling of White native speakers' /θ/ or /ð/ as stops were returned. Still more evidence corroborating the Immigrant Origin Hypothesis is that 30 years later we do find stopping in the mouths of speakers of native NYCE. A prime literary attestation can be found in Stephen Crane's 1893 novel *Maggie, a Girl of the Streets,* in which the characters are lower class New Yorkers. What follows is a short example has both /θ/ and /ð/ with relevant words in bold:

> "Ah, what **deh** hell" cried Jimmie. "Shut up er I'll smack yer **mout'**. See?" (p. 5)

This is the usual way that Crane indicates his characters' utterances of these phonemes. Crane is a more literarily significant author than Alger, and his use of dialect has attracted scholarly attention. Slotkin (1992) argues in favor of the accuracy of his representations:

> [Crane] is especially sensitive to the nuances of dialect, realizing that even within a basically monodialectal novel, social stratification and characterization can be achieved through careful selection of a few instances of both dialectal and idiolectal usage.

Bailey (2012) also believes that Crane was able to render dialect well. Again, contemporaneous periodicals provide corroborations. Jonathan Lighter in response to my ads-l query supplied this example:

> A can of benzene exploded in a Bowery eating house the other day and the proprietor yelled down the kitchen companion way: "If yer spill any more of **dat** coffee I'll massacre yer" (*Tid-Bits,* January 15, 1887)

A slightly earlier example containing stopping with *with* but not with *the* was contributed by George Thompson:

> [jokers on the Fulton Ferry begin a clamor of shouts typical of the old fire department] Another yelled "Jump her, boys Jump her" Another, "Bust her Let her go Yer goin asleep. Turn on the water Turn it off Lend us your bouquet- holder Give us a blast Hit him **wid** a spanner (*NY Commercial Advertiser,* January 29, 1881, p. 3, col. 4)

A final piece of support for the Immigrant Origin Hypothesis comes in first dialectological account of NYCE (Babbitt 1896). Babbitt notes that in the 1890 census that eighty percent of New Yorkers are immigrants or children of immigrants and directly ascribes /θ/ and /ð/ stopping to the influence of their heritage languages. It therefore seems quite likely that stopping appears as a NYCE feature only with the generation born to German, Irish, Italian, and Jewish immigrants beginning in the late 19th century. Of course, to finally confirm this hypothesis, it would be useful to find still more converging evidence from different sources, but it seems a good fit to the data available now.

The case of stopping suggests the fruitfulness of mining literary and periodical attestations for earlier stages of NYCE, but the history in NYCE of pronoun *youse* shows their limitations. The question is not the provenance of the form. Montgomery (2001) states that it comes from Irish English to the US with Irish immigrants. Instead, the question is how it was used in late 19th and early 20th Century NYCE. That question arises because *yehs* (*yeh* is equivalent to the reduced from now usually written *ya*) is attested in variation with *you* and *yeh* not only as a plural but also in singular address. Stephen Crane provides these examples in *Maggie*:

-   "Run, Jimmie, run Dey'll get **yehs**, screamed a retreating Rum Alley child (p. 2)
-   If yer mudder raises 'ell all night **yehs** can sleep here (p. 9)
-   I spent me money here fer t'ree years an now **yehs** tells me yeh'll sell me no more stuff. T'hell wid yeh (p. 24)

Taken at face value, these attestations suggest that *yehs* could function in either plural or singular capacity. Use of an originally plural form as singular is not unprecedented. *You,* for instance, originated as a 2PP pronoun. The problem is that *youse* does not seem to be used that way currently, and loss of previously existing singular usage would be surprising based on known patterns of language evolution. As a general principle, when a form expands its functions in this way, it does not usually revert to its previously limited range. Nevertheless, supporting Slotkin's and Bailey's attestations of Crane's ability to render dialect, he also his speakers use forms that are recognizably NYCE:

-   Dat Johnson **goil** is a puty good looker.
-   Dere **was a mug come in** deh place de odder day wid an **idear** he wus goin' the own de place. (p. 15)
-   "**Gawd**," he said, "I wonner if I've been played for a duffer."

Also, Crane is not alone in providing attestations of *youse* with a singular referent. Joel Berson, again in response to a query on the American Dialect Society Listserv, found numerous examples, some dating to 1854. Here are three:

-   "T'roth, Rosie Deasey, **youse is** th' foinest gurrul in th' War-r-d to be callin' on a could night " (1887 caption in *Puck* (New York), p. 192/2)

- ”Ef **youse is** man 'nuff ter kill dat dorg, you is all right, I reckon." (1888, "Andersonville violets: a story of northern and southern life", Herbert W. Collingwood, p. 59)
- **"Yous is** not the nice lady that blisse joutleman was to marry ?" cried the woman ... "No, I was with Nathan Mudge. My name was Kate Godwin." (1854. "Easy Nat; or, the Three Apprentices. A Tale of Life in New York and Boston, but 'Adapted to any Meridien'", by A. L. Stimson, page 267)

Intriguingly, *youse* appears in these cases with the singular verb form *is,* as it does with *tells* in one of Crane's examples. Nevertheless, this evidence is not definitive. First, there is the unlikeliness of a putative later reversion to plural only usage. Second, there are suggestions within *Maggie* that Crane's linguistic accuracy has its limits. When one of the characters is drunk he slurs his /ð/ in a way unexpected from someone with dh-stopping:
- Les have **nozzer** drink, **zen** (p 52)
- **Zat** fler [=fellow] damn fool. (p. 52)

The slurring here involves the wrong place of articulation of a fricative, not a stop. Drunkenness would not have changed a stop articulation to [z]. Finally, there are possible explanations for inaccurate attestations in Crane's work in Crane's own artfulness. Crane mixes singular uses of *yeh* in with *yehs* and plural uses of both. Inconsistent uses in real life are simply variation, but in literature they can portray a speaker as careless or even degraded, which fits Crane's presumed goals in this novel. More generally – and with particular reference to vignettes – singular *youse* might be based on stereotypes of working class speech not understood by observers. Outsiders may have been struck by the existence of *youse* without realizing that it was limited to plural contexts. Many inaccurate portrayals of the speech of stigmatized communities have been documented (see e.g., Barrett 2014 for erroneous depictions of AAE). On this point, although Crane had experience in poor New York communities, he does not show the kind of empathy for his characters that Alger does. So it follows that his interest lay in more portraying his themes than drawing accurate verbal portraits. In the end, although I am skeptical regarding the accuracy of Crane and others' portrayals of the usage of *youse* at the turn of the 20th century, the question must also be left open. Evidence in the form of non-literary usage in documents and letters and potentially other sources would be needed to settle it.

7.2 Research on NYCE and Recent Developments

In principle, NYCE history should become easier to recount after the emergence of recording technology, but this resource was not exploited until the analysis of the Atlas of the United States and Canada recordings in the 1930s.[3] By contrast, dialectological work emerges 40 years earlier with a short article by Babbit (1896). Labov (in SSENYC) and Bailey (2012) are quite admiring of his efforts. They observe that, unlike his successors, Babbitt includes the speech of working class New Yorkers and the children of immigrants in his description. Also, Babbitt addresses a number of features that would be hard for untrained observers to notice and depict. Most notably he describes the short-A split in part as a change in progress:

> æ is very high, pretty close to *e* of the normal scale and never mixed, – being thereby clearly distinguished from the New York *e (>ə)*. Among the older New Yorkers, this very high vowel is used in all the set of words pronounced in New England with the broad vowel (*ask, half, pass*, etc.), and is really higher in these words than in *man, cab*, etc. But this distinction is now lost, and the general vowel has overtaken the special one (*hend* hand, *keb* cab, *dense* dance, *fef pest* half past). In *can*, the weak form is *kin,* which is often kept even under accent. (Babbit 1896: 455–464)

Babbit also discusses some pronunciations that have vanished, such as a backing in the nucleus of FACE. On the other hand, Babbitt's report on NYCE is not close to comprehensive; for example, he does not discuss the lax part of the short-A split. Also, not mentioned is any evidence of THOUGHT tensing and raising. It is not clear whether this absence is because it had not progressed enough to stand out or it just did not make it to this short description.

After Babbitt, more than 30 years passed before Trager (1930), the next examination of NYCE appeared. The list below summarizes the relevant studies that appeared between that time and SSENYC. A more complete review of their contributions is found in SSENYC:

- Trager (1930, 1940): These two studies are discussions of the phonological status of short-A in NYCE and other dialects (the author actually mentions Nebraska), pointing to the phonemic split hypothesis.
- Thomas (1932, 1942, 1947): These mostly brief studies are based on college students and assume a prescriptivist stance.
- Frank (1948), Kurath (1949, 1972), Atwood (1953), Wetmore (1959), Kurath and McDavid (1961): All this work is based on the *Linguistic Atlas of the United States and Canada.* The work most focused on NYCE is Frank's doctoral dis-

---

3 There are almost certainly unexplored early recordings in various archives that could provide information on the dialect of New Yorkers born in the early to mid 19th Century.

sertation. Labov is quite critical of it in SSENYC. These works document the decline of regionally specific lexicon is as discussed earlier.

– <u>Hubbell (1950)</u>: Labov (SSENYC: 26) finds this comprehensive description of NYCE phonology "over-representative since no one actually uses all the contrasts shown." Another limitation is that Hubbell used informants mostly from Columbia University, although he added what he called "less cultured" informants too. Hubbell also made use of Atlas recordings. Despite its limitations, no other study comes close to Hubbell in descriptive detail.

– <u>Bronstein (1962)</u>: This study reexamines some variables as derived from interviews with Queens College students of years prior to the study. Of particular note (commented on by Labov) is his discussion of the short-A split. Also worth mentioning is Bronstein's citation of the backing of PRIZE, but he does not explore phonological conditions or view the distinct vowel qualities as symptomatic of a split.

These works provide starting points necessary for any study of NYCE in terms of time depth, again despite their methodological limitations.

7.2.1 Labov's *Social Stratification of English in New York City*

SSENYC first appeared in 1966, and quickly became programmatic for the emerging field of variationist sociolinguistics. Of course, that work also documents the features Labov examined. In terms of evolution, Labov discusses the slow loss of r-lessness and dates the origins of this process to the change in what was considered the prestige variant after World War II. Elite New Yorkers raised in the prewar period were r-less, as can be heard most prominently in recordings of Franklin Roosevelt. Another change discussed in Chapter 3 and in SSENYC is the raising of BATH and THOUGHT, with PALM following behind THOUGHT in the NYC Chain Shift (see Chapter 3) among Whites. Many of these changes are also discussed in Labov, et al. (1972) and in some of his other studies, in particular Labov (1994).

In 2006 Labov issued a second edition that adds some data gathered after the initial study and eliminates sections that have not withstood the test of time. The most significant addition is a series of retrospective reflections interpolated throughout the text made in light of the subsequent 40 years of variationist work. I noted in Chapter 1 that SSENYC was designed to establish the theoretical fact of sociolinguistic variation in terms of orderly heterogeneity, and in the second edition (SSENYC: 18) justifies the choice NYCE for that goal. He says New York provides "a classic case" of dialect variation in which "it is not possible at any one time to predict which of several alternatives an individual will adopt in the stream of speech." All dialects by definition show this same order-in-variation, but what makes NYCE particularly apt as an illustration follows from the stigma associated with it. New Yorkers' linguistic embarrassment leads to greater than usual efforts to avoid local forms and so sets up variation that is particularly salient and clearly motivated. Through the clarity of its motives, NYCE provides a particularly convincing case study to make the point that variation is "an aspect of linguistic structure rather than the absence of it" (SSENYC: 18).

Social motivation for variation has appeared throughout this book, but how the study of variation contributes to the understanding of human language as a system is also a significant contribution from SSENYC. As described in Chapter 3, Labov concentrated on two vowel variables (oh) – i.e., THOUGHT and (aeh) – i.e., BATH. Linguistically, Labov describes these two vowels as fitting into a larger subsystem of *in-gliding vowels*, and this entire system became the subject of the final chapter of SSENYC. So it is fitting that discussion of this structure form part of the present book as well.

The system, laid out below in Figure 7.1, uses Labov's variable notation but adds Wells's keywords. It assumes complete r-lessness because when an /r/ is pronounced, the subsystem collapses into mainly BATH-(aeh) and THOUGHT-(oh) (see Chapter 3). Although there are six vowels in Figure 7.1, this full system can be described as an irregular pentagon because BATH-(aeh) is located in the middle of one of the laterals, not at its own point.

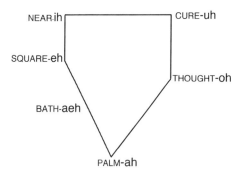

Figure 7.1: Maximal NYCE Ingliding Vowels

In comments on the second edition Labov refers to several diagrams included in the first edition that portray the interaction of social stratification with the internal linguistic structure manifested by this subsystem. The diagrams are quite complex and can be difficult to process visually, and Labov mentions being tempted to remove them. He then explains his decision to keep them as follow:

But on reflection, I find that these intricate assemblies of triangles, pentagons, and rect-angles, have considerable success in capturing the way in which patterns of style shifting and social stratification intersect with the phonemic system. They have been retained and might well have appeared on the front cover of this second edition (SSENYC: 345).

Figure 7.2 is based on one those diagrams (SSENYC: 368), which shows the effects of style shifting on the lower middle class pattern. It relies on solely Labov's variable notation without Wells' keywords because otherwise the diagram – complicated enough as it is – becomes too cluttered. I have added the letters at the left to indicate the various levels of style shifting.

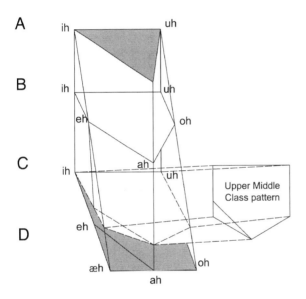

Figure 7.2: Labov's Structure of NYC Vowel System: stylistic variation

Level D represents the pattern used by Lower Middle Class when speaking with the greatest attention to speech. Level C shows their system at less attention, which matches the speech of the upper middle class, which is extracted to the right. Levels D and C show the same six vowels that appear in Figure 7.1 but differ in that in that in D BATH-(aeh) and THOUGHT-(oh) have moved farther from SQUARE-(eh) and CURE-(uh) than in C. Labov describes the D pattern as "hypercorrect" because it goes beyond the uses of the most prestigious group. Like Shakespeare's lady that doth protest too much, level D reveals mainly insecurity.

Level B involves a further reduction in formality compared to C. At this level BATH-(aeh) moves to join SQUARE-(eh) – i.e., it comes to be pronounced [ɛə] the

BATH word *bad* becomes homophonous with the SQUARE word *bared,* as [bɛᵊd] ('beh-uhd'). This means that the pentagon now becomes regular with SQUARE-(eh)/BATH-(aeh) at the equivalent position in the front as THOUGHT-(oh) ('thaw-uht') is in the back. At level A, the most relaxed pattern, the combined BATH-(aeh)/SQUARE-(eh) move up the front join NEAR-(ih) and the THOUGHT-(oh) merges with CURE-(uh), to form a triangle. As a result, the NEAR word *beard* is now homophonous with *bared* and *bad,* as [brᵊd] ('bi-uhd') and the THOUGHT (or NORTH) word *shore* become homophonous with *sure* as [ʃʊᵊ] ('shu-uh').[4] Since PALM-(ah) remains at the bottom – though presumably moving towards the back chasing THOUGHT in the NYC Chain Shift – the in-gliding vowel subsystem only has three exponents: high front BATH-(aeh)/SQUARE-(eh)/NEAR-(ih) versus high back THOUGHT-(oh)/CURE-(uh) versus low PALM-(ah). This integration of social and linguistic patterns captures the primary mission of variationist research: to understand how social and linguistic factors interact to produce language variation and change.

7.2.2 Research since SSENYC

The history of the study of NYCE since Labov left for Philadelphia in 1971 was recounted briefly in Chapter 1. Before he left, one significant study was completed by his student Paul Cohen (1970) in the remarkable masters thesis on the short-A split cited in Chapter 3. Independently of Labov, two other early studies are Berger's (1968) account of the NYCE vowels and Silverman's (1975) brief account of the influence of AAE on the emerging dialect spoken by Puerto Ricans. Both are within the dialectological tradition more than the then emerging field of variationist sociolinguistics. A much more complete variationist study of the same topic as Silverman's is Wolfram's (1974) study of youths from Spanish Harlem. As discussed earlier Wolfram found that Blacks and Puerto Ricans had high rates of consonant cluster deletion, but that for Puerto Ricans with Black friends, these rates were particularly high.

As also mentioned in Chapter 1, little variationist research appeared in the quarter century after that study, with work such as Tannen's (1981, 1984) study of discourse and Urciuoli (1996), and Zentella's (1997) studies of bilingualism taking up the slack. Cutler's (1999/2003, 2007, 2008, 2010) studies that combine variationist and discourse concerns mark the resurgence of interest in variation

---

4 This chart was produced before the relations between (ohr) and (oh) – NORTH and THOUGHT – were determined to be not a merger but a near merger (see Chapter 3). This would change the details but not the basic theoretical point of the diagram.

as such. The primary support for this resurgence lies with three sociolinguists at NYU: John Singler, Gregory Guy, and Renee Blake. Although their primary research focuses have been outside New York, they have contributed to the study of NYCE through mentoring doctoral students' conducting classes and encouraging even non-students. I personally owe them considerable debt, particularly to John, whose professional generosity knows no limits.

Of their students, Becker's work has been prominently featured here, as has Wong's (2007, 2010, 2013) studies of Chinese Americans, Coggshall's (Becker & Coggshall 1999, Coggshall & Becker 2010) cross-ethnic comparisons. These studies show how African American and Latinos, are increasing use of classic NYCE variants such as raised and ingliding THOUGHT. The adoption of these classic NYCE traits appears to be occurring simultaneously with some tendency to lower these forms among Whites (particularly in Manhattan) and Asians. Blake and Shousterman (2010) study Black West Indian New Yorkers, and most recently Newlin-Lukowicz's (2013) has examined of Polish New Yorkers. More work from these sociolinguists is ongoing and can be expected to appear in the next few years.

In addition to this work from NYU, Labov et al.'s (2006) *Atlas of North American English* provides data mainly on vowel systems, noting for example the recent fronting of GOOSE in the environment of coronal consonants. This work also notes the general conservative nature of the NYCE vowel system. My research has focused on variation and race in post-immigrant groups including Latinos (Slomanson & Newman 2004, Newman 2010) and East Asians (Newman and Wu 2011). Similar to Cutler, I have also conducted ethnographic studies of discourse involving rap artists (e.g., Newman 2001, 2005). In addition, as discussed in Chapter 3, Mather (2012) also provides the third replication of the Department Store Study.

Other variationist research has included NYCE in regional studies including Johnson (2010) on the northeast, Coyne (2009) on New Jersey, and Olivo (2013) on Long Island. Olivo points to the development of an allophonic distinction particularly in Long Island between checked (followed by a consonant) and free (syllable ending) upgliding vowels: FLEECE, FACE, GOAT, and GOOSE. Finally, NYCE phonology has attracted the attention of theoreticians in that field including most prominently Benua (1995), Silverman (2002), and Kaye (2012). Other sociolinguistic studies involving NYCE have also appeared, such as Angermeyer's (2005) examination of bilingualism.

One theme throughout this book is how much research still needs to be done to really understand NYCE. Since the early 2000s, a number of variationists have undertaken two large-scale coordinated studies of the English spoken in London in the wake of population movements of locals out of the city core and the influx of immigrants who replaced them. The first is known as the Linguistic Innovators project, which focused on adolescents in two neighborhoods, and the second is the Multicultural London English project (e.g., Torgersen, Kerswill, & Fox 2006; Fox 2007; Kerswill, Cheshire, Fox, & Torgersen 2007; Kerswill, Torgersen, & Fox 2008; Cheshire & Fox 2009). These studies along with studies of the English spoken by London South Asians (Sharma & Sankaran 2011) provide an enviable data set and deeper understanding of multicultural immigrant London. Somewhat later, a similar approach has gotten underway in Toronto (Hoffman & Walker 2010, Nagy, et al. 2014). The Philadelphia Neighborhood Corpus, with Labov in the lead (e.g., Labov, Rosenfelder & Fruehwald 2013) is the longest standing of these "big data" projects since it began soon after Labov's arrival at the University of Pennsylvania in the 1970s. As yet, nothing comparable has been undertaken in New York, although plans are beginning to be formulated by a number of my colleagues at CUNY. That work, if successfully carried out, has the potential to fill in the many gaps identified in the previous chapters, provide new insights, and return the city to the forefront of the exploration of language variation and why it matters.

8 Conclusion

8.1 New York City English and Prominence of Race

In the introductory chapter, I stated that NYCE needs to be defined plurally. Throughout the following chapters race – as constructed by New Yorkers – was presented as the most prominent factor implicated in this multiplicity. In Chapter 2, for instance, New Yorkers were shown to be highly conscious of racial-dialectal differentiation and at times looked to enforce it among those who, they felt, did not comply with their expectations in that regard. In each of the descriptive chapters differentiation based on racial identity appeared for phonology, morphosyntax, discourse, and lexicon.

However, exclusive emphasis on racial categories can erase other important distinctions including social class, gender, and affiliation categories like professions, political stances, religion, and subculture. *Intersectionality,* the fact that people express multiple social identities simultaneously is something sociolinguist researchers should always keep present. A New Yorker can be Black and Catholic and Middle Class and middle aged and male and gay or Asian and Latino and atheist and female and rich.

These social categories interact. From the "first wave" perspective, for example, social class plays a prominent role in setting up racial categories and filling them with meaning. One way, for instance, that class informs race in New York involves a division between Blacks and Latinos, on the one hand, and Whites and Asians on the other. This *super-racial* opposition corresponds to gross patterns of socioeconomic stratification in New York as in America generally and increasingly to residential patterns (Logan & Stults 2011). An interrelated web of class-infused stereotypes concerning criminality, popular cultural production and expectations, and educational achievement fall out along it. Certainly, White and Asian low-wage workers, welfare recipients, hip-hop artists and low-grade criminals exist in multitudes alongside Latino and Black professionals, preppies, geeks, and millionaires. However, it appears that for many New Yorkers, including many of the very people in question, those individuals exist at least to a certain extent against type or at least as exceptions. Discrimination in the form of racial profiling and limited access to many public resources continues to disproportionally to affect Latinos and Blacks while privilege and benefit of the doubt gets accorded with equal unfairness to Asians and particularly Whites. Not surprisingly then, linguistic exponents of this super-racial binary can be found in NYCE as well, some of which are listed in Table 8.1.

Table 8.1: Latino/Black vs. White/Asian pattern

Feature	Blacks and Latinos	Whites and Asians
2nd person plural	*You-all* based forms	*You guys* based forms
PRIZE	monophthongal	diphthongal
Non-standard AAE syntax (e.g., invariant *be*, completive *been*, non-inverted modal questions)	Variably present	Largely Absent
Direction of changes in progress	Maintenance of r-lessness, increase in THOUGHT height	Decline in r-lesses, lowering of THOUGHT height

By contrast, it is hard to find linguistic commonalities shared only, say, by Whites and Latinos or Blacks and Asians. Nevertheless, it is clear that each racialized group studied so far has certain characteristic features not generally shared with other groups:

- East Asians: Voice quality distinctiveness (Newman and Wu 2011)
- Whites: Backing of the nucleus of PRIZE and fronting of that of MOUTH (Chapter 3)
- Latinos: Raising of PRICE and pre-voiceless variants of MOUTH (i.e. Canadian Raising), Spanish substrate features such as clear /l/, syllable timing, and elision or weakening of voiced stops in certain contexts. (Chapter 3, Sloman-son & Newman2004, Newman 2010)
- Blacks: The lack of near merger of NORTH and THOUGHT, different behavior of (th) and (dh), lack of linking-R.

Finally, there are other features that appear to distinguish subracial ethnic groups. Lexical usages concentrated among Jews and Italians were discussed in Chapter 5, and ultraorthodox Jews have been the subject of a number of studies (Jochnowitz 1968, Fader 2007). Greater rhoticity distinguishing Jamaicans from African Americans was found by Blake and Shousterman (2010). The distinctive behavior of Darryl and Kendrick of the BQ-16 regarding dh-stopping suggests the possibility for still further distinctions involving Jamaican and Haitian Americans vis-à-vis African Americans and possibly other Black groups. In the same vein, the responses of some judges in Newman and Wu (2011) suggest that there are per-ceptible though not always perceived differences between Koreans and Chinese. It is likely that a similar phenomenon affects Latinos of different national origins as well (Shousterman, personal communication).

Of course, not all members of ethnic and racial groups conform to these neat racial or ethnic profiles. Those exceptions along with additional permutations become visible when zooming one step in to a "second wave" perspective that examines microsocial groups. Wolfram (1974) finds that Nuyoricans with African American friends showed a greater consonant cluster simplification than Nuyoricans without such cross-racial socializing and African Americans themselves. Labov, et al. (1968a) finds that "lames," youths isolated from mainstream low SES African American social life, showed less dense AAE features in their Harlem studies. My own work (Slomanson and Newman 2004) shows differences between Latinos affiliated to Black oriented cultures versus as Hip-Hop and White ones such as Metal and Nerd. However, these subcultural affiliations do not eliminate Spanish substrate variants. Similarly, racially tinged speech patterns persist despite the cross-racial socializing at UAA as illustrated in Figure 2.9.

Still more information and a deeper understanding of super-racial, racial, and subracial ethnic dialectal differentiation appear with a fully zoomed in third-wave approach. Cutler (2008, 2010, 2014) shows a limited and careful deployment of AAE origin variants among White participants in hip-hop peer culture. Successful incorporation of these variants into a personal style entails not attempting to use AAE systematically because such an effort would invite accusations of inauthenticity. At the same time one of Cutler's (2010) participants defies the policing from a White non-Hip-Hop oriented peer to maintain stricter adherence to White racial norms. Similarly in Chapter 2, class distinctions, particularly for White participants such as Andy Sullivan and Janet Krebbs, were recast in racial terms. "Sounding White" was defined as an upper class variety from outside New York. "Sounding Black," not surprisingly held an opposing indexical valence to "sounding White." However, the difference although influenced by class-related distinctions cannot be reduced entirely to them. So whereas middle class Blacks tended to use less dense forms of AAE, AAE features were systematically avoided by Evan, the African American nerd. Significantly, Evan also avoided other Hip Hop stylistic elements associated with his childhood community. He framed this move as a rejection of collective norms *per se* by claiming that people should follow their own personal interests rather than those they may have been pressured to accept by a social group or community. In other words, Evan's avoidance of what might be seen as Black identity markers was constructed as a radically individualist stance. Yet ironically, this supposedly individualist stance itself is associated with what is ultimately a shared collective set of values, i.e., nerd ideals of defying peer cohort values (Bucholtz 1999). As a final fillip, Evan could not completely escape AAE variants, which given his origins in South Jamaica, must have comprised a considerable portion of his childhood linguistic input. Evan's case reveals the large number factors that combine to produce the various forms NYCE takes, including those visible at all three waves of variationist study, such as:

- original dialects and languages spoken and heard in childhood,
- social network organization and microsocial peer-culturally affiliated communities
- individual styles and circulating discourses and norms about on racial identity and its relation to class, peer-cultural and personal identity.

It is the task of future variationist sociolinguistics to untangle the roles each plays in other cases.

8.2 The Sociolinguistics of Diversity and Superdiversity

This book will close with some thoughts on the study of NYCE, including its past accomplishments and future goals and challenges in light of the issues raised in the previous section. To begin at the beginning, the idea of NYCE arises out of dialectology. The basic dialectological premise is, after all, that linguistic features cluster in specific regions in such a way as to support thinking of the speech of those regions as constituting nameable varieties. Variationist sociolinguistics emerged as a response to one of the limitations to this understanding: variation within dialects. This response consists of applying three insights first made by Labov in SSENYC:

- It was possible to account for variation in NYCE – and so by extension other dialects – by employing a more sophisticated linguistics that incorporates orderly heterogeneity.
- Socioeconomic factors play a major role in providing the order.
- The NYCE speech community should properly be defined in terms of common norms more than common features.

In other words, geography defines NYCE by delineating its territory; social stratification governs variation within it; and the noise stratification creates is reduced by placing the community – in the form of norms – ahead of the individual. However, another form of social variation, ethnicity and particularly race, complicates this elegant model. In SSENYC Labov's response is to note minor differences between Italians and Jews, but exclude African Americans from many analyses. This removal reflects two dynamics. First, differences in actual feature usage make analyses that include both Whites and Blacks difficult to interpret. Second, to a large extent the norms governing linguistic evaluation diverge along racial lines:

> The African American informants … are separated from the rest of the sample population by more than a quantitative difference in trends. In almost all respects, the African Americans reverse the pattern of attitudes shown by the others. … While most white New Yorkers thought that outsiders disliked New York City speech, almost all of the African Americans who expressed an opinion thought that out-of-town residents did not dislike the speech of the city. While most white New Yorkers showed negative attitudes toward the New York speech pattern themselves, only three of twenty AA respondents expressed this opinion, and nine reported that they liked it (SSENYC: 336).

Although Labov claims that New York City is a single speech community, he acts in terms of these analyses as if that community is divided racially in ways that disrupt that singularity. In subsequent research, Labov describes AAE across the US as a unitary dialect with limited geographic variability (Labov 1994, 2001, 2008b). On that view, dialects can be defined either ethnically or geographically, albeit with some level of interaction between these dimensions. In the case of Whites, the definition is largely geographic although admitting ethnic trends. In the case of Blacks, the dominant criterion is racial with only secondary geographic effects. More recent studies, however, have challenged this still relatively simple model as the racial diversity of the US in general and New York in particular has increased substantially. A number of studies including second and third wave studies show considerable interaction between race and geography (see Becker 2010, Coggshall & Becker 2010).

In the introduction, I mentioned a theoretical challenge associated with new immigration and other developments associated with globalization and post-industrial society. Sociolinguists such as Blommaert (2010) Blommaert and Rampton (2011, 2012) adopt Vertovec's (2007) claim that diversity in metropolises such as New York achieves a qualitatively different level, referred to as superdiversity. Under such conditions Blommaert (2010: 4) concludes that variationist approaches are inadequate. For one thing, he believes, they maintain a "superficial" conceptualization of "space and time." For another, he argues that variationists maintain an antiquated "modernist" model of language traceable to early 20th century structuralism. He is particularly concerned that this structuralist treatment examines language ahistorically and independently of its social functions. Essentially, this is a criticism of looking at language structure as an autonomous object exclusively in present time rather than as structure in use in a given historical context. Instead of analyzing structural elements of language in their own terms, Blommaert (2010) and Blommaert and Rampton (2011, 2012) examine the linguistic repertoires deployed by different groups, circumstances, and activities. These authors certainly do speak of dialects, but dialects, along with linguistic variation generally, are seen entirely in terms of social meanings, often called indexicalities, or what such forms point to.

It should be clear from a number of discussions in previous chapters that analyzing the indexicalities of variants is perfectly compatible with the purportedly modernist axioms regarding the relative independence of structure. One area this has been particularly prominent is in "third wave" variationist sociolinguistics (e.g., Eckert 2008, 2012). This combination is also implicit in a proposal by Benor (2010). In a review of a wide range of sociolinguistic research, Benor notes that in case after case members of ethnic groups employ sometimes one associated trait, sometimes another, sometimes several, and sometimes the entire set of possibilities. Benor concludes that the consequent absence of systematicity in this deployment means that these ethnic based traits fail to fulfill the orderly heterogeneity that defines dialectal unity. For that reason, rather than thinking in terms of ethnic dialects or ethnolects, Benor argues, we should properly consider ethnically marked features as constituting ethnolinguistic repertoires. This proposal emphasizes the social meaning of features, through the emphasis on indexicality, much as Blommaert proposes. However, Benor does not abandon the principle of the crucial role of structure or the importance of investigating it. It is just that in Benor's view, ethnic variation differs from geographic based variation or SES influence on that geographic variation, where systematicity remains a major consideration.

Cases like Evan's, which show not entirely successful attempts to avoid racially marked features suggest that there can be aspects of such usage that go beyond the ability of an individual to control (see Coupland 2007). This inability to deploy features to express a desired and even strongly assumed identity strongly suggests dialectal status rather than a repertoire (see also Cutler 1999, 2007, Fix 2014). My own work with Latino English (Newman 2010) also shows levels of systematicity in racially-marked speech forms. Some Latino participants in that study appeared to be operating with repertoire-like deployment of Spanish substrate variants, whereas for others the variants showed clear signs of orderly heterogeneity. Following upon work in London by Sharma and Sankaran (2013), it may be that substrate-origin forms develop into sociolinguistic variants only when given enough time (they suggest three generations) and sufficient community isolation. Repertoire-like feature use may arise initially and then be maintained given motives to do so such as ideological commitment to identity-based speech styles and lack of the isolation needed to allow systems to develop. Then as they are learned by the next generation, they can be reorganized into systematic dialectal variants.

More evidence in favor of this hypothesis can be found zooming out now to a first wave view of Black New Yorkers. There are aspects of ethnic related speech in these New Yorkers' English that are probably too subtle to be deployable in identity work. One case is the lack of a NORTH/THOUGHT near merger only among

Blacks in the BQ-16 (see page 65). The whole concept of near merger depends, after all, on maintenance of a distinction that is not accessible to conscious awareness. A similar argument can be made for the lack of linking-R also among Blacks (see page 50), which seems a dubious candidate for an index because of its dependence on very subtle phonological conditioning. A third is the different behaviors noted for (th) and (dh), which is also relatively subtle. There appear to be cases here of systematic differences that operate at a different level than a repertoire is likely to function. These more obscure features exist simultaneously with the use of salient variants that index a NYCE identity: raised NORTH/THOUGHT, AAE high rates of r-lessness, and less clearly social class (th) stopping.

In sum, it appears that further exploration of the relationship between indexing and systematic unconscious aspects of language in (super)diverse urban centers like New York is warranted. Dismissing the relevance of variationist approaches in favor of those that exclusively explore indexing and identity would actually be counterproductive if the goal is to understand how people do identity work with language. If nothing else, the absence of so-called "modernist" understandings embedded in variationist analyses of language will constitute an obstacle determine the hard limits of such abilities. By contrast, variationist assumptions, theories, and methods as used in New York can be expected to yield significant findings on the interface of language and society going forward just as they did at the time of Labov's first explorations on the Lower East Side. In this spirit, it can only be hoped that the survey of NYCE provided in this book will not only serve as a reference on the social and linguistic factors associated with NYCE but will identify new areas for research. The following provide just a sample of the types of questions this future research can explore:

- To what extent do the children of White transplants adapt to NYCE norms? What factors lead to greater or lesser accommodation?
- What are the contributions of still unexamined groups including Middle Easterners, South Asians, non-Chinese East Asians, and Africans? Do they have identifiable ethnolinguistic features? Are they changing NYCE discourse patterns?
- How do intonation and stress patterns vary along social dimensions in NYCE? What about between NYCE and other regional forms of US English?
- Cutler (1999/2003, 2007, 2008, 2010, 2014) shows that *not* sounding White has advantages on a social level. Is this change in prestige helping to reverse the stigma associated with NYCE if as Andy, Laura, and Janet seem to imply traditional NYCE is not seen as White?
- How do social factors impacting NYCE resemble and differ from other diverse megalopolises? Can we speak of a sociolinguistics of the 21st Century megacity? On this point, it would be particularly interesting to compare New York

with its peers such as London, Cairo, Shanghai, Mexico City, Mumbai, Lagos and São Paulo.

– What is the role of identity versus simple contact in producing dialectal features?

– Have there been changes in discourse features? And how can variation be described in that domain of language?

– How did NYCE develop historically beyond the minimal number of traits examined so far?

– What changes in progress are continuing in NYCE? What is the extent of deregionalization?

– How extensive are the splits described by Kaye (2012) involving PALM and LOT and PRICE and PRIZE? What are their lexical distributions? What are their respective social correlates?

In other words, the future looks bright for investigations of NYCE.

9 Appendix A: Short Biographical Descriptions of the BQ-16

- Mandie John is the daughter of Chang John and so is a third generation Chinese American. She was a student at Queens College and had strong interest in classical music and had friends who spanned a number of racial groups. She does not speak Chinese. The data were taken from her interviews with her father and Carl Pisapia.
- Chang John was born in Brooklyn but raised in Queens, and is second generation Chinese American. Somewhat unusually, his parents came before the 1965 Immigration Act and so he grew up in a largely non-Asian community. His interests were not focused on Chinese culture, and he grew up to become a lawyer. He is dominant in English. He was interviewed by his daughter.
- Clara Chin was born in Venezuela to parents who had immigrated there from China but the family moved to New York when she was a baby. She does not speak Spanish or much Chinese but is close to her extended family. She is a college graduate and as an active Evangelical Christian she went on a mission to India the year after her college. She was interviewed by a QC student.
- Rashid Lewis grew up in South Jamaica from a low-income family and largely absent father. He was my student as 9th grader at UAA, and I would say the most difficult student I had. However, most teachers felt he had calmed down considerably since ninth grade, and he was relatively popular with other students. A number pointed out how intelligent he was and no one was afraid of him. The interview was, at least content wise, by far the most interesting I had before or since covering multiple topics including Hip-Hop, drugs, school, race, and social changes. He reminded me of "Larry" the Harlem gang member whose discussions of god and race informed Labov's (1972a) polemic against the view that the African American inner city residents were verbally deprived.
- Kendrick Pierre was a Haitian American Queens College senior at the time of the interview. His father had been a teacher in Haiti but became an electrician in New York, and Kendrick had always been successful at school. He was interested in rap and although bilingual in Haitian Creole felt himself to be English dominant. I was the interviewer.
- Diondre Davis had an Afro-Panamanian father and African American mother who raised her. She identified as African American and knew no Spanish. She had trained to be a chef at an elite cooking school but felt discriminated against because of her sex, and so was studying nursing at the time of the interview done with a QC student who was a co-worker.

- Darryl Hanson was a student at UAA but entered after I left. He was also rap artist who I call *Cherub* in Newman (2001, 2005). He was Jamaican American but I never heard him speaking Patois with friends. He went on to college, and at last contact he was considering grad school while earning money from producing and selling beats. I interviewed him.
- Delia Figueres was also a student at UAA who entered after I left. She was born in New York and was fluently bilingual and biliterate. Her parents were working class. She was a successful student, and I interviewed her when she was a senior waiting to hear which colleges had accepted her. She was interested in becoming an elementary school teacher and was volunteering as a tutor at a local school.
- Colton Vega was a college student and third and fourth generation Nuyoriquen. He knew little Spanish. He grew up and still lived in a rough part of Bushwick and his experience with violence there was a motivation for him to move after college to Florida. He was active in gymnastics and was becoming involved in freerunning, a form of street acrobatics. I interviewed him.
- Missy Ibáñez was an older college student studying to be a teacher. She was raised by her single Dominican mother. She was also a single mother but at the time of the interview was with a boyfriend. She is bilingual and attended ESL as child but was raising her child in English. She is an active Evangelical Catholic. She was interviewed by a student.
- Johan Aranda was also a college student who was highly involved in technology although majored in Urban Studies. He came to the US as a small child. He was bilingual and biliterate, and his parents were working class. He grew up in an area of Queens with a large Indo-Caribbean population and had friends from that community. At the time of the interview he was very active politically. I interviewed him.
- Carl Pisapia was a music major and childhood friend of Mandie John, who interviewed him. He grew up in an area of Flushing that was becoming increasingly Asian and had Asian friends from early on, along with White ones. Both his parents were college graduates.
- Laura Feldman had a Jewish father and Italian mother but was raised Catholic and identified more with the Italian side of the family and went to a Catholic high school. Her parents were lower-middle class. She described her neighborhood, Howard Beach, (as discussed later) as "a bubble." It is a white largely working class area with older New York families, and an unfortunate history of racism, which, while not forgotten seems to have eased. She planned to be teacher but later entered a Speech Pathology master's.
- Andy Sullivan is a friend and neighbor of Laura's and they went to high school together. His parents were Irish and Italian and working class. He reported

that he was pursuing teaching as a profession. He is also gay, although he came out publically only after the interview, which I did with him.

– Janet Krebbs was a student of mine at UAA. She had a working class background and was mixed White, and she was not academically oriented. Her interests centered on theatre. I interviewed her.

– Sharon Rosen was a student at Queens College. Her parents had a professional background involved in education. She is Modern Orthodox Jewish, and was planning on getting an MA in Speech Pathology. She was interviewed by a student, who was a friend.

10 Appendix B: Transcriptions of NYCE Speakers

10.1 Rashid Lewis

The following quote is the complete version of Rashid's answer to my question on p. 41

> R: It depends on the community. Namean [=know what I mean]. I found it growing up. Like see me personally, I am from South Jamaica, and that's a low-income neighborhood, and I am not afraid to say it. Some people are. Now they's White kids in this school. Now in my neighborhood for a twenty-block radius, they probably be like five White kids. Now that's between about fifty sixty houses, a couple of projects, namean. So that's crazy. Those white kids there, they be just like us, cuz that's the way they raised, and there is no love lost [=no hatred]. I grew up with you; you may be a little white, but I am a little black too; it's the same difference, namean. Now, had me personally my black self go to Long Island, namean then, it might be, it might be a little shaky, cuz those people are not used to seeing me. They used to seein' they kind of black people; they not used to seein me. So I might come over there, and I might say somethin' that'll offend them, and they might say somethin' that'll offend me, because we not used to bein' around the same surroundings. Just like bein' in school. I only know a certain amount of white kids in this school, 'namean. I mean not in this school in my neighborhood when I came to this school I started seeing all types of stuff. I was basically a prisoner of the ghetto. I never left my neighborhood, I went to Junior High School in my neighborhood, I almost went to High School in my neighborhood, I mean I stayed in my neighborhood I never really came to Manhattan or the Bronx, Brooklyn, never really went out there, stayed in that lil' area of Queens and it was crazy in there, but as I came out here to [UAA's neighborhood], I realized whoa these kids in here... like in my neighborhood it's due or die you make money if you got to there is nothin' bad there is nothin' bad with sellin' drugs. And marijuana is barely even illegal nowadays in my neighborhood, I mean if police see ya smokin', marijauna they be like "Ah, let 'em live ya know. I used to do it too, it's not even worf the paper work. I mean let's catch somebody sellin' it or let's get the shootout or somin'.' Then they go crazy, that's how it is in my neighborhood, but out here it's more stricter, it's a different variety of kids. I got a lot of [incomprehensible] in my neighborhood, so that's nothing to worry about, but I seen white kids with chains hangin' down to they ankles from they pockets attached to they wallets, now I am thinkin' in my head, "you got a chain connected to your pants that goes all the way down to the floor connected to your wallet, and you don't want nobody to steal your wallet, that's the object of the chain right? but with the chain they know you got a wallet. Chances is they still stick you up anyway. They'll take it right off your pants." And that was always crazy to me. I see a lot of kids with purple hair, stickin' up all different ways, but then again I guess, then again, they got black kids in their neighborhood doin' stupid shit. Or not only that, maybe that't how things going over there. I never been in [incomprehensible] before. I never seen... I never... what else ain't I never seen? I never really seen like girls kiss girls, and boys kiss boys till I came out here. Never seen that. It's not that it's hated in part of my own neighborhood; it'just that you just don't see it. Namean. You just don't see it . Maybe it's hidden. Out here it's real crazy though. A different atmosphere, a lot of cultural diffusion out here. They's a lot of, a lot of

different peoples hangin out together and a lot of different races 'namean, and it's beautiful, that's what I like. Like me, to take the white kids in this school personally, like if they walked down a block in my neighborhood, it's not worf my time to say, "how's it goin?" cuz I probably never see 'em again but kids here, I mean it's worf my time, I can say "watsup" cuz I know I might see 'em again. And it's like that, 'naught I mean ya meet kids with different views and different opinions different everything. And some kids, like my friend White Mike, I don't call him White Mike to be racist. He knows I call him White Mike. I call him White Mike because their was a Black Mike and there was a White Mike cause there was another Mike. They was two Mikes, and it was hard every time you say Mike bof of them turn around. So I's like listen, you White Mike, you Black Mike, and Black Mike ain't here no more, so he's stuck with the name.

10.2 Gay Latinos: Kicked Out of Victoria's Secret

Jonny: I got kicked out of Victoria's Secret.

John: What did you? That's a women's store. You sick bastard.

Jonny: I wasn't putting on clothes. I was in there with like a few of my female friends, and you know I was in there and the security there kept on giving me dirty looks, like I shouldn't be there. Like, I don't care, I'm just there for my friends. I'm not trying nothing on. Come on. Not like somebody else over here.

John: What?

Jonny: You and your thongs.

John: I don't try my thong on in the store Joey. I buy it then go home. Do a little work then wear my thong. My pleasure.

Jonny: So he was looking at me funny. So I took this little pink thing off the coat thing. And I was like, "You would look so cute in this, Mr. Officer." And he kicked me out. I can't go back to Victoria's Secret on Steinway.

10.3 Andy Sullivan and Laura Feldman

Andy and Laura describe class relations and racialization as Whites in terms of the class differences at their catholic high school. The description how people from their neighborhood avoided organized sports is reminiscent of Penny Eckert's (1988) study of Jocks and Burnouts in a Detroit area high school. However, both Andy and Laura went to college. There are a number of important NYCE features including many (r-0)s and THOUGHT raising.

Andy: My cousins are from Franklin Square and they like, they sound like more proper and more White than like I do. And like my brothers, they all sound like, you can tell, like an accent like

MN: You mean sound white. What is White? Can you imitate it at all?

Andy: Can I? I can't imitate I'm terrible with... You, know more proper, like you know

MN: OK

Andy: Like kinda Connecticut, like that. Laura: Yeah

MN: Yeah, I understand. You mean more preppy?

Andy: Yeah more preppy.

Laura: That's how my friend Lauren speaks, when my friend first, when I first spoke to her like ever, she was like, "Where are you from," she was like. She speaks like she's from the Manor, I don't know if you know like Douglaston Manor.

MN: Ok,

Laura: It's like they think like they're, I don't know where they think they're from. [laughs] She is like uhm, she was, she has like a very, everything's very proper, it's like very Connecticut, it is. It's like preppy, like they all sail their little boats and stuff. So, I I like, I don't relate to that stuff. I feel like we're like. Like she goes, she's like a swimmer, and they do tennis, and whoever doesn't do tennis, they sail, and we, like I don't, walk the Boulevard. It's like we grew up doing [all laugh]. No one really has like, like a hobby. Some people, a lot of the boys will play like baseball, maybe basketball, no one really has

Andy: Not on a team, in the streets.

Laura: Yeah, yeah. No one, No one in [their school] who was in [their school] who was in Howard Beach, maybe, of all the us, there's like fifteen, maybe three played football. There was, it just wasn't, no one played organized sports. It was like no one wanted to be bothered. It was all just very, on the Boulevard. That's what we did.

MN: What's the Boulevard.

Laura: Cross Bay Boulevard. It's like where the stores are. It's like that what you did when you were little. Walked the Boulevard. You thought you were cool.

10.4 Johan Aranda

Johan discusses his interest in Reguetón. His speech has considerable Spanish substrate influence. Particularly noticeable is the rhythm, the elision of final /d/ and /t/ and some weaking of intervocalic voiced stops /b/, /d/. He also devoices final voiced fricatives.

Johan: They rap about, sing about deeper meaning you know about love about different things that's going on in the community, so that's interesting. And it's changing, and you know, for a certain time, the Reguetón used to be like one beat, you know one sound, and now you know it's changing into different things. You know they're adding mambo music, they're adding salsa, they're adding merengue. They're adding a lot of things to it, you know.

MN: So do you, do you do anything with it? Do you make any music?

Johan: In freshman year in high school, I used to write lyrics, you know, but that was just like a hobby. It was just like I was takin' the train and put out a notepad and just started writing.

MN: And you stopped?

Johan: Yeah, I stopped. There was no point of it because I was into my studies. I was into school. I just put that aside

References

Alger, Horatio. 1867. *Ragged Dick; or, Street Life in New York with the Bootblacks.* Authorama. http://www.authorama.com/ragged-dick-1.html.

Alger, Horatio. 1872. *Phil the Fiddler; or, The Story of a Young Street Musician.* Classic Reader: http://www.classicreader.com/book/3121/

Alim, H. Samy. 2003. We are the streets: African American Language and strategic construction of street conscious identity. In *Black Linguistics: Language Society and Politics in Africa and the Americas,* S. Makoni, G. Smitherman, A. Ball, and A. Spears (eds.), 40–59. New York/London: Routledge.

Alim, H. Samy. 2004a. *You know my steez: An ethnographic and sociolinguistic study of styleshifting in a Black American speech community.* Chapel Hill, NC: Duke University Press/ American Dialect Society.

Alim, H. Samy. 2004b. Hip Hop Nation Language. In Edward Finegan and John Rickford (eds.) *Language in the USA: Perspectives for the 21st Century.* Cambridge, UK/NY: Cambridge University Press.

Alim, Samy. 2006. *Roc the Mic Right The Language of Hip Hop Culture.* London: Routledge.
Alim, Samy. 2009. Translocal style communities: Hip hop youth as cultural theorists of style, language, and globalization. *Pragmatics* 19(1). 103–128.

Alim, H. Samy and Geneva Smitherman. 2012. Articulate While Black: Barack Obama, Language, and Race in the U.S. NY/Oxford, UK: Oxford University Press

Allen, Irving Lewis. 1993. *The City in Slang: New York Life and Popular Speech.* Oxford, UK/NY: Oxford University Press.

Angermeyer, Philipp S. 2005. Spelling Bilingualism: Script Choice in Russian American Classified Ads and Signage. *Language in Society* 34(4): 493–531.

Atwood, Elmer B. 1953. *A Survey of Verb Forms in the Eastern United States.* Ann Arbor: U. of Michigan Press.

Babbitt, Eugene H. 1896. The English of the lower classes in New York City and vicinity. *Dialect Notes* 1: 457–464.

Bailey, Benjamin. 2000a. The language of multiple identities among Dominican Americans. *Journal of Linguistic Anthropology,* 10(2), 190–223.

Bailey, Benjamin. 2000b. Language and negotiation of ethnic/racial identity among Dominican Americans. *Language in Society, 29*, 555–582.

Bailey, Benjamin. 2002. *Language, Race, and Negotiation of Identity: A Study of Dominican Americans.* New York: LFB Scholarly Publishing.

Bailey, Benjamin. 2007. Language Alternation as a Resource for Identity Negotiations. In Peter Auer and Werner Kallmeyer (eds.), *Social Identity and Communicative Styles -An Alternative Approach to Variability in Language.* pp. 29–56. Berlin and New York: Mouton de Gruyter.

Bailey, Richard. 2012. Speaking American: A History of English in the United States. UK/NY: Oxford University Press.

Baker, Adam, Diana Archangeli, & Jeff Mielke. Variablity in American English s-retraction suggests a solution to the actuation problem. *Language Variation and Change,* 23: 347–374.

Bakht, Maryam. 2010. Lexical Variation and the Negotiation of Linguistic Style in a Long Island Middle School. Unpublished Doctoral Dissertation. NYU

Baranowski, Maciej. 2002. Current usage of the epicene pronoun in written English, *Journal of Sociolinguistics*, 6(3): 378–397.

Barrett, Rusty. 2014. African American English and the promise of code-meshing. In Ashanti-Young, Vershawn, Rusty Barrett, YShanda Young-Rivera, and Kim Brian Lovejoy (Eds.) *Other People's English: Code-Meshing, Code-Switching, and African American Literacy*. NYC: Teachers College Press.

Baugh, John, 1983. Black Street Speech. University of Texas Press, Austin, Texas.

Baugh, John. 1999. *Out of the mouths of slaves: African American language and educational malpractice*. Austin, TX: University of Texas Press.

Becker, Kara & Amy Wing Mei Wong. 2009. The short-a system of New York City English: An update. University of Pennsylvania Working Papers in Linguistics. Volume 15, Issue 2 Article 3. pp: 10–20. http://repository.upenn.edu/pwpl/vol15/iss2/3/

Becker, Kara & Elizabeth L. Coggshall. 2009. The Sociolinguistics of Ethnicity in New York City, *Language and Linguistic Compass*, 3(3): 751–766.

Becker, Kara. 2009. /r/ and the construction of place identity on New York City's Lower East Side *Journal of Sociolinguistics*. 13(5): 634–658.

Becker, Kara. 2010. *Regional Dialect Features on the Lower East Side of New York City: Sociophonetics, Ethnicity, and Identity*. Unpublished Doctoral Dissertation, NYU.

Becker, Kara & Amy Wing Mei Wong. 2009. The short-a system of New York City English: An update. University of Pennsylvania Working Papers in Linguistics. Volume 15, Issue 2 Article 3. pp: 10–20. http://repository.upenn.edu/pwpl/vol15/iss2/3/

Benor, Sarah B. 2008. Towards a new understanding of Jewish language in the twenty-first century. *Religion Compass* 2: 1062–1080.

Benor, Sarah B. 2009. Do American Jews speak a 'Jewish language'? A model of Jewish linguistic distinctiveness. *The Jewish Quarterly Review* 99: 230–269.

Benor, Sarah B. 2010. Ethnolinguistic repertoire: Shifting the analytic focus in language and ethnicity. *Journal of Sociolinguistics* 14: 159–183.

Benor, Sarah B. 2012. *Becoming Frum: How Newcomers Learn the Language and Culture of Orthodox Judaism*. New Brunswick, NJ: Rutgers University Press.

Benua, Laura. 1995. Identity effects in morphological truncation. In J.Beckman, L. Walsh-Dickey & S. Urbanczyk (eds), *University of Massachusetts Occasional Papers in Linguistics* 18, *Papers in Optimality Theory*, GLSA, Amherst.

Berger, Marshall D. 1968. The internal dynamics of a metropolitan New York vocalic paradigm. *American Speech* 43.33–9.

Blake, Renée and Cara Shousterman. 2010. Second generation West Indian Americans and English in New York City. *English Today*, 26(3): 35–43

Blommaert, Jan. 2010. The Sociolinguistics of Globalization. Cambridge, UK/NY: Cambridge University Press.

Blommaert, Jan & Ben Rampton. 2011. Language and Superdiversity. *Diversities*, 13(1): 1–22. www.mmg.mpg.de/diversities and www.unesco.org/shs/diversities

Blommaert, Jan & Ben Rampton. 2012. *Language and Superdiversity. MMG Working Paper 12–05*. Göttingen: Max-Plank Institute for the Study of Religious and Ethnic Diversity. http://www.mmg.mpg.de/workingpapers.

Bonfiglio, Thomas Paul. 2002. *Race and the Rise of Standard American*. New York: Mouton de Gruyter.

Brodkin Sacks, Karen. 1999. How Jews became white folks and what that says about race in America. In Steven Gregory and Roger Sanjek (eds.) *Race*. Rutgers, NJ: Rutgers University Press. pp. 78–102.

Bronstein, Arthur. 1962. Let's take another look at New York City speech. *American Speech*, 37, 13–26.

Brown, Penelope, & Levinson, Steven. 1978. Universals in language usage: Politeness phenomena. In Edward.Goody (ed.), Questions and politeness: Strategies in social interaction. Cambridge, UK/NY: Cambridge University Press

Bucholtz Mary. 1999. "Why be normal?": language and identity practices in a community of nerd girls. *Language in Society*, 28(2):203–23

Butters, Ronald R. 1974. Variability in Indirect Questions. *American Speech 49 (3/4): 230–234*.

Butters, Ronald R. 1976. More on Indirect Questions. *American Speech* 51(1/2): 57–63.

Cheshire, Jenny & Sue Fox. 2009. Was/were variation: A perspective from London. *Language Variation and Change*, 21, 1–38.

Carver, Craig M. 1987. American regional dialects: A word geography. Ann Arbor, MI: University of Michigan Press.

Clarke, Sandra. *Newfoundland and Labrador English*. Dialects of English Series: Edinburgh, Scotland: Edinburgh University Press.

Coggshall, Elizabeth and Kara Becker. 2010. The vowel phonologies of white and African American New York Residents. In Malcah Yaeger-Dror and Erik R. Thomas (eds.) *African American English Speakers And Their Participation In Local Sound Changes: A Comparative Study. American Speech Volume Supplement 94, Number 1*. Chapel Hill, NC: Duke University Press. pp: 101–128.

Cohen, Paul. 1970. The Tensing and Raising of Short [a] in the Metropolitan Area of New York City. (Master's thesis, Columbia University).

Coon, Carleton S. 1939/1962. *The Origin of Races*. New York: Knopf, 1962.

Corona, Víctor, Luci Nussbaum & Virginia Unamuno. 2013. The emergence of new linguistic repertoires among Barcelona's youth of Latin American origin. *International Journal of Bilingual Education and Bilingualism*,16(2): 182–194

Coye, Dale. 2009. Dialect Boundaries in New Jersey *American Speech*, 84(4) 414–452

Crocker, Andrew. 2014. "Chef, Carnal, Baby": A Study of Employees' Address Terms Usage in a Manhattan Restaurant. Ms. Queens College/CUNY.

Cutler, Cece. 1999/2003. Yorkville crossing: White teens, hip hop and African American English. *Journal of Sociolinguistics*, 3(4):428–442. Reprinted in V. Stroud-Lewis (Ed.), *Language, Ethnicity & Race: A Reader* (pp. 314–327). Oxford: Routledge.

Cutler, Cece. 2007. Hip-hop language in sociolinguistics and beyond. *Language and Linguistics Compass*, 1(5): 519–538.

Cutler, Cece. 2008. Brooklyn Style: hip-hop markers and racial affiliation among European immigrants. *International Journal of Bilingualism*, 12(1–2), 7–24.

Cutler, Cece. 2010. Hip-Hop, White Immigrant Youth, and African American Vernacular English: Accommodation as an Identity Choice. *Journal of English Linguistics*. 38(3) 248–269.

Cutler, Cece. 2014. *White Hip-Hoppers, Language and Identity in Post-Modern America*. Milton Park, UK/NY: Taylor and Francis.

Dávila, Arlene. 2000. Talking Back: Hispanic Media and U.S. Latinidad. CENTRO Journal, 12(1): 37–47

Dillard, Joey L. 1992. *American English*. London/ NY: Longman.

Dinkin, Aaron and Michael Friesner. 2009. Transmission or Diffusion: NYC-like short a in Southeast Florida and the Hudson Valley. Talk presented at *NWAV 38* 23 October 2009 Ottowa, Ontario. http://www.ling.upenn.edu/~dinkin/ShortAhandout.pdf

Dinkin, Aaron. 2010. The Present-Day Dialectological Status of the Hudson Valley. *International Linguistic Association Annual Conference*, New Paltz, N.Y. 17 April 2010. http://www.ling.upenn.edu/~dinkin/HudsonValleyHandout.pdf

Durian, David. 2012. *A New Perspective on Vowel Variation across the 19th and 20th Centuries in Columbus, OH*. Doctoral Dissertation, The Ohio State University. http://www.ling.ohio-state.edu//~ddurian/Dissertation/

Eckert, Penelope. 1988. Adolescent social structure and the spread of linguistic change. *Language in Society.* 17 (2): 183–207.

Eckert, Penelope. 2008. Variation and the indexical field. *Journal of sociolinguistics.* 12.453–76.

Eckert, Penelope. 2012. Three waves of variation study: The emergence of meaning in the study of variation. *Annual Review of Anthropology*, 41.87–100.

Edwards, Walter F. 2004. African American English: Phonology. *A handbook of varieties of English: V. 1 Phonology*, Berlin: Mouton DeGruyter, pp. 383–392.

Fader, Ayala. 2007. Reclaiming Sacred Sparks: Linguistic Syncretism and Gendered Language Shift among *Hasidic Jews in New York. Journal of Linguistic Anthropology*, 17(1): 1–22.

Feinstein, Mark. 1980. Ethnicity and topicalizations in New York City English. *International Journal of the Sociology of Language 26,* 15–24.

Fessenden, Ford. 2012. A Portrait of Segregation in New York City's Schools. *New York Times*. Published May 12. http://www.nytimes.com/interactive/2012/05/11/nyregion/segregation-in-new-york-city-public-schools.html (Retrieved January 19, 2014).

Fischer, David Hackett. 1989. Albion's Seed: Four British Folkways in America. New York: Oxford University Press.

Fix, Sonia. 2014. AAE as a bounded ethnolinguistic resource for white women with African American ties. *Language and Communication*. http://dx.doi.org/10.1016/j.langcom.2013.11.004

Fought, Carmen. 1999. A majority sound change in a minority community: /u/-fronting in Chicano English. Journal of Sociolinguistics 3:5–23.

Fought, Carmen. 2003. *Chicano English in Contact*. NY: Palgrave/Macmillan.

Fought, Carmen. 2006. *Language and Ethnicity*. Cambridge, UK/NY: Cambridge University Press.

Fowler, Joy. 1986. The social stratification of (r) in New York City department stores, 24 years after Labov. New York: New York University unpublished manuscript.

Fox, Susan. 2007. *The demise of Cockneys*? Language change in London's 'traditional' East End. Ph.D. dissertation, University of Essex.

Frank, Yakira. 1948. *The Speech of New York City*. University of Michigan Dissertation. Gold, David, 1986. On Jewish English. *Jewish Language Review*. 6: 121–135.

Goodfriend, Joyce. 1992. *Before the Melting Pot: Society and Culture in Colonial New York*. Princeton, NJ: Princeton University Press.

Gordon, Matthew. 2004. "New York, Philadelphia and other Northern Cities" in Kortmann, Bernd & Schneider, Edgar W. (Eds.) A Handbook of Varieties of English: Volume 1: Phonology. Berlin: De Gruyter.

Gordon, Matthew. 2013. Labov: A Guide for the Perplexed. London/NY: Bloomsbury

Grabe, Esther. and Low, Ee Ling. 2002. Durational variability in speech and the rhythm class hypothesis. In C. Gussenhoven & N. Warner (Eds.), *Laboratory Phonology* 7 (pp. 515–546). Berlin: Mouton de Gruyter.

Green, Lisa. 2002. *African American English: a linguistic introduction*. Cambridge: Cambridge University Press.

Hall-Lew, Lauren and Malcah Yaeger-Dror. 2014. New Perspectives on Linguistic Variation and Ethnic Identity in North America. In Lauren Hall Lew & Malcah Yaeger Dror, Eds., Special Issue: "New Perspectives on Linguistic Variation and Ethnic Identity in North America." Language and Communication 35(1): 1–8.

Halle, Morris & K. P. Monahan. 1985. Segmental phonology of Modern English. Linguistic Inquiry, 16: 57–116.

Herzog, Marvin, Vera Baviskar, Andrew Sunshine, Ulrike Kiefer, Robert Neumann, Wolfgang Putschke, Uriel Weinreich. 1992. The Language and culture atlas of Ashkenazic Jewry, Vol. 1. NY: YIVO/ Tübingen: Max Niemeyer Verlag.

Hoffman, Michol and Walker, James. 2010. Ethnolects and the city: Ethnic orientation and linguistic variation in Toronto English. *Language Variation and Change*, 22: 37–67.

Hoyt, Edwin P. 1974. *Horatio's Boys*. Chilton Book Company

Hualde, José Ignacio. 2006. *The Sounds of Spanish* Cambridge, UK/NY: Cambridge University Press.

Hubbell, Allan F. 1950. *The Pronunciation of English in New York City*. NY: Farrar, Strauss, and Giroux.

Huddleston, Ronald and Geoffrey Pullum. 2001. *The Cambridge Grammar of the English Language*. Cambridge, UK/NY: Cambridge University Press.

Ibrahim, Awad. 1999. Becoming black: Rap and Hip-Hop, race, gender, identity, and the politics of ESL learning. *TESOL Quarterly* 33 (3): 349–369.

Ibrahim, Awad. 2001. "Hey, whadap homeboy?" Identification, desire & consumption: Hip-Hop, performativity, and the politics of Becoming Black. *Taboo: Journal of Culture and Education,* 5(2), 85–102.

Ibrahim, Awad. 2004. One is not born Black: Becoming and the phenomenon(ology) of race. *Philosophical Studies in Education,* 35, 89–97.

Irving, Washington. 1809. *Knickerbocker's History of New York.* http://www.gutenberg.org/files/13042/13042-h/13042-h.htm

Jacobs, Harrison, Andy Kiersz & Gus Lubin. 2013. The 25 Most Segregated Cities In America. *Business Insider,* April 25, 2013 (Retrieved January 19, 2014) (Maps created by Eric Fisher) http://www.businessinsider.com/most-segregated-cities-census-maps-2013-4#new-york-ny-most-of-manhattan-is-white-south-of-125th-street-with-the-exception-of-chinatown-south-brooklyn-is-mostly-white-with-pockets-of-asians-and-hispanics-and-northeast-brooklyn-going-into-queens-is-heavily-black-queens-and-the-bronx-are-highly- diverse-19

Jacobs, Neil G. 2005. *Yiddish: a Linguistic Introduction*. Cambridge, UK: Cambridge University Press.

Jochnowitz, George. 1968. Bilingualism and Dialect Mixture among Lubavitcher Hasidic children. *American Speech* 43(3): 188–200.

Johnson, Danel Ezra. 2010. *Stability and Change along a Dialect Boundary*. Publication of the American Dialect Society 95.

Kaplan, Thomas. 2012. A Complex at Aqueduct Is Risk-Free, Cuomo Says. *New York Times,* January 20, http://www.nytimes.com/2012/01/20/nyregion/cuomo-portrays-queens-convention-center-plan-as-risk-free.html?ref=nyregion.

Kasinitz, Philip, Mollenkopf, John. H., Waters, Mary. C. & Holdaway, Jennifer. 2008. *Inheriting the City: The Children of Immigrants Come of Age*. New York: Russell Sage Foundation.

Kachadurian, Kyle. 2013. Intensifiers are mad dispersed! Where in the world are intensifiers hiding? Ms. Queens College.

Kaye, Jonathan. 2012. Canadian Raising, eh? In *Sound Structure and Sense: Studies in Memory of Edmund Gussmann*. Eugeniusz Cyran, Henryk Kardela, Bogdan Szymanek (eds.) Lublin: Wydawnictwo KUL. Pp. 321–352

Kerswill, Paul, Eivind Torgersen, and Sue Fox. 2008. Reversing drift: Innovation and diffusion in the London diphthong system. *Language Variation and Change*, 20, 451–491.

Kerswill, Paul, Jenny Cheshire, Sue Fox, & Eivind Torgersen. 2007. *Linguistic Innovators: the English of Adolescents in London: Full Research Report ESRC End of Award Report*, RES-000-23-0680. Swindon ESRC. http://www.esds.ac.uk/doc/6127%5Cmrdoc%5Cpdf%5C6127uguide.pdf

Kilgannon, Corey. 2012. Character Study: A gentile who lives for Yiddish. *New York Times, January 29,* http://www.nytimes.com/2012/01/29/nyregion/shane-baker-raised-episcopalian-lives-for-yiddish-theater.html?ref=nyregion

Kretzschmar, William, McDavid, V.G., Lerud, T.K. and Johnson, E. (eds.). 1994. Handbook of the Linguistic Atlas of the Middle and South Atlantic States. Chicago: University of Chicago Press.

Kurath, Hans. 1928. 'The origin of the dialectal differences in spoken American English'. Modern Philology 25, 385–95.

Kurath, Hans. 1949. *A Word Geography of the Eastern United States*. Ann Arbor: U. of Michigan Press.

Kurath, Hans. 1972. *Studies in Aerial Linguistics*. Bloomington, Indiana: Indiana University Press.

Kurath, Hans and Raven I. McDavid. 1961. *The Pronunciation of English in the Atlantic States*. Ann Arbor: University of Michigan Press.

Labov, William. 1966/2006. *The Social Stratification of English in New York City* 2nd Edition. Cambridge: Cambridge University Press.

Labov, William. 1972a. The logic of non-standard English. *Language in the Inner City: Studies in the Black English Vernacular*. Philadelphia, PA: University of Pennsylvania Press.

Labov, William. 1972b. *Sociolinguistic Patterns*. Philadelphia, PA: University of Pennsylvania Press.

Labov, William. 1994. *Principles of Linguistic Change. Volume 1: Internal Factors*. Oxford: Basil Blackwell.

Labov, William. 2001. *Principles of Linguistic Change. Volume II: Social Factors*. Oxford: Blackwell.

Labov, William. 2007. Transmission and diffusion. *Language* 83(2): 344–387

Labov, William. 2008a. Mysteries of the substrate. In Miriam Meyerhoff and Naomi Nagy (Eds.) *The Social Lives of Language and Multilingual Speech Communities: Celebrating the work of Gillian Sankoff*. Amsterdam/Philadelphia: Benjamins. (pp. 315–326)

Labov, William. 2008b. Unendangered Dialects, Endangered People. In King, K., N. Shilling-Estes, N. Wright Fogle, J. J. Lou, and B. Soukup (eds.), *Sustaining Linguistic Diversity: Endangered and Minority Languages and Language Varieties* (Georgetown University Round Table on Languages and Linguistics Proceedings). Georgetown University Press, pp. 219–238.

Labov, William. 2009. *A Life of Learning: Six People I Have Learned From*. The 2009 Charles Homer Haskins Prize Lecture. American Council of Learned Societies. Published exclusively in electronic format. http://www.acls.org/publications/audio/labov/default. aspx?id=4462

Labov, William. 2011. *Principles of Linguistic Change. Volume III: Cognitive and Cultural Factors*. Oxford: Wiley Blackwell.

Labov, William, Sharon Ash, and Charles Boberg. 2006. *Atlas of North American English: Phonetics, Phonology and Sound Change*. Berlin: Mouton De Gruyter.

Labov, William, Paul Cohen, Clarence Robins, and John Lewis. 1968a. A study of the Non-Standard English of Negro and Puerto Rican Speakers in New York City, V. 1: Phonological and Grammatical Analysis. Washington, DC: Office of Education, Bureau of Research/ERIC.

Labov, William, Paul Cohen, Clarence Robins, and John Lewis. 1968b. A study of the Non-Standard English of Negro and Puerto Rican Speakers in New York City, V. 2: The Use of Language in the Speech Community. Washington, DC: Office of Education, Bureau of Research/ERIC.

Labov, William, Mark Karen, and Corey Miller. 1991. Near mergers and the suspension of phonemic contrast. *Language Variation and Change*, 3(1): 33–74.

Labov, William, Malcah Yaeger, & Richard Steiner. 1972. *A Quantitative Study of Sound Change in Progress*. Philadelphia: U. of Pennsylvania Press.

Labov, William, Ingrid Rosenfelder and Josef Fruehwald. 2013. One Hundred Years of Sound Change in Philadelphia: Linear Incrementation, Reversal, and Reanalysis. *Language*, 89(1): 30–65.

Levon, Erez. 2006. Mosaic Identity and Style: Phonological variation among Reform American Jews. *Journal of Sociolinguistics,* 10(2): 181–204.

Lo, Adrienne and Angela Reyes. 2009. Introduction: On Yellow English and Other Perilous Terms. In Reyes, Angela and Adrienne Lo, eds. *Beyond Yellow English: Toward a linguistic anthropology of Asian Pacific America*, New York: Oxford University Press: 3–17

Logan, John R. and Brian Stults. 2011. The Persistence of Segregation in the Metropolis: New Findings from the 2010 Census. Census Brief prepared for Project US2010. http://www.s4.brown.edu/us2010/Data/Report/report2.pdf (Retrieved January 19, 2014)

Mather, Patrick-André. 2012. The Social Stratification of /r/ in New York City: Labov's Department Store Study Revisited. *Journal of English Linguistics*.

McCloskey, James. 2006. Questions and questioning in a local English. In: Raffaela Zanuttini, Héctor Campos, Elena Herburger & P. Portner (eds*.)*. *Crosslinguistic Research in Syntax and Semantics: Negation, Tense, and Clausal Architecture,* Washington, DC: Georgetown University Press, 87–126

McNally, Therese A. 2009. *The accents of the 5 boroughs of NYC – a how to by a native – the real deal* . Youtube Video http://www.youtube.com/user/vigwig#p/a/u/2/1hrA9-6o4tl.

Mendoza-Denton, Norma. 2008. *Homegirls: Language and Cultural Practice among Latina Youth Gangs*. Malden, MA: Blackwell.

Meseck, Birgit. 1992. Speech Cosmetics in New York; or, How to Lose the New York Accent. *Amerikastudien / American Studies*, 37(1):141–150

Montgomery, Michael. 1996. Was colonial American English a koine? In Juhani Klemola, merja Kytö, and Matti Riassanen (eds.) *Speech Past and Present: Studies in English Dialectology in Memory of Ossi Ihalainen*. University of Bamberg Studies in English Linguistics 38. Frankfurn am Main and Bern: Peter Lang, pp. 213–235.

Montgomery, Michael. 2001. British and Irish antecedents of American English,' in John Algeo (ed.) *The Cambridge History of the English Language, v. 6: English in North America.* Cambridge, UK/NY: Cambridge University press. pp. 89–151.

Montgomery, Michael. 2004. Solving Kurath's Puzzle. in Raymond Hickey (ed.) Legacies of Colonial English: *Studies in Transported Dialects.* pp. 310–325.

Mufwene, Salikoko. 2008. *Language Evolution: Contact, Competition and Change.* NY: Continuum.

Nagy Naomi, Joanna Chociej, and Michol F. Hoffman. 2014.Analyzing Ethnic Orientation in the quantitative sociolinguistic paradigm. Language & Communication (in press)

Newlin-Lukowicz, Luiza. 2013. TH-stopping in New York City: Substrate effect turned ethnic marker, *University of Pennsylvania Working Papers in Linguistics 19(2) Selected Papers from NWAV 41*: 151–160.

Newman, Michael. 1997. What pronouns can tell us: a case study of epicenes in English, II Studiesin Language, 22: 2, 353–390.

Newman, Michael. 1998. Epicene pronouns: the linguistics of a prescriptive problem. Outstanding dissertations in linguistics' series. NY: Garland

Newman, Michael. 2001. 'Not Dogmatically/ It's about me': contested values in a high school rap crew *Taboo: a journal of culture and education*, 5 (2):51–68.

Newman, Michael. 2005. Rap as literacy: a genre analysis of Hip-Hop ciphers. *Text* 25(3): 399–436.

Newman, Michael. 2010. Focusing, implicational scaling, and the dialect status of New York Latino English. *Journal of Sociolinguistics,* 14(2): 207–239.

Newman, Michael. 2011. The NYC Short-A system: Continuity and Change over the Generations in a Complex Phonological System. Paper presented at New Ways of Analyzing Variation-40. Georgetown University, Washington, DC: October 28.

Newman, Michael, Adriana Patiño-Santos, & Mireia Trenchs-Parera. 2013. Linguistic reception of Latin American students in Catalonia and their responses to educational language policies, *International Journal of Bilingual Education and Bilingualism.* 16(2): 195–209.

Newman, Michael & Angela Wu. 2011. Do you sound Asian when you speak English. *American Speech,* 86(2): 152–178.

New York City Department of Parks and Recreation. 2000. *Spuyten Duyvil Creek.* http://www.washington-heights.us/history/archives/spuyten_duyvil_creek_23.html

Niedzielski, Nancy and Dennis Preston. 2003. *Folk linguistics.* Berlin: Mouton de Gruyter.

O'Hare, Kieran Michael. 2010. Your you're your life. *New York Times,* October 25, http://www.nytimes.com/interactive/2010/10/25/nyregion/20101025-reader-subway-maps.html?ref=nyregionspecial&_r=0#/kieran_michael_ohare-14/

Olivo, Ann Marie. 2013. The Strong Island Sound: Sociolinguistic evidence for emerging American ethnicities. Unpublished Doctoral Dissertation, Rice University.

Omi, Michael and Howard Winant. 1994. *Racial Formation in the United States*. New York: Routledge.

Otheguy, Ricardo. 2011. Functional Adaptation and Conceptual Convergence in the Analysis of Language Contact in the Spanish of Bilingual Communities in New York. *Handbook of Hispanic Sociolinguistics.* Hoboken, NJ: Wiley.

Otheguy, Ricardo & Nancy Stern. 2011. On so-called Spanglish. *International Journal of Bilingualism* 15:(1) 85–100.

Painter, Nell Irwin. 2010. *The History of White People.* NY: W. W. Norton & Company.

Payne, Arvilla C. 1980. Factors Controlling the Acquisition of the Philadelphia Dialect by Out-of-State Children. In W. Labov (ed.) *Locating Language in Time and Space*. New York: Academic Press, 143–178.

Pederson, Lee. 2001. Dialects. In John Algeo (ed.) *The Cambridge History of the English Language, v. 6: English in North America*. Cambridge, UK/NY: Cambridge University press. pp. 253–290.

Pennycook, Alastair. 2003. Global Englishes, Rip Slyme, and performativity. *Journal of Sociolinguistics*, 7 (4): 513–533.

Pennycook, Alastair. 2007. Language, localization and the real: hip-hop and the global spread of authenticity. *Journal of Language, Identity and Education* 6(2).

Pennycook, Alastair & Alim, H. Samy. 2007. Glocal linguistic flows: Hip Hop Culture(s), identities, and the politics of language education. *Journal of Language, Identity and Education* 6(2):

Popik, Barry. 2004. *Why is New York Called the Big Apple* http://www.barrypopik.com/index.php/new_york_city/entry/summary_why_is_new_york_called_the_big_apple/ accessed April 24, 2012.

Poplack, Shana. 1980. "Sometimes I Start a Sentence in English y termino en español": Toward a Typology of Code-Switching. *Linguistics* 18 581–618.

Potowski, Kim and Janine Matts. 2008. Interethnic language and identity: MexiRicans in Chicago. *Journal of Language, Identity and Education*, 7 (2): 137–160.

Rahman, Jacquelyn. 2012. The N Word: Its History and Use in the African American Community. *Journal of English Linguistics* 40(2) 137–171.

Reitano, Joanne. 2006. *The Restless City: A Short History of New York from Colonial Times to the Present*. NY/London: Routledge.

Rickford, John and Russell Rickford. 2000. *Spoken Soul: The story of Black English*. NY: Wiley.

Rickford, John R., 1999. African American Vernacular English: Evolution, Educational Implications. Blackwell, Cambridge, Massachusetts.

Roberts, Sam. 2006. Mayor's Accent Deserts Boston for New York. *New York Times*. January 16. http://www.nytimes.com/2006/01/16/nyregion/16accent.html?pagewanted=all

Roberts, Sam. 2009. Yiddish Resurfaces as City's 2nd Political Language. *New York Times*. http://www.nytimes.com/2009/07/21/nyregion/21yiddish.html?scp=1&sq=Yiddish%20Resurfaces%20as%20City's%202nd%20Political%20Language.%20By%20SAM%20ROBERTS&st=cse

Roberts, Sam. 2010. Unlearning to Tawk Like a New Yorker. *New York Times*. November 19 http://www.nytimes.com/2010/11/21/nyregion/21accent.html?pagewanted=all

Roberts, Sam. 2011. A Racial Attack That, Years Later, Is Still Being Felt. Cityroom. *New York Times*. http://cityroom.blogs.nytimes.com/2011/12/18/a-racial-attack-that-years-later-is-still-being-felt/?scp=1&sq=howard%20beach&st=cse.

Robertson, Roland. 1995. 'Glocalization: Time-Space and Homogeneity-Heterogeneity', in Featherstone, Lash & Robertson (eds), *Global Modernities*, London, Sage,

Romaine, Suzanne. 2001. Contact with other languages. in John Algeo (ed.) *The Cambridge History of the English Language, v. 6: English in North America*. Cambridge, UK/NY: Cambridge University press. pp. 154–183.

Roudometof, Victor. 2005. "Translationalism, Cosmopolitanism, and Glocalization". *Current Sociology* 53 (1): 113–135.

Sanjek, Roger. 1996. The enduring inequalities of race. In Steven Gregory and Roger Sanek (eds.) *Race*. New Brunswick, NJ: Rutgers University Press. Pp. 1–17.

Santa Ana, Otto. 1996. Sonority and syllable structure in Chicano English. *Language Variation and Change, 8(1): 63–90.*

Santa Ana, Otto and Robert Bayley. 2004a. Chicano English: Phonology. *A handbook of varieties of English: V. 1 Phonology,* Berlin: Mouton De Gruyter, pp. 417–434.

Santa Ana, Otto and Robert Bayley. 2004b. Chicano English: Morphology and Syntax. *A handbook of varieties of English: V. 2 Morphology and Syntax,* Berlin: Mouton De Gruyter, pp. 374–390.

Sapir, Edward. 1921. *Language: An Introduction to the Study of Speech.* New York: Harcourt.

Scheltema, Gajus and Westerhuijs, Heleen. 2011. *Exploring Historic Dutch New York.* Museum of the City of New York/Dover Publications, New York.

Schieffelin, Bambi. 1994. Codeswitching and Language Socialization: Some Probable Relationships. In *Pragmatics: From Theory to Practice,* ed. by Judith Felson Duchan, Lynne E. Hewitt, and Rae M. Sonnenmeier, pp.20–42. Englewood Cliffs, NJ: Prentice Hall.

Schiffrin, Deborah. 1984. Argument as Sociability. *Language in Society*, 13(3): 311–335.

Schneider, Edgar. 2007. *Postcolonial English: Varieties Around the World.* Cambridge, UK: Cambridge University Press.

Selesky, Harold E. 2006. Neutral Ground of New York. *Encyclopedia of the American Revolution: Library of Military History.* Ed. Harold E. Selesky. Vol. 2. Detroit: Charles Scribner's Sons, 796–797.

Sharma, Devyani & Lavanya Sankaran. 2011. Cognitive and social forces in dialect shift: Gradual change in London Asian speech. *Language Variation and Change,* 23(3): 399–428.

Shorto, Russell. 2004. *The Island at the Center of the World: The Epic Story of Dutch Manhattan and the Forgotten Colony That Shaped America.* NY: Random House.

Silverman, Daniel. 2002. Dynamic versus static phonotactic conditions in prosodic morphology. Linguistics 40(1), 29–59.

Silverman, Stuart. 1975. The learning of Black English by Puerto Ricans in New York City. In Joey Dillard (ed.) *Perspectives on Black English.* The Hague: Mouton.

Slomanson, Peter, and Newman, Michael. 2004. Peer Group Identification and Variation in New York Latino English Laterals. *English World-Wide* 25: 199–216.

Slotkin, Allan. 1993. *You* as a multileveled dictional device in Stephen Crane's representation of Bowery Dialect in Maggie, A Girl of the Streets. *South Central Review*, 7(2): 40–53

Spears, Arthur. 2001. "Ebonics" and African-American English. In Clinton Crawford (ed.) *The Ebonics and Language Education of African Ancestry Students.* Brooklyn, NY: Sankofa World Publishers. pp. 235–247.

Steinmetz, Sol. 1981. Jewish English in the United States. *American Speech*, 56.1: 3–16.

Szmrecsanyi, Benedikt & Bernd Kortmann. 2009. Vernacular universals and angloversals in a typological perspective. In: Filppula, Markku, Juhani Klemola & Heli Paulasto (eds), *Vernacular Universals and Language Contacts: Evidence from Varieties of English and Beyond.* London/New York: Routledge, 33–53

Tannen, Deborah. 1981. New York Jewish Conversational Style. *International Journal of the Sociology of Language,* 30: 133–149.

Tannen, Deborah. 1984. *Conversational Style.* Oxford, UK/NY: Oxford University Press.

Thomas, Charles. K. 1932. Jewish dialect and New York Dialect. American Speech 7(5). 321–6.

Thomas, Charles. K. 1942. Pronunciation in downstate New York. American Speech 17(1).30–41.

Thomas, Charles. K. 1947. The place of New York City in American linguistic geography. *Quarterly Journal of Speech* 33(3). 314–20.

Thomas, Erik. 2001. *An Acoustic Analysis of Vowel Variation In New World English*. PADS 81. Durham, NC: Duke University Press and the American Dialect Society.

Thomas, Erik R. 2007. Phonological and Phonetic Characteristics of AAVE. Language and Linguistics Compass 1:450–75.

Thomas, Erik R. 2011. Sociophonetics: An Introduction. Basingstoke, U.K./New York: Palgrave.

Thomas, Erik R., and Phillip M. Carter. 2006. Rhythm and African American English. English World-Wide 27.331–55.

Thomas, Erik & Tyler Kendall. 2007–2012. The Vowel Normalization and Plotting Suite. North Carolina State Unverisity. http://ncslaap.lib.ncsu.edu/tools/norm/norm1.php

Thomas, Erik and Alicia Bedford Wassink. 2007. Variation and Identity in African American English. In Carmen Llamas and Dominick Watt (Eds.) *Language and Identity*. Edinburgh, Scotland: Edinburgh University Press. pp. 157–165.

Tillery, Jan, Tom Wikle, & Guy Bailey. 2000. The Nationalization of a Southernism. *Journal of English Linguistics*, 28(3): 280–294

Torgersen, Eivind, Paul Kerswill, and Sue Fox. 2006. Ethnicity as a source of changes in the London vowel system. In F. Hinskens (ed.). *Language Variation – European Perspectives. Selected Papers from the Third International Conference on Language Variation in Europe (ICLaVE3)*, Amsterdam: Benjamins. 249–263.

Toribio, Almeida Jacqueline. 2000. Language variation and the linguistic enactment of identity among Dominicans. *Linguistics: An Interdisciplinary Journal of the Language Science*s 38, 1133–1159.

Toribio, Almeida Jacqueline. 2003. The social significance of language loyalty among Black and White Dominicans in New York. *The Bilingual Review/La Revista Bilingüe* 27.1, 3–11.

Trager, George L. 1930. The pronunciation of short s in American Standard English. *American Speech, 5,* 396–400.

Trager, George L. 1940. One phonemic entity becomes two: the case of 'short a' *American Speech, 15,* 255–258.

Trenchs-Parera, Mireia, and Michael Newman. 2009. Diversity of language ideologies in Spanish-speaking youth of different origins in Catalonia. Journal of Multilingual and Multicultural Development 30(6): 509–24.

Trudgill, Peter. 1992. Dialect typology and social structure. In Ernst Jahr (ed.) *Language Contact and Language Change*. Berlin/New York: Mouton de Gruyter. 195–212.

Trudgill, Peter. 2004. *New-Dialect Formation: The Inevitability of Colonial Englishes*. Edinburgh: Edinburgh University Press.

Trudgill, Peter & Jack Chambers. 1991. *Dialects of English: Studies in grammatical variation.* Berlin: Mouton De Gruyter.

Twist, Alina, Adam Baker, Jeff Mielke, Diana Arcangeli. 2007. Are covert /ɹ/ allophones really indistinguishable? *University of Pennsylvania Working Papers in Linguistics*, v. 17.2: Selected Papers from NWAV 35. (207–216).

Uffmann, Christian. 2007. Intrusive [r] and optimal epenthetic consonants. *Language Sciences* 29: 451–476.

Urciuoli, Bonnie. 1996. *Exposing Prejudice: Puerto Rican Experiences of Language, Race, and Class*. Boulder, CO: Westview.

US Census Bureau. 2010. http://2010.census.gov/2010census/how/interactive-form.php accessed July 16, 2010.

Vertovec, Steven. 2007. Super-diversity and its implications. *Ethnic and Racial Studies*, 30(6): 1024–1054.

Vaux, Bert and Scott Golder. 2003. *The Harvard Dialect Survey*. Archived Versions accessed May 5, 2014 http://dialect.redlog.net/. Question 50: "Which word(s) do you use to address two or more people?" Map generated by Emily Tucker Prud'hommeaux.

Wells, John C. 1982. *Accents of English*. Cambridge: Cambridge University Press. ISBN 0-521-22919-7 (vol. 1)

Welmore, Thomas H. 1959. *The Low-Back and Low-Central Vowels in the Eastern United States*. American Dialect Society Publication No. 32. Tuscaloosa: University of Alabama Press.

Wolfram, Walt. 1969. *A Sociolinguistic Study of Description of Detroit Negro Speech*. Washington, DC: Center for Applied Linguistics.

Wolfram, Walt. 1974. *Sociolinguistic Aspects of Assimilation: Puerto Rican English in NYC*. Washington, DC: Center for Applied Linguistics.

Wolfram, Walt. 1991. Dialects and American English. A Publication of Center for Applied Linguistics. Englewood Cliffs, NJ: Prentice-Hall.

Wolfram, Walt. 2007. Sociolinguistic Folklore in the study of African American English. *Language and Linguistic Compass*, 1(4): 292–313.

Wong, Amy Wing-mei. 2007. Two Vernacular Features in the English of Four American-born Chinese. In *University of Pennsylvania Working Papers in Linguistics: Selected Papers from NWAV 35*. 13(2): 217–230. http://repository.upenn.edu/pwpl/vol13/iss2/17/.

Wong, Amy Wing-mei. 2010. New York City English and second generation Chinese Americans. *English Today*, 26(3): 3–11.

Wong, Amy Wing-mei. 2012. "The Lowering of Raised-THOUGHT and the Low-Back Distinction in New York City: Evidence from Chinese Americans," University of Pennsylvania Working Papers in Linguistics: Vol. 18: Iss. 2, Article 18. Available at: http://repository.upenn.edu/pwpl/vol18/iss2/18

Wong, Amy Wing-mei and Lauren Hall-Lew. 2014. Regional variability and ethnic identity: Chinese Americans in New York City and San Francisco. Language & Communication (in press)

Yavas, Mehmet. 2006. *Applied English Phonology* Malden, MA/Oxford, UK: Blackwell

Yaeger-Dror, Malcah and Erik R. Thomas (eds.) *African American English Speakers And Their Participation In Local Sound Changes: A Comparative Study*. American Speech Volume Supplement 94, Number 1. Chapel Hill, NC: Duke University Press. pp: 101–128.

Zacks, Richard. 2012. *Island of Vice: Theodore Roosevelt's doomed question to clean up sin-loving New York. NY: Doubleday*

Zentella, Ana Celia. 1997. *Growing Up Bilingual*. London: Blackwell.

Index